•••••• BRIEF CONTENTS

Preschool
APPROPRIATE PRACTICES

Janice J. Beaty

Elmira College

Harcourt Brace Jovanovich College Publishers

Fort Worth   Philadelphia   San Diego   New York   Orlando   Austin   San Antonio
Toronto   Montreal   London   Sydney   Tokyo

Publisher	Ted Buchholz
Acquisitions Editor	Jo-Anne Weaver
Project Editor	Angela Williams
Production Manager	J. Montgomery Shaw
Art & Design Supervisor	Vicki McAlindon Horton
Text and Cover Designer	CIRCA 86, Inc.
Cover Photographer	Donna Buie

Thanks to all of our cover models *(Annalise, Harrison, Keith, Davona, Chelsea, and David)* and their "stage moms."

Library of Congress Cataloging-in-Publication Data

Beaty, Janice J.
   Preschool: appropriate practices / Janice J. Beaty.
      p.   cm.
   Includes bibliographical references.
   ISBN 0–03–047524–4
      1. Education, Preschool—Curricula.   2. Education, Preschool—
   Activity programs.   3. Classroom learning centers.   4. Child
   development.   I. Title.
   LB1140.4.B43   1991
   372.19—dc20   91–11442
                                                          CIP

ISBN: 0–03–047524–4

Requests for permission to make copies of any part of the work should be mailed to: Permissions Department, Harcourt Brace Jovanovich, Publishers, 8th Floor, Orlando, Florida 32887.

Address for editorial correspondence: Harcourt Brace Jovanovich, Inc., 301 Commerce Street, Suite 3700, Fort Worth, TX 76102.

Address for orders: Harcourt Brace Jovanovich, Inc., 6277 Sea Harbor Drive, Orlando, Florida 32887. 1-800-782-4479, or 1-800-433-0001 (in Florida)

PRINTED IN THE UNITED STATES OF AMERICA

2 3 4 5   016   9 8 7 6 5 4 3 2 1

•••••• CONTENTS

LIST OF TABLES AND FIGURES

LIST OF CHANTS

••••••• PREFACE

"Let the learning environment do the teaching" is the overall theme of this textbook. By advancing the idea that the preschool child learns best through playful exploration of classroom learning centers, this book suggests a curriculum that speaks to children's developmental needs as well as the teacher's task of choosing appropriate activities for each learning center. Readers will learn how to arrange the physical environment of a preschool classroom in order for individual children of ages three to five to become deeply involved in their own learning through a self-directed learning environment.

"Let the teacher be a facilitator of learning" is a second theme that helps teachers understand how to set up learning centers, serve as behavior models in these centers, observe children's developmental levels, and then make plans for individuals. Readers will learn how to determine children's developmental levels of manipulation, mastery, and meaning by observing children's interactions with materials and with one another.

"Let the children learn to care" is a third overall theme, referring to the behavior children will learn to exhibit in the classroom that then carries over into their lives: caring about themselves, caring about one another, and caring about their materials and environment.

The textbook is organized into chapters based on ten learning centers within today's preschool classroom: blocks, computer, manipulative/math, story, writing, art, music, science, dramatic play, and large motor. Each chapter discusses how to set up the center so that children can use it on their own, which activities to provide in order to support specific development in children, and how to observe in order to determine an individual child's development and needs.

Several unique aspects of the textbook include: the use of children's books to motivate a youngster's involvement in learning activities in the various centers; the use of a simple but effective observation tool, the Child Interaction Form, to help teachers determine a child's developmental level; the use of the computer as an interactive learning tool responding to children's exploratory play; the inclusion of preschool math activities in the Manipulative Center; the inclusion of a Writing Center to support children's natural emerging literacy; chapters full of original learning activities, especially those featuring large motor skills inside the classroom; and finally, the use of the Child Interaction Form to help teachers make plans for individual children.

•••••• ACKNOWLEDGMENTS

Many thanks to Elmira College colleagues: Bonny Helm, who read the manuscript and offered many meaningful suggestions; Linda Pratt, whose creativity always shines forth in new educational endeavors; the Elmira College administration, who provided the time necessary to complete the project; my husband, Dale Janssen, for listening to and making thoughtful responses to the manuscript; the Romulus Central School prekindergarten staff and school administrators; the parents, staff, and children of the Helm Nursery School and the Gingerbread House Day Care Center for allowing their children to be photographed, and Joan Hibbard, the Center's director; Sue Bredekamp of NAEYC for her work in developing and promoting "developmentally appropriate practice" in classrooms for young children; and Donna Zeigler for composing original music to accompany the chants. Finally, I would like to thank the reviewers of this text: Deborah Andrews, Tidewater Community College; Ruth Barnhart, Iowa State University; Audrey Beard, Albany State College; Clifford Brooks, Bowling Green State University; David L. Brown, East Texas State University; Rhoda Chalker, Florida Atlantic University; Diane Cromwell, American River College; David Kuschner, University of Cincinnati; Carol Mellsom, New York University; Marcia Oreskovich, University of Northern Colorado; and Janice Wood, University of North Florida.

Janice Beaty

To Mary Klein Maples

*A special friend, colleague,
and early childhood advocate*

1

THE SELF-DIRECTED
LEARNING ENVIRONMENT

COME IN *(Action chant)*

Walk up the sidewalk,	(march in place throughout)
Knock at the door,	(knock with hand)
Peak through the window,	(hand over eyes)
Gaze at the floor,	(look down)
Hand on the doorknob,	(turn with hand)
Should you begin?	(stop all motion)
Open the door wide!	(pull "door" open)
COME RIGHT IN!	(jump forward)

· · · · · · · · · ·**Expectations of Teachers and Children**

As students and teachers in the field of early childhood education, we are all engaged in a remarkable endeavor: that of guiding young children through their very first group learning experience. We want desperately to succeed. We want children to come into our classrooms with delight on their faces and excitement in their eyes. We ourselves want to be excellent teachers who offer outstanding education to the three-year-olds, four-year-olds, and five-year-olds who come into our programs. We want to be able to solve all their problems and meet all their needs.

It is such a new experience for them. They come into our classrooms with such high anticipation, with such great expectations. Will we like them? Will they be able to do what we expect of them? Will they like school? Will they find a friend?

It is such an important experience for us. Will we be able to provide the quality programs that their parents expect of us and that we expect of ourselves? Will we be able to handle a whole classful of some twenty lively youngsters? Will we be able to reach and satisfy those children with special needs?

This textbook offers IDEAS + that can make such a learning experience happen for teachers and children. It discusses the how's and why's of learning psychology in terms that the teacher can relate to. It offers ideas for converting the classroom into an active and attractive learning environment with freedom for the teacher to direct and support and with confidence for the child to choose and accomplish the learning tasks necessary for both to succeed. It gives suggestions for providing appropriate activities and materials for the age level and learning stage level of every child in your class.

As you read this textbook, try to put yourself in the place of the child in your classroom. What would make the environment comfortable for you? What kinds of activities would you choose to be involved with? What kind of support would you appreciate from those in charge? Use the answers to these questions as guidelines for your work with young children. They will appreciate this concern on your part, and they will respond in the way that you hoped they would.

• • • • • • • • • • What We Know About Teaching and Learning

Research has shown us that the more direct involvement young children have with learning activities, the more effectively they learn. The studies of Jean Piaget and the cognitive psychologists who followed him all point to the fact that young children learn best when they are actively involved in sensory exploration of materials and activities. Teachers of young children agree. Whenever they set up their classrooms so that the children can become directly involved with materials, all kinds of exciting interactions take place. So intensely do young children interact with their favorite materials and activities, in fact, that it is difficult to pull them away.

You may well agree with this observation, but you may also wonder: "Is this really teaching? If I set up the classroom environment so that the children get deeply involved in the activities, then what am I supposed to do? Isn't a teacher supposed to teach?"

"Yes, of course," is the answer. But *teaching* in an early childhood classroom is a very special skill, performed for a very special audience. The teacher in an early childhood classroom is a guide or *facilitator of learning*. This means that the teacher sets up the classroom so that the children can teach themselves. That's right. Children below age seven, we have learned, create their own knowledge by direct, hands-on interaction with the materials, activities, and people in their environment. Thus, such children must have an especially rich environment full of materials, activities, and people who relate well to their ages and stages of development if they are to learn.

When the teacher sets up the classroom so that children can become involved on their own, then she or he is free to work with individual children, observing them and taking note of those who need special help and support. She can then provide the materials and the interaction with individuals or small groups who may need this help or who may need redirection when their interest flags. That is the *appropriate practice* for preschool teachers.

We also know that young children learn best when they learn as individuals rather than in a total group situation. Although they will sit still and listen when the teacher talks to the entire class, this is not how young children develop cognitively, physically, socially, or emotionally. To learn to understand the world around them and their part in it, young children need to have hands-on interaction with materials and equipment on their own, either as individuals or in small groups. That is the *appropriate practice* for preschool children.

The National Association for the Education of Young Children believes, in fact, that "the major determinate of program quality is . . . the degree to which the program is *developmentally appropriate*." A two-part definition of developmental appropriateness follows:

1. Age appropriateness. Human development research indicates that there are universal, predictable sequences of growth and change that occur in children during the first nine years of life. These predictable changes occur in all domains of development—physical, emotional, social, and cognitive. Knowledge of typical development of children within the age span served by the program provides a framework from which teachers prepare the learning environment and plan appropriate experiences.

2. Individual appropriateness. Each child is a unique person with an individual pattern and timing of growth, as well as individual personality, learning style, and family background. Both the curriculum and adults' interactions with children should be responsive to individual differences. Learning in young children is the result of interaction between the child's thoughts and experiences with materials, ideas, and people. These experiences should match the child's development abilities while also challenging the child's interest and understanding. (Bredekamp, 1986)

• • • • • • • • • • Creating a Self-Directed Learning Environment

In order to provide a curriculum that speaks to the needs of individual young children in this appropriate manner, we need to create a *self-directed learning environment* within our program. That is, we need to provide, assemble, and arrange a physical classroom environment that allows children to: 1) perceive which activities are available, 2) make their own choices of activities to pursue, and 3) become deeply involved in their own learning.

In the preschool classroom, it is the learning environment itself that is the curriculum. The choice and arrangement of the equipment and materials we provide set the stage for whatever is to happen. The wise teacher, who understands how young children learn, arranges her environment so that the child can direct his energies into the learning areas of greatest interest to him. The teacher can then spend time working with individuals and small groups in the various classroom learning centers, observing and recording their accomplishments in order to support these children in their growth and development.

If we as preschool teachers are to provide a curriculum that speaks to the needs of individual children of various ages and stages, then we must *let the learning environment do the teaching*. This then frees us as teachers to work with individual children and small groups. We must arrange this environment carefully so that individual children can use it on their own without much direction on our part. We must ensure that it contains materials and activities appropriate for the wide range of individual interests and abilities that a class of preschool children possesses. And we must ensure that although each learning center stands on its own, each one is also integrated into the total curriculum in an appropriate manner.

• Providing Learning Centers

Your first appropriate task, then, in teaching a class of three-, four-, and five-year-old children is to set up such a *self-directed learning environment*. How will you do it? First, you must become aware of the curriculum areas that your program supports. They are often described in terms of topics or subjects, that is, language arts, social studies, science, mathematics, physical activities, art, and music. Sometimes they are described in terms of child development aspects, that is, social, emotional, physical, cognitive, language, and creative.

Next, you must convert these curriculum or child development topics into classroom learning centers. That is, you must plan physical space for each of the curriculum topics that your program includes. Because the classroom arrangement and all that happens in it *is* the curriculum in an early childhood program, this text is arranged by chapters that have converted the curriculum subjects into the following classroom centers:

Curriculum Topic	Learning Center
Language Arts	Story Center
	Writing Center
	Computer Center
Social Studies	Block Center
	Dramatic Play Center
Science	Science Center
	Computer Center
Mathematics	Manipulative/Math Center
	Computer Center
	Block Center
Physical Activities	Large Motor Center
	Manipulative/Math Center
	Block Center
Art	Art Center
	Writing Center
	Computer Center
Music	Music Center
	Large Motor Center

In this text, the six major aspects of child development are treated in each of the ten learning center chapters. For example, Chapter 3, "Block Center," discusses social, emotional, physical, cognitive, language, and creative growth of children through self-exploratory interaction with blocks.

• Locating and Spacing Learning Centers

Once you know which learning centers your classroom (that is, your curriculum) should include, then you can begin to plan your locating and spacing of them. It was once believed that early childhood classrooms should be arranged so that active or noisy activities would not be adjacent to passive or quiet activities. The Appropriate Practices Curriculum takes a different point of view. Because many classrooms are not large enough for the noisy/quiet theory to make that much difference, the arrangement of learning centers can be based on other concerns, for example, how learning centers relate to one another.

Children will be moving from one activity to another. They may be engaged in block building, but they may want to see the photos of the field trip taken at the bridge construction site last week. Those photos happen to be displayed in the Writing Center because other children are writing spontaneous stories in *personal script* about their last week's field trip experience. Or the children may want to move from the Block Center to the Dramatic Play Center because the children there are pretending to be construction workers building a bridge.

Ten curriculum areas are described in this text: blocks, computer, manipulative/math, story, writing, art, music, science, dramatic play, and large motor. To **arrange a classroom based on these ten areas,** it is important to consider how each of them relates to the others before a classroom can be arranged so that it will be used most appropriately.

One way to approach this task is to take each learning center at a time and jot down on paper any other center in the classroom to which it has a strong relationship. You can also rank these learning centers in an informal order of their importance in the relationship. For example, Dramatic Play is first in importance in its relationship to Blocks because children often represent what they have experienced on a field trip to both the Dramatic Play and Block Centers. What might result is a list like the following:

Learning Center	Related Center
1. Blocks	Dramatic Play
	Writing
	Art
	Large Motor
	Manipulative/Math
	Story
	Writing

Learning Center	Related Center
2. Computer	Writing
	Manipulative/Math
	Art
	Story
3. Manipulative/Math	Computer
	Blocks
	Science
	Large Motor
4. Story	Writing
	Dramatic Play
	Blocks
	Computer
	Science
	Music
5. Writing	Computer
	Story
	Dramatic Play
	Blocks
	Art
6. Art	Computer
	Dramatic Play
	Writing
	Blocks
7. Music	Large Motor
	Story
	Manipulative/Math
8. Science	Story
	Manipulative/Math
	Computer
9. Dramatic Play	Blocks
	Art
	Writing
	Story
10. Large Motor	Blocks
	Music
	Manipulative/Math
	Dramatic Play

Looking, then, at the Block Center as a case in point, six learning centers seem to relate to block building. At the top of the list is Dramatic Play. Dramatic Play also lists Blocks at the top of its list. Thus, you might decide to locate the Block Center and the Dramatic Play Center adjacent to each other. In a like manner, the Computer Center that lists Writing first and the Writing Center that lists Computer first might well be located near each other.

To **make it simpler** for yourself, make ten small squares of paper with the name of the learning center in large letters on each, and the name of one or two of the most important areas having a relationship to it in small letters. Then, take a sheet of paper to represent the floor plan of the classroom, and move the squares around on it so that centers that have an important relationship in your program are close to one another. Obviously, the size and shape of the classroom, the doors, the sink, and other special features must be taken into consideration as you design your *self-directed learning environment.*

The space allotted to each learning center depends upon the kinds of activities that will occur in the center and the number of children expected to use the center at one time. Arrangements of particular centers will be discussed in detail in the chapters describing those centers.

• Perceiving the Activities Available

In order to become *self-directed* in the classroom, young children need to be able to recognize what is available to them. Your spacing of activities into definite centers through use of room dividers, shelves, tables, and other means will help them to understand where certain activities are to occur. For instance, two shelves of blocks against a wall does not really define the Block Center. Pulling the two shelves away from the wall and placing them at right angles to the wall and to each other marks off the area in a much more definite manner. All the learning centers in your classroom can be defined in a similar way. The learning center chapters to follow tell how.

• • • • • • • • • • Learning Center Labels

Children also recognize what is available through **picture and sign labels**. Colorful cutouts of each of your curriculum centers can be mounted on the wall or room divider of the center at children's eye level. Use construction paper of various colors to make your labels attractive. One method for making learning center labels is to trace objects from the area onto differently colored pieces of paper; cut out the objects and mount them on a large, white backing paper with words printed at the top designating the area. For example, trace unit blocks of various types (half-unit, ramp, arch, cylinder) on paper of different colors for each block. Then cut them out and paste them on the sign like a collage of blocks. Letters indicating Block Center can be cut out of colored construction paper or can be printed with colored felt-tip markers.

FIGURE 1–1 Floor Plan

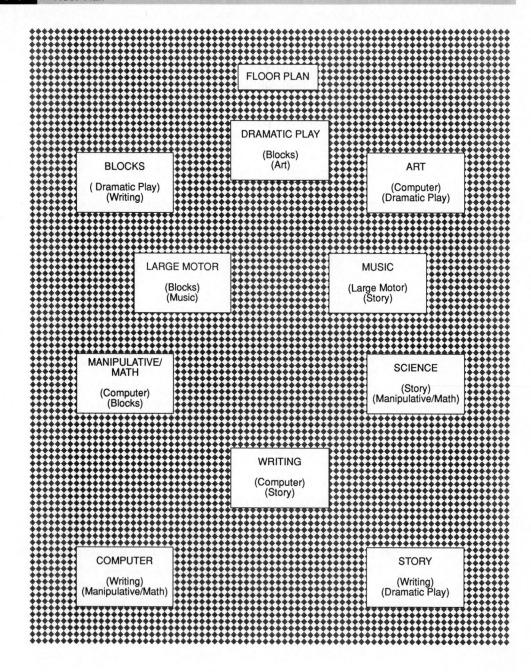

Another method is to **use a logo** for each center. An orange arch can represent Block Center, a blue floppy disk can represent Computer Center, purple puzzle pieces can represent Manipulative/Math Center, and so on. The backing paper of the sign itself can represent the area better if it is cut into the shape of the area. You might want to color-code each area by making the sign itself a certain color, having the objects on the sign in white. Then, you can cut out smaller duplicates of the same center-shaped signs and paste them on a large floor plan of the room. Use both written and graphic symbols for your signs, as children need to know how we express our names for things in words as well as in pictures.

You can find many other interesting ways for making learning center signs. **Take photos** of each learning center, enlarge them, and mount them on signs, for instance. Look in your professional library for illustrated books on each of the learning centers, make a photocopy of a relevant illustration, and then enlarge it for a sign. Or do the same with children's books showing pictures of a nursery school. The time you spend preparing the environment for the children to use is well worth your effort. Some of the most stimulating and significant hours you and your staff will occupy during the year can be those spent preparing the environment so that children will want to use it on their own. In making the classroom environment inviting for children, you will also make it inviting to work in for yourself.

• • • • • • • • • • Learning Center Maps and Schedules

Once the centers are labeled, you can make a large **illustrated floor plan** of the classroom to be mounted near the door so that children as well as visitors can identify the various centers. Be sure to mount it at the children's eye level. Children are intrigued with maps. This is a map of their classroom. They will need to learn how to read it. Introduce it to individuals and small groups at first, explaining what it is and how you will be using it. If you have pasted small colored cutouts of the learning center signs onto this floor plan as suggested above, the children will be able to match the center on the map with the center in the room designated by a larger, similar sign. However you label your learning centers, you can use a similar small label on your floor plan so that children can more easily identify the centers.

This floor plan or map is a symbol for the children. It represents or symbolizes the classroom. The children will enjoy learning to "read" this illustrated symbol of their room. They will feel proud to be able to point out to parents or visitors the various learning centers represented on it. It is only one of the many symbols they will find in a classroom following the Appropriate Practices Curriculum.

Another type of symbolization for both children and visitors is the Daily

+   Schedule of activities. This, too, can be an **illustrated schedule chart** with the learning centers shown as small, cutout signs of the center. Make this chart one that can be taken off the wall easily for discussion at morning circle time or whenever you bring the children together. The children can learn to "read" this chart, too. It will tell them what is happening in their classroom for the day and is another means for making them aware of what is available for them to choose to do in their *self-directed environment*. Let them try to match the cutout learning center symbols on the chart with the actual labels in the various centers.

An illustrated Daily Schedule should contain all the activities available for children to do during each of the time slots sequenced throughout the day. The chart can be divided into sections such as *arrival, activities, snack, outdoors, lunch, nap, activities,* and *departure*. Each section of the chart will show illustrations of the centers having special activities. If your Daily Schedule is on a bulletin board, then the cutout signs for the centers can be changed or moved around from day to day with thumb tacks as the activities change. To make the schedule more meaningful for the children, let them be the ones to move the signs on the chart. Once you begin to develop a schedule for the children to "read" daily, it will become a dynamic part of your classroom and not just a permanent list of activities tacked to the wall for your supervisor to check. See Chapter 13, "Planning for Individuals," for more information on developing this movable feast of activities.

· · · · · · · · · ·**Making Own Activity Choices and Becoming Deeply Involved**

Why should children make their own choices of the activities in a classroom? Wouldn't it be simpler for the teacher to assign children to a center or to an activity? Probably. Most children would certainly accept the teacher's assignment. After all, three-, four-, and five-year-olds are used to being told what to do by adults. Why should this program be any different?

This program may be different because it is based on current research and child development theory that says young children learn most effectively when they become deeply involved in their own learning. To become deeply involved means that they must be interested in the activity. A teacher-assigned activity may or may not be of interest to an individual child. A child's own choice is much more likely to interest him or her deeply.

A child entering a classroom for the first time may see a number of materials or activities that interest him. But in order for the child to choose to become involved in any of them, he or she must first have developed a sense of trust in himself, in the teacher, in the other children, and in the classroom itself. A new classroom, a large group of lively peers, or new adults as teachers can be quite overpowering for a three-year-old who has never been out of the family circle for long.

• • • • • • • • • • • Trust in Self

Such a child needs to learn, first of all, that she can trust herself in the classroom. That is, she needs to learn self-confidence. Will she know what she is supposed to do in the classroom? Will she be able to succeed at any of the activities? Will the teacher like her? Will the other children like her? Most of your children have these questions, doubts, and even fears, whether or not they are expressed.

To learn self-confidence, a young child needs to succeed at the activities you provide. If you have been observing the developmental levels of every child, you will be providing a wide range of activities at a variety of difficulty levels. Your support in helping the children to choose activities that interest them will send them in the right direction. Your patience in waiting for children who are not yet ready to become involved in activities will give them a chance to develop the confidence necessary to make choices in this fascinating new environment. And your provision of a **self-regulating method** to   +
help them choose activities on a rotating basis or to take turns with activities when the one they want is already occupied will help them to understand about others' needs.

The young child is highly egocentric, or self-centered. He or she looks at everything in terms of him- or herself. Yet your classroom must serve more than a dozen other children. You could spend most of your time trying to regulate individual children's behavior when more than one want to play with a certain material or activity at the same time. On the other hand, you could set up your classroom so that the children can regulate their own behavior. Children who learn to use self-regulating devices develop trust in their own abilities and confidence to explore the classroom on their own.

You can, for instance, have **tickets** for children that are color-coded for   +
each learning center. You can make as many colored tickets as there are children allowed in the center. The tickets can be placed in envelopes at the entrance to the center for the children to take as they enter. You might have six orange tickets for the Block Center, for example, that children would attach to arm bracelets. When children are ready to leave the area, they return the tickets to the envelope; or they might want to trade their orange ticket with another child who has a blue ticket for the Computer Center.

Tags are also interesting for children to use. Laminated name tags with a   +
piece of Velcro or a hole punched in one end can be hung on one of the hooks or fastened on a Velcro tab at the entrance to a center. The number of hooks or fasteners in a center would help to control the number of children using the center. Children can get their name tags from a hook or fastener on their cubby or from a tag board and hang it in the learning center of their choice. A **photo tag picture of each child** can also be made and laminated   +
with a clear contact-type paper to be used as a self-regulating device in the same manner.

For self-regulation, this classroom has a chart with Velcro-backed figures for children to remove and to place on the corresponding Learning Center chart of their choice.

+   Still another popular device is a **learning center necklace:** a yarn necklace with the learning center symbol or color code that can be worn by children while they are in a particular center. When they leave the center, they take off the necklace and return it to one of the hooks at the center entrance. Colored chips (from card games) or colored pieces (from board games) can also be selected by each child and used as a self-regulator to gain admittance into a center. Your own ingenuity and that of the children will help you to design other self-regulating devices that give children the freedom to make their own activity selections and, thus, to learn to trust themselves in this exciting new environment.

· · · · · · · · · · **Trust in the Teacher**

The child needs to learn that he can trust the teacher to allow him to make his own choices and to support him in them. He needs to feel secure that the teacher will not try to make him change his mind or place him somewhere else. ("Those puzzles are too hard for you, Jeffrey. Why don't you play with this table game?") Not only will the teacher support him in the choice he makes, but she will also support him in doing his chosen activity. Suppose he has made an activity choice that is too difficult for him. The sensitive teacher will keep an eye on his progress. If he seems to need help, she will offer it without intruding. If he seems to need direction, she will help him find the way himself, perhaps by offering alternatives. If he seems to need peer support, she may suggest to another child that he and Jeffrey work together on the activity. But if Jeffrey prefers to work alone, she will accept this preference as well.

Whatever Jeffrey does in the classroom, the teacher needs to **accept him unconditionally**. She will rejoice in his successes, help him to go on to   + something else when his chosen task is finished, and not turn against him, even when he loses self-control. She is there to support him under all conditions. She herself does not lose control when something that he does annoys her. She helps him to get back on the right track without guilt or recriminations.

Another way the teacher can help youngsters trust her is to **give them enough time** to get involved with the materials or activities of their choice.   + Too often, teachers regulate classroom activity time to suit their own convenience or their particular expectations of children. What if children need more time with an activity in order to understand and learn from it? Is it more important that everyone in the class get a turn on the computer every day, for instance, or would it be more meaningful for a few youngsters to spend an extended time with the computer once their interest is aroused? Children will learn to trust the teacher if they see that she accepts their self-regulation of time in the activities they have chosen to explore.

A final way the teacher can help the child to trust her is through her attitude and actions regarding the child's home and family. Does she **show delight when she meets one of the child's parents**? Does she show interest   + when the child talks about his home? Does she refrain from correcting his speech because she realizes this is an indirect reflection on his family? Will she allow (and even welcome) him to **bring a toy from home**? Helping a   + youngster to make the sometimes difficult transition from home to school is an important service the preschool teacher must perform for each of the children.

When the child learns through experience that he or she can trust the teacher like this, then that child will feel free to make choices in the classroom and become deeply involved in his or her learning.

· · · · · · · · · · **Trust in Peers**

Equally as important to the novice preschooler is being able to trust his or her own peers. How will the other youngsters feel about her, she may wonder on the first days or first weeks in the classroom. What if they don't like her? What if they don't play with her? What if they don't let her play with them? It is so difficult for two or three young children to let a stranger into their midst for long. As it is, many of the youngest children may relate more easily to adults than to other children since their previous experience has been principally with adult caregivers.

What can be done? Again, it is up to the teacher or other staff member to help the child become involved with peers if this is her choice. If she is ready to build with others in the Block Center, to work with a partner on the computer, or to join the dramatic play—but doesn't know how—then it is up to the teacher to give her assistance. **Gaining access to ongoing play** is especially difficult for some children of this age. Either they are too shy to intrude or too aggressive to be accepted by others. The sensitive teacher needs to help such a child find a middle ground.

Perhaps shy Betsy can do a task for the teacher with another child. If these two youngsters are compatible, then perhaps they can work together with the blocks or the computer. If Betsy is still not yet ready for the over-powering presence of a group, then the teacher may help her set up a similar activity parallel to the group activity. Parallel play like this has been found to be one of the most effective ways for preschoolers to gain entrance to ongoing group activities when they are ready. (Smith, 1982, 130)

On the other hand, if the child is too aggressive and pushy in trying to join a group, the teacher could help her to gain access by assigning her a role in the ongoing dramatic play or asking her to perform a task for the teacher that will include playing with the group. (Can she count the number of items on the "grocery store" shelf and tell the "cashier"?)

The child who displays self-confidence and trust in the teacher is usually ready to join a group. All she may need is your brief assistance in gaining group access. When the others see that you support her, they may well extend their own support. Thus, she will develop trust in her peers that will eventually free her to make her own choices and become deeply involved in her own learning.

• • • • • • • • • • Trust in the Environment

Finally, if a young child is to make choices and become deeply involved in the activities of the classroom, he must develop trust in the environment. This trust translates into: 1) an awareness of the choices available; 2) an interest in the materials; 3) a freedom to explore; and 4) time to become deeply involved. Your setting up of the environment so that young children understand it and how to use it is the first step, already mentioned. Your giving the children the freedom to explore the materials on their own and the time to become deeply involved adds immeasurably to their developing of trust in the environment.

Once young children are aware of the choices available, they need to develop an interest in the materials. Are they familiar materials? Are they appropriate for the ages and developmental levels of the children? Teachers following the Appropriate Practices Curriculum will want some of the **materials** in their classroom environments to be **similar to those found in** the **homes** of the children. Although many classroom activities will be new, different, and challenging to three-, four-, and five-year-olds, some should also be familiar. Water play, bubbles, and dough making are activities the youngsters may have first encountered at home. Teachers can set up such familiar activities early in the year to put the children at ease and then add new twists in water play and dough making as the year progresses.

The dramatic play family area with its kitchen furnishings is another familiar center that should help children build trust in the classroom environment. Later, other role-play areas can be added. Home-type furnishings such as mats or rugs, wall hangings, an easy chair or rocker, pictures, and pillows are all appropriate accessories because they help young children feel at home in school. If the children's homes are ethnic or multicultural, your classroom furnishings can reflect this as well. A Mexican serape, a native American blanket or rug, a Caribbean woven mat, a fishing net, or a paper lantern can decorate the classroom walls. If children have handicapping conditions, your materials may need special knobs or handholds.

Are the materials exciting ones? Put yourself in the place of a three-, four-, or five-year-old child coming into a new classroom. What kinds of things would you want to play with? Your children will be attracted to colorful objects, to things that look the right size and shape, to materials that look as if you can do something "neat" with them.

Teachers with programs with little money for new materials can make their own. **Homemade materials** are often the best ones anyway, since they are created for personal tastes and thus are used more frequently. Bring in empty food boxes of all sizes (cereal boxes, package mix boxes, boxes from sugar, salt, tea, or rice, for example). Let the children paint them over and then cut out pictures from magazines to be glued on them. What can they be used for? Science collections? Decorations in the family area? Pretend treasure boxes? Let the children decide.

If the learning environment is expected to help children develop trust, then one important message it can convey at the outset is: **This classroom cares** for you. It has been arranged carefully for you to understand what is available and to choose by yourself the activities that interest you most. It will also provide materials to help you to feel at home and wanted: stuffed animals for comfort while you look at a book in the Story Center, dolls to care for in the Dramatic Play Center, a box of little cars and figures of people and animals to select and hold during rest time. The pictures on the wall are at your eye level, and some designs in the Block Center are on the baseboard for you to see when you are playing on the floor.

Some classrooms go a step farther and offer children a basket of **tiny toys**
+ **to borrow** one at a time for overnight. Other programs have a second set of
+ children's **picture books for home lending**. This is yet another way to help children trust the environment by making an easy transition from home to school. Children are encouraged to take home a school material, but they are expected to return with it the next day. Such a practice builds not only great anticipation for the day ahead, but also the child's own care for materials in his or her environment.

· · · · · · · · · · · **Setting the Stage for Learning**

The self-directed learning environment is thus a dramatic one that sets the stage for learning by offering appropriately arranged learning centers responsive to the individual child's interests and needs. With this setting in place, the children can begin their exciting learning adventure of creating their own knowledge through interaction with the people and materials in their environment. The teachers can begin observing children in order to provide appropriate activities and support for the youngsters' continued growth and development. And the Appropriate Practices Curriculum to follow will evolve naturally as children and teachers work together in an atmosphere of trust and caring.

IDEAS+
in CHAPTER 1

1. *Arranging a classroom based on ten centers*
   a. Make a floor plan with cutouts. (p. 7)

2. *Helping children recognize what is available*
   a. Provide picture and sign labels. (p. 7)
   b. Use a logo. (p. 9)
   c. Take photos for signs. (p. 9)
   d. Make an illustrated floor plan. (p. 9)
   e. Make an illustrated schedule chart. (p. 10)

3. *Developing a child's self-regulating method*
   a. Use tickets. (p. 11)
   b. Use tags. (p. 11)
   c. Use a photo tag of each child. (p. 11)
   d. Use learning center necklaces. (p. 12)

4. *Developing a child's trust in the teacher*
   a. Accept the child unconditionally. (p. 13)
   b. Give children enough time to become involved. (p. 13)
   c. Show delight in meeting parents. (p. 13)
   d. Have children bring a toy from home. (p. 13)

5. *Developing a child's trust in peers*
   a. Help the child gain access to ongoing play. (p. 14)

6. *Developing a child's trust in the environment*
   a. Have materials similar to those in the home. (p. 15)
   b. Make homemade materials. (p. 15)
   c. Demonstrate that this classroom cares. (p. 15)
   d. Provide tiny toys to borrow. (p. 16)
   e. Provide picture books for home lending. (p. 16)

REFERENCES CITED

Bredekamp, S. (Ed). (1986). *Developmentally appropriate practice* (pp. 5–6). Washington, DC: National Association for the Education of Young Children.

Smith, C. A. (1982). *Promoting the social development of young children: Strategies and activities.* Palo Alto, CA: Mayfield Publishing Company.

OTHER SOURCES

Ackerman, P. L., Sternberg, R. J., & Glaser, R. (1989). *Learning and individual differences: Advances in theory and research.* New York: W. H. Freeman.

Beaty, J. J. (1990). *Observing development of the young child.* Columbus, OH: Merrill Publishing Co.

Beaty, J. J. (1992): *Skills for preschool teachers.* Columbus, OH: Merrill Publishing Co.

Buzzelli, C. A., & File, N. (1989). Building trust in friends. *Young Children, 44* (3), 70–75.

Ideas that work with young children: Child choice—another way to individualize—another form of preventive discipline (1987). *Young Children, 43* (1), 48–54.

Ideas that work with young children: Integrating individualizing into your program (1987). *Young Children, 42* (2), 18–19+.

Kantrowitz, B., & Wingert, P. (1989, April 17). How kids learn. *Newsweek,* pp. 50–57.

Lindberg, L., & Swedlow, R. (1985). *Young children exploring and learning.* Boston: Allyn & Bacon.

Myers, B. K., & Maurer, K. (1987). Teaching with less talking: Learning centers in the kindergarten. *Young Children, 42* (5), 20–27.

NAEYC position statement on developmentally appropriate practice in early childhood programs serving children from birth to age 8 (1986). *Young Children, 41* (6), 3–19.

NAEYC position statement on developmentally appropriate practice in programs for 4- and 5-year olds (1986). *Young Children, 41* (6), 20–29.

Safford, P.L. (1989). *Integrated teaching in early childhood: Starting in the mainstream.* White Plains, NY: Longman.

Siegler, R. S. (1986). *Children's thinking.* Englewood Cliffs, NJ: Prentice-Hall.

CHILDREN'S BOOKS

Cole, J., & Cole, P. (1988). *Hank and Frank fix up the house.* New York: Scholastic, Inc.

Cohen, M. (1971). *Will I have a friend?* New York: Collier Books.

Gwenda Turner's playbook. (1985). New York: Viking Kestrel/Penguin Books.

Lloyd, D., & Dale, P. (1986). *The stopwatch.* New York: Harper and Row.

Maris, R. (1983). *My book.* New York: Puffin Books.

Rockwell, H. (1984). *My nursery school.* New York: Puffin Books.

TRY IT
YOURSELF

1. Make a classroom floor plan for your program showing learning centers arranged according to the ideas presented under "Locating and Spacing Learning Centers."

2. Design picture and sign labels for all of your learning centers according to the ideas presented under "Learning Center Labels."

3. Make an illustrated schedule chart showing the Daily Schedule of activities in your program according to the ideas under "Learning Center Maps and Schedules."

4. Provide a self-regulating method for helping children to choose activities in your classroom according to the ideas discussed under "Trust in Self."

5. Carry out one of the ideas under "Trust in the Environment" to show that "this classroom cares for you." Use one that has not already been done in your classroom.

2

THE TEACHER'S ROLE

TEACHER *(Action chant)*

Good morning, teacher,	(march in place throughout)
How do you do?	(right hand wave)
Good morning, teacher,	
I'm fine, too!	(left hand pat top of head)
Good afternoon, teacher,	
I want to state:	(arms outstretched)
Good afternoon, teacher,	
I feel GREAT!	(jump)

• • • • • • • • • • •The Teacher in the Self-Directed Learning Environment

As a teacher in a *self-directed learning environment,* your role is different from that of a teacher in a traditional classroom. You have already read in Chapter 1 how to set up such a learning environment so that children can make choices and become deeply involved in their own learning. You have read how to help children make independent choices of activities through their development of trust in themselves, the teacher, their peers, and the environment. Now it is necessary to consider one of the most important tasks that a teacher in a *self-directed learning environment* must perform: that of providing appropriate curriculum materials and activities based on curriculum goals and the children's developmental levels.

This is the teacher's principal chore in a program in which the learning environment does the teaching: to provide appropriate learning materials and then to support the children in their use of them. How does she or he do it? The chapters to follow discuss ideas and activities for each of the classroom learning centers. This chapter discusses: 1) how a teacher can determine the developmental stages of the children so that the activities and materials provided will be appropriate for children at various levels of their growth; and 2) how a teacher can support the children in their interaction with the self-directed environment.

• • • • • • • • • • •Children's Developmental Levels

We recognize that young children grow and develop physically in a well-defined chronological sequence as they mature from year to year. We also realize that children simultaneously progress through certain stages of psychological, intellectual, social, language, and creative development. Growth within these ages and stages of development is not always even. Some children progress more rapidly than others, while some exhibit developmental lags. How can we help them?

One three-year-old may be speaking in expanded sentences, while another may be talking baby talk. How can we meet the needs of both these children in our classrooms? Another child may be five years old chronologically but only three years old in her social development. How will we know? And how will we know what to do about it? In order to provide appropriate materials and activities to promote the growth and learning of all the children in our classrooms, it is necessary to assess the developmental level of each child.

Determining Children's Developmental Levels

A great deal has been written about the developmental levels of children. Researchers have examined children's physical, cognitive, social, emotional, and language development, among other things. They have come up with large motor rating scales, self-concept measures, personality projective techniques, perceptual-motor surveys, language inventories, learning profiles, observational checklists, and numerous other devices for assessing the level of the young child's development. Many of these techniques are good. Some are excellent when used by trained people for their intended purpose. Few, however, speak to the practical needs of the classroom teacher or the college student preparing to become a teacher.

Early childhood classroom personnel use such tools to determine each child's developmental level in order to provide materials and activities that are appropriate for the individual. To be appropriate, such materials and activities should: appeal to his or her current interest level and ability, stimulate and prolong her involvement, challenge the child physically and intellectually, and be neither too difficult nor too easy. A big bill to fill, indeed!

Lists, scales, surveys, and inventories are fine when used by the experts. However, most classroom staff members would prefer to use a simple, sure method for determining a child's level of development on the spot . . . some easy-to-see clues that can be translated on the spot into curriculum ideas for that particular child . . . some easy-to-use observational method that takes little time but makes a great deal of sense to busy child-care workers.

The 3-M Method for Observing Interaction

Such a method is available. It is based on the research of Jean Piaget and the cognitive psychologists who followed, but it also speaks to the findings of Italian educator Maria Montessori as well. This text has adapted such information about children's cognitive and affective development and translated it into an easy-to-apply observational scheme that will help students and teachers determine a child's developmental level in the activity area in which he is working or playing. We call it **the 3-M method for observing child interaction with materials: manipulation, mastery, and meaning**.

We find it to be a practical and invaluable method for determining a child's level of involvement with materials and activities. It is the key to planning and setting up the *self-directed learning environment* so that children can choose and use the activities on their own, thus giving the teacher time to work with individuals. In addition, it speaks to the developmental level of the individual child, giving him an opportunity to interact with materials appropriate to his own age and stage of development.

Most psychologists and child-care specialists have come to agree with the premise that the child does, indeed, construct his own knowledge as Piaget's studies have shown us, and that the child proceeds through sequential stages of development as he interacts with his environment and as he matures. According to Piaget, this knowledge is of three types: physical knowledge, logico-mathematical knowledge, and social knowledge (Wadsworth, 1989, 20–21). For young children, the principal means through which they construct this knowledge is playful interaction with objects, activities, and people in their environment.

The important aspect of these findings for the child-care practioner is the *how. How* do children carry out this interaction with the objects, activities, and people in their environment that results in their acquisition of knowledge? That is the key to determining their level of development. We soon come to realize that in almost every instance, children progress through certain *sequential* and *observable* interaction stages that are directly tied to their level of maturity and development. If the teacher can recognize these stages, then she will know the child's level of development.

Stages of Interaction

Children from birth to about age seven progress through three distinct stages of playful interaction with the objects and activities that they encounter in their environment. Cognitive psychologists often speak in terms of *exploratory play*, *practice play*, and *symbolic play*. We have translated these terms into three words more meaningful for our particular use in observing children in the preschool classroom: *manipulation*, *mastery*, and *meaning*, the three M's.

Manipulation is the earliest stage of children's playful interaction with the things in their environment. They do not yet know what the objects are for, how they are supposed to work, or what they can do with them. Young children and even infants begin by manipulating objects. The infant picks up a rattle and puts it in her mouth. She drops it and kicks it with her feet.

She picks it up again and puts it in her mouth. Then she bangs it on the crib or the floor. It makes an interesting noise, so she bangs it again. This is the manipulation stage of interaction with an object. Cognitive psychologists often call this *exploratory play.* All young children, regardless of their ages, go through this *manipulation* stage with new and unfamiliar materials.

Once the infant has discovered that the best thing you can do with a rattle is to shake it or bang it so that it will make an interesting noise, she begins shaking it over and over again. She has reached the *mastery* stage of interaction. Cognitive psychologists often call this *practice play.* In order to master an object, the infant or young child repeats the appropriate actions over and over. In order to be able to shake the rattle in the first place, however, an infant must be physically mature enough to be able to hold the rattle and shake it. In addition, she must be cognitively mature enough to understand that the shaking of the rattle is what makes the noise. Thus, she needs to repeat the same action if she wants to hear the noise. Once she has reached this *mastery* stage of interaction, the infant seldom goes back to her earlier manipulation stage for long.

Most infants do not progress beyond *mastery* to the *meaning* stage of interaction. Their condition has not yet developed to the point at which they can apply their own meaning to the object or the action.

Most preschoolers, on the other hand, progress through all three stages of interaction while working with materials and activities in the classroom. They may begin at the easel, for example, by smearing paint around randomly at the *manipulation* stage, later filling their papers over and over with lines and ovals at the *mastery* stage, and eventually drawing a person at the *meaning* stage.

Thus it is possible, if you can identify the child's interaction stage, to recognize the youngster's level of development. Or, as noted by Johnson et al. in their book on play and development, "Children engage in the type of play that matches their level of cognitive development." (Johnson, Christie, & Yawkey, 1987, 8)

What a unique idea for an effective observation technique! Simply **watch children at work or play** in one of your activity areas, **and identify which of** + **the** three **interaction stages they are using**: *manipulation, mastery,* or *meaning.* This will tell you the developmental level they have reached.

Does such a system really work? Can these three stages be applied to all of the many activities that occur in a busy preschool classroom? Let's try it.

• • • • • • • • • • Manipulation

Manipulation, the first of the interaction stages, is concerned with the beginning explorations of the child with an object or activity with which he is unfamiliar. Because he does not know how the thing works, he will try it out in a variety of ways until he learns what it does and how to do it.

Take block building with unit blocks, for instance. A child in the manipulation stage often fills up containers with blocks and then dumps them out. He or she tries handling blocks in all sorts of ways but does not really build with them.

In dramatic play, a child in the manipulation stage will use new implements and paraphernalia in various strange and sometimes funny ways until he figures out how they work and what he can do with them. He may talk or shout into the sounding end of a stethoscope as if it were a microphone. He may use the round, silver eye examiner as a patch over his eye or to blow through.

Art activities readily reveal a child's manipulative stage. In the beginning, she may splash one color of paint on top of another until it covers the paper or merely swish the same color around and around in scribbles. Writing activities also begin with scribbles for the child in the manipulative stage—although many children are aware of the difference between their art scribbles and their writing scribbles.

· · · · · · · · · · **Mastery**

Once a child begins to control the medium he is working with, he spontaneously progresses to the mastery stage and seldom returns to the same manipulation. *Mastery* is often called *practice play* by cognitive psychologists. It refers to the tendency of the child to repeat the action again and again, almost as if he were practicing or drilling himself.

With blocks, a child in the mastery stage will stack one block on top of another in a tower, knock it down, and then build it over, again and again. Or he may build a long line of blocks on the floor and then build a similar line parallel to the first one or on top of it, like a wall.

In dramatic play, the two-year-old who has progressed through manipulation of the baby doll and the cradle may now put the baby to bed in the cradle, cover it with the blanket, rock the baby, and then take everything out of the cradle and do it all over again—many times.

Once children have gained control of an art medium through manipulation, they will repeat the same operation over and over, such as painting parallel lines on several easel papers or making nothing but rows and rows of cookies out of play dough.

· · · · · · · · · · **Meaning**

The more advanced stage of children's interaction with materials occurs when the children have finally gotten control of the medium through *ma-*

nipulation and *mastery.* Now they are ready to add their own *meaning* to the activity if their cognitive development is advanced enough. It is fascinating to observe how children do this. More often than not, children in completely different programs who are in the meaning stage of interaction will spontaneously use materials in the same way.

With unit blocks, children build the same kinds of buildings. In dramatic play, most children play doctor by giving shots. With painting or drawing materials, children around the world all draw their first spontaneous human as a "tadpole man" with arms and legs attached to the big head/body. Even with computer programs, children in different nursery schools and kindergartens make up their own, almost identical games after mastering a similar piece of computer software (Beaty, 1987). It seems as though we human beings are certainly stamped out of the same mold, doesn't it?

Time Frame

How long are children in each of these three interaction stages? "As long as is necessary" is the best answer we can give at present. Observe your own children and keep track of how long they do fill-and-dump manipulation-type activities in the Block Center before they begin to build the mastery-stage towers or roads over and over. It may differ with every child.

It is true that the 3-M interaction stages are loosely tied to age, that is, the younger the child is, the longer he or she seems to stay in the earlier stages. Maturity plays an important part, but so does practice. Children need the opportunity and time to interact with both familiar and unfamiliar materials and activities. Because children progress through the three interaction stages at differing rates, be sure to give them the time necessary for this spontaneous, self-taught learning to occur.

But, would it not be more helpful for the teacher to show the immature child how to build with blocks or draw with paints? He could then progress through the stages more quickly and catch up with his more advanced peers. No. The way that the young child constructs knowledge is through his *own* interaction with materials, activities, and people in his environment. For a teacher to show him how does not really add to his understanding, and it may, in fact, detract from his accomplishments. He needs to pursue the activities on his own and in his own way. That is the whole point in having a *self-directed learning environment.* The teacher's task is something quite different.

The Teacher's Task

The learning environment is in place. The children have chosen activities to pursue. Everyone is busily engaged. Now, what does the teacher do? The

The teacher makes specific observations of particular children to see how they are getting along, to listen to what they are saying, and to determine their level of involvement.

teacher or teaching team in such a classroom has four distinct tasks to perform:

1. Observe and listen to children in learning centers.
2. Record the observations.
3. Respond to individuals as they work and play.
4. Serve as a behavior model for the children.

• Observing Children's Interactions with Materials

As the teacher circulates around the room, she or he will first make general observations to be sure that children are comfortable with their self-selected activities. Then, she will begin specific observations of particular children to see how they are getting along, to listen to what they are saying, and to determine their level of involvement.

How good is your observer's eye? You will need to keep it carefully focused on what children are doing with materials and with one another. In a *self-directed learning environment*, it is this ongoing, focused observation that reveals whether the curriculum is working. The teacher who has carefully arranged the environment and supplied the materials to meet the learning and developmental needs of her children now needs to find out whether children are really able to become involved in activities in meaningful ways.

What will you look for? First of all, try to determine whether a child is interacting with materials at the manipulative, mastery, or meaning level of involvement. When you see three-year-old Ben pull all the blocks off the shelf, load up the large wooden dump truck with them, and then dump them out, you will recognize that he is interacting at the manipulative stage of learning. You will want to make a note of this on a *Child Interaction Form* observation tool as described on page 32.

When you see that Julie at the easel is making blue circles all over her paper, then tearing off the paper and beginning again with another page of blue circles, you will realize that she is at the mastery level of drawing skills because she is performing the same task over and over.

At a nearby table, Paul is having trouble making a puzzle on a puzzle board. He picks up a puzzle piece and tries to force it into a hole. When it does not fit immediately, he does not rotate the piece to match it with the hole or try it in another hole. He leaves it on the board and picks up another piece to try. Soon he is frustrated, dumps all the pieces on the table, and leaves.

Because he is actually trying to make the puzzle rather than playing randomly with the pieces, you realize that he is past the manipulative stage of puzzle making. Had he struggled awhile until he finally got it right, you might then see him doing the puzzle over again as children often do at the mastery level. Should you intervene or not? It will depend on the circumstances as well as on your knowledge of Paul and the puzzle.

You might decide to sit with Paul awhile, handing him a piece at a time and encouraging him to try each one in different ways. On the other hand, you may realize from previous observations of Paul and of the puzzle's use that this particular puzzle is simply too difficult for him. You may, instead, encourage him to try a simpler puzzle. Be sure to record Paul's efforts, whatever happens.

• Observing Children's Interactions with One Another

In addition to observational data about the children's stages of interaction with materials, you will want to **note how children are interacting socially with one another**. Social play categories you may want to observe   +
include some originally described by Parten (1932):

1. Unoccupied behavior
2. Onlooker behavior
3. Solitary, independent play
4. Parallel activity
5. Cooperative play

Children who are new to a preschool classroom sometimes begin with *unoccupied behavior* rather than getting involved with activities. They may stay in one spot, follow the teacher around, or simply wander around the room. The sensitive teacher understands that they may need time to gain self-confidence before they become involved with classroom activities. She will note this on her observational record but will not pressure the child to join in.

As the unoccupied child becomes more at ease in the classroom, he or she may exhibit *onlooker behavior,* that is, spending time watching what other children are doing, but not joining in. If the teacher realizes that such behavior is the next step in the child's development of social skills, she will again not make an issue of it and force the child to join in, but simply encourage him to choose an activity that he might like to try on his own awhile, yet leave him alone if he does not.

Solitary, independent play is the next level of social interaction. Many children play by themselves in the early childhood classroom, especially the younger or more inexperienced youngsters. Even more mature children at the mastery or meaning stages of art activities frequently like to paint, draw, or construct things on their own. You should make note of this and then observe whether these children ever interact with others.

As children become more aware of what others are doing, they may begin to play close to them in a *parallel activity.* A great deal of the play that goes on in an early childhood classroom is of this parallel nature. Two children will build block houses side by side but not interact with each other in any other way.

Cooperative play is easy for the teacher to identify when she notes several children playing together with the same materials, each adding to the play or following what the others have decided to do. Again, this interaction can be recorded on the Child Interaction Form.

• Listening to What Children Say

How good is your observer ear? You need to **keep it carefully tuned to what children are saying as they interact** with both the materials and one another. Some children may seem to be talking to themselves, saying over and over just under their breath what it is they are doing, in a kind of self-talk. Other children may talk to their neighbors, asking questions, making statements, or giving directions. Sometimes they wait for a reply, sometimes not. Some of the children are carrying on a true conversational dialogue with other children.

In all these situations, the children's words may give you a clue to their thinking or their level of development. A child's words may help you decide whether she needs more practice in her self-selected activity or whether she is ready to extend her learning with new materials. If you can do it unobtrusively, try to record this talk verbatum.

Observing children's actions and listening to their words is another key to the self-directed environment. Because children are in control of their own learning, teachers need to spend a great deal of time observing and listening in order to plan for individuals. From their observations, teachers can learn:

1. What is the child's interaction level (manipulation, mastery, or meaning)?
2. What is the child's social involvement (unoccupied, onlooker, solitary, parallel, or cooperative)?
3. What should the teacher do next (intervene or not, make comments or ask questions, bring in new material, etc.)?

• Recording Observations

It is important that you **make on-the-spot recordings of the child observations** you are performing during the activity period. If you wait until later, you will have lost the moment. So many things occur with even one child alone that it is nearly impossible to remember all that you have seen and heard unless you write it down.

As a facilitator of learning in a self-directed classroom, your task is to observe and record each child every day. How else will you know whether your curriculum is working? How else will you discern what to arrange next for the children? You may want to repeat certain activities day after day. On the other hand, the Science Center may need expanding. Ben may need a set of table blocks and boxes to give him other manipulative experiences with blocks before he is ready for actual building. Julie may need a whole pad of paper and a box of watercolors to give her additional practice in her mastery of a brush and paint. Paul may need simpler puzzles to work on and you to sit beside him while he tries. How would you know all of this (and so much more) if you had not observed and recorded it?

The teacher in a recent NAEYC videotape states: "For me the key to creating an effective curriculum is constant observation of the children" (NAEYC, 1989). This is so true. The teacher in the Appropriate Practices Curriculum is not at the front of the classroom teaching. She or he is circulating throughout the room, watching how children are interacting with the materials and activities that she has so carefully set up for them. Most importantly, she is **writing down how each of the children is using the materials, interacting with peers, and talking about it**.

• The Child Interaction Form

Using an observation tool for data collecting helps observers focus on particular aspects of child behavior. Because you will be looking for child interaction with materials in the learning centers as well as children's interactions with one another, an observation form that features such data is especially helpful. Use of the one-sheet *Child Interaction Form* can be made by observers in each of the learning centers, either for individual children or for all the children in a particular learning center on a particular day.

A number of these blank forms can be located on the tops of cabinets and shelf dividers or on clipboards in each learning center. Observers can then record what individuals are doing in each center on a particular day. A different sheet can be used for each child in the learning center, or one sheet can be used to record the actions of all the children in that center.

If the child moves on from one learning center to another, you may want to carry the form along with you to record his or her words and actions. It is also helpful for more than one observer to record data on a single form in a cumulative manner. If you are using one form to record what happens to all the children in a particular learning center, that form will, of course, be left in that center.

On the back of each Child Interaction Form is space to record an individual child's *Accomplishments* and *Needs* as well as your *Plans* for the child or for the learning center. This **interpretive information can be recorded at the time that the observation is made or later**, say, at the end of the day if this is more convenient. All the data collected can then be gone over at the end of the day to give you and the staff feedback about individual children and particular learning centers. In addition, **this data serves as the basis**

FIGURE 2–1	Child Interaction Form

Child_____   Observer_____

Center_____   Date_____

CHILD INTERACTION FORM
With Materials

Manipulation Level   Actions/Words
(Child moves materials around
without using them as intended.)

Mastery Level   Actions/Words
(Child uses materials as
intended, over and over.)

Meaning Level   Actions/Words
(Child uses materials in
new and creative ways.)

With Other Children

Solitary Play   Actions/Words
(Child plays with
materials by self.)

Parallel Play   Actions/Words
(Child plays next to others with same
materials but not involved with them.)

Cooperative Play   Actions/Words
(Child plays together with
others and same materials.)

+   **for individual planning** during weekly or monthly sessions as discussed in
    Chapter 13, "Planning for Individuals."

    Each of the following chapters discusses use of the Child Interaction
    Form in a particular learning center. Kinds of behavior to look for as the
    child interacts with materials and other children are presented as exam-

ples. Interpreting the observations and making individual plans are then featured in Chapter 13, "Planning for Individuals."

• Responding to Individual Children as They Work and Play

Not only does the teacher in the self-directed learning environment observe and record child behavior, she or he also responds to individuals in the learning centers. **Her response** may be in words or in actions, but its intention **is to give the child support, encouragement, and direction** in the activity he has chosen. The teacher remembers that her role is not to teach in the traditional sense of the word, but to facilitate learning so that the child can learn from the environment. In other words, the child teaches himself.

This teacher-child interaction, however, is equally as important as any other feature of the classroom. It takes skill and practice on the teacher's part to respond appropriately. Because of the teacher's thoughtful response, the child's thinking should be challenged, his self-confidence should be reinforced, and his learning should be extended to new levels. It is obvious, then, that the teacher's response to a child in the Appropriate Practices Curriculum is not simply small talk or empty praise. It is, instead, carefully thought-through comments in the form of statements that reflect the child's actions. Or it may be in the form of carefully worded questions that help the teacher learn what the child is doing or thinking or that help the child reformulate his own ideas.

• Making Comments that Reflect the Child's Actions

As the teacher observes in the Manipulative/Math Center, she notices that Adrianne is carefully lining up all the dominoes so that the dots or blanks on half of one domino match the dots or blanks on the next domino. Adrianne has to search at some length to find domino blocks whose dots match. The teacher has not seen her performing at this level before. She wonders whether Adrianne has ever played the game before—at home, for instance. Before making a comment, the teacher spends more time observing and then carefully thinks through what she is going to say.

She could ask, "Where did you learn to play dominoes, Adrianne?" But this question assumes that Adrianne was taught by someone else, which may not be the case. What if Adrianne taught herself, for instance?

This teacher knows that her statements and questions should first of all be supportive of what children are doing, not prying or trying to elicit the "correct" answer. She also knows that empty praise is not really helpful in support of what the child is doing. This teacher realizes that one of the best ways of supporting what a child is doing is to **make a comment that reflects**

+ **specifically what the teacher sees**. This usually prompts the child to reply in a way that illuminates the experience for both teacher and child.

"Adrianne, I see that you are putting together dominoes that have the same number of dots. You have a long line of dominoes that match one another."

Although this statement seems very matter-of-fact and not particularly full of praise, the teacher's tone of voice expresses her excitement.

Adrianne looks up with a smile and answers, "I found all the dominoes, even 'six.' My brother can't count to six. He's only two." Then she goes back to work finding more dominoes to put at the end of her line.

The teacher's comment, reflecting what she sees the child doing, has helped in three ways: 1) It summarizes what the child is doing, which clarifies things for both teacher and child; 2) it prompts the child to respond, which gives the teacher insight into the child's thinking; and 3) it indirectly encourages the child to continue.

The teacher jots down on the Child Interaction Form under *Mastery:* "Adrianne is matching a long line of dominoes accurately." On the back of the form, under *Accomplishments,* she notes: "Matching dominoes by numbers of dots; first time." Under *Needs,* she writes: "Play with other children." Finally, under *Plans,* she writes; "Suggest she play dominoes with someone else tomorrow."

The teacher realizes that the dominoes on the manipulative shelf have never been used as a game in the classroom. Most of the children merely stack them up at a manipulative level. Tomorrow, the teacher will set up a table for a dominoes game with Adrianne, if she is interested, and with another child who would choose to play. This would not be a game with rules for the children to win or lose, but an opportunity to try out their matching skills at a mastery level.

The teacher then wonders how Adrianne will eventually play dominoes at the meaning level—maybe by making up her own game. This teacher knows that she will need to find other number and matching games that will extend Adrianne's learning. She is even more excited about setting up the dominoes game in the Manipulative/Math Center for the next day to see who else will choose to play and who may exhibit mastery skills in matching like Adrianne.

Another way a teacher could respond to a child after observing her actions is to **ask a question in a way that will elicit a statement from the**
+ **child about her work**. She needs to be careful not to ask the question bluntly. For instance, she should avoid a question such as: "What are you doing, Adrianne?" Adrianne, who has been interrupted, may not even answer, or she may reply only: "I'm playing dominoes." Far better is the specific and detailed question: "Can you tell me what you are doing with the domino blocks, Adrianne?" Or the teacher may challenge the child: "What other way could you match those dominoes, Adrianne?"

As you note, the purpose for a teacher's verbal response to a child's work in a learning center should be:

1. To give support and encouragement
2. To challenge his thinking
3. To extend his learning
4. To help the teacher decide what to do next to support the child or extend his learning

She will avoid terms of judgment, such as: "That's very good, Roger" or "I like the way you did that." Instead, she will describe specifically and non-judgmentally what the child is doing: "Roger, you are stacking the blocks up very high today!" The teacher should also avoid comparisons of one child with another, although she may compare a child's current actions with previous ones: "Roger, you stacked your blocks more evenly today than you did yesterday." She hopes that Roger will reply to her as well, which she can then note on her observation form as an indicator of his thinking. If she feels that it is appropriate (based on previous observations of Roger), the teacher may then respond: "What other ways could you stack blocks?" He may be used to this kind of challenge from his teacher and take her up on it. On the other hand, he may not be finished building his tower, since children in the mastery stage seem to need a certain amount of practice of a particular skill before they move on.

It is not necessary for the teacher to respond to every child every time she sees him. As she circulates around the room, she will be observing and recording carefully the actions and words of each child. She then needs to use her good sense of timing on when to intervene with a comment or a question, and when not to intervene. With a child who is deeply involved in a project of his own, she may not want to interrupt. On the other hand, some children may need her help or redirection to continue an activity or to start something new.

In reviewing her recorded comments at the end of the day, the teacher will have an idea about which children she needs to interact with, which children she needs to make a comment to, and which children may be better off not being disturbed. For Brian, who has finally stopped following her around and has joined the children at the water table for the first time, it would be foolish for her to make a comment that could divert his attention back to her again. Experience and practice in this type of classroom interchange is the best way for the teacher to learn when to respond to individual children and when to leave them alone.

• Serving as a Behavior Model for the Children

A fourth important task for the teacher in a self-directed learning environment is to serve as a behavior model for the children. The Appropriate

Practices Curriculum presented here follows three thematic ideas intertwined throughout this textbook:

1. *Let the learning environment do the teaching* because the preliterate child learns best through independent exploration of self-selected activities arranged by the teacher.

2. *Let the teacher be the facilitator of learning* by observing children's developmental stages in the activity areas, by supporting children's growth and learning through her responses, and by serving as a behavior model for learning in the various classroom areas.

3. *Let the children learn to care* by following the teacher's example in learning to care about themselves, about one another, and about their environment.

• Facilitator of Learning

To be a successful facilitator of learning in such an environment, the teacher needs to **put herself or himself in the place of the child** as often as possible. In order to set an example as a learner, she needs to understand what it feels like to be a learner in a self-discovery environment. She needs to try out (or think about how it would be to try out) the various activities from the point of view of a three-, four-, or five-year-old child. What would she do with the materials upon encountering them for the first time? How would she find out how to use them? What questions would she want answered? What help would she elicit from her classmates?

She can discover the answers to such questions by observing what the children do or ask. Then, she will know how to behave as a learning model herself. When someone asks her how to play dominoes and she finds she does not know, she might respond as a child would: "Let's make up our own game. How would you like to play it?" When someone asks her a math or science question with which she is unfamiliar, she might answer: "Let's see if we can find the answer together. Where will we begin?"

The teacher in such a classroom adopts the *curiosity* of a child about finding out how things work and what they are for. Above all, such a teacher needs to take on the *enthusiasm* of the child who has encountered a new object or a new idea for the first time. Learning is one of the great adventures of life. It should be as thrilling and exciting as you can make it!

• A Model of Caring

Finally, the teacher needs to **set the stage and lead the way about caring**. Children need to learn to care about themselves, about one another, and about their environment. Their behavior will reflect how they care. If they care about themselves, they will show it by being self-confident, helpful, happy, and cooperative. They will not do things that are destructive to themselves, such as disregarding safety practices.

If children care about one another, they will work and play together cooperatively. They will "help each other toward constructive work," says Sally Cartwright in her article on group endeavor. "In a relaxed, noncompetitive atmosphere, they come to be warmly responsive to one another" (Cartwright, 1987, 8, 10). They will not be aggressive toward one another nor destructive with another child's possessions. They will share, help one another, and take turns peacefully.

If children care about their environment, they will participate in keeping it in good shape, in not being destructive to materials, and in helping to pick up and clean up.

The teacher can serve as a behavior model in all three of these regards, first by caring for herself. She (or he) can **present herself as a happy, confident person** who enjoys her job. She can dress attractively: Whether in jeans or a dress, she can be neat, clean, and well-groomed. Children like colorful clothing. Let the teacher wear a bright blouse or shirt to show that she or he likes to look nice for the children. Working with active young children is physically draining for an adult. The teacher can keep herself healthy by eating nutritiously and getting enough sleep so that she is peppy and alert for the day's activities.

The teacher also needs to demonstrate her care for others: first of all, her care for the children in the classroom. By **showing her delight in what they are doing**, in what they are wearing, in the interesting things that are happening in their families, by showing her concern over their health, over the things that are bothering them, over problems facing their families, she will help children realize that the teacher cares about them. **By listening seriously** to what the children have to say, **by not "talking down"** to children but conversing with them as she would with a friend, the teacher lets them know she cares. She can also demonstrate her care for others in the classroom **by treating the assistants or student interns as she would like to be treated herself**.

Finally, the teacher needs to show her care for the environment of the classroom, the building, and the playground by helping to keep it clean, in order, and beautiful. What can you do to **add beauty to your learning environment**? Perhaps a plant or a picture will spruce it up. A coat of paint on the walls or varnish on the shelves may help. During cleanup time, you can lead the way by helping pick up materials and arrange them attractively on the shelves. Perhaps the children will help you plant a tree on the playground. They could help you frame their own art for display in the halls or office.

The chapters to follow are full of suggestions for caring: for yourself, for one another, and for the environment. When teachers and children work to-gether toward these goals, an Appropriate Curriculum will evolve almost on its own.

IDEAS +
in CHAPTER 2

1. *Determining children's developmental levels*
   a. Use the 3-M method for observing child interaction: manipulation, mastery, and meaning. (p. 23)
   b. Watch children at work or play and identify which of the three interaction stages they are using. (p. 24)
   c. Note how children are interacting socially with one another. (p. 29)
   d. Keep carefully tuned to what children are saying as they interact. (p. 30)

2. *Recording child observations*
   a. Make on-the-spot recordings of child observations. (p. 30)
   b. Write down how child uses materials, interacts with peers, and talks about it. (p. 31)
   c. Use an observation tool to help focus. (p. 31)
   d. Record interpretive information at time of observation or at end of day. (p. 31)
   e. Use this data as basis for individual planning. (pp. 31–32)

3. *Responding to individual children*
   a. Give support, encouragement, direction. (p. 33)
   b. Make comments that reflect specifically what you see. (pp. 33–34)
   c. Ask questions in a way that will elicit a statement about a child's work. (p. 34)
   d. Avoid using terms of judgment. (p. 35)

4. *Serving as a behavior model for the children*
   a. Put yourself in the place of the child. (p. 36)
   b. Set the stage and lead the way about caring. (p. 36)
   c. Present yourself as a happy, confident person. (p. 37)
   d. Show your delight in what children are doing. (p. 37)
   e. Listen seriously to children. (p. 37)
   f. Avoid "talking down" to children. (p. 37)
   g. Treat assistants and interns as you would like to be treated. (p. 37)
   h. Add beauty to your learning environment. (p. 37)

REFERENCES CITED

Beaty, J. J., & Tucker, W. H. (1987). *The computer as a paintbrush.* Columbus, OH: Merrill Publishing Company.

Cartwright, S. (1987). Group endeavor in nursery school can be valuable. *Young Children, 42* (5), 8–11.

Johnson, J. E., Christie, J. F., & Yawkey, T. D. (1987). *Play and early childhood development.* Glenview, IL: Scott, Foresman.

NAEYC. (1989). *Developmentally appropriate practice: Curriculum—the role of the teacher* (video #856). Washington, DC: National Association for the Education of Young Children.

Parten, M. B. (1932). Social participation among pre-school children. *Journal of Abnormal and Social Psychology, 27,* 243–269.

Wadsworth, B. J. (1989). *Piaget's theory of cognitive and affective development.* New York: Longman.

OTHER SOURCES

Beaty, J. J. (1990). *Observing development of the young child.* Columbus, OH: Merrill Publishing Company.

Beaty, J. J. (1992). *Skills for preschool teachers.* Columbus, OH: Merrill Publishing Company.

Feeney, S., Christensen, D., & Moravcik, E. (1987). *Who am I in the lives of young children?* Columbus, OH: Merrill Publishing Company.

Hitz, R., & Driscoll, A. Praise or encouragement? New insights into praise: Implications for early childhood teachers (1988). *Young Children, 43* (5), 6–13.

Lay-Dopyera, M., & Dopyera, J. (1987). *Becoming a teacher of young children.* New York: Random House.

Rogers, D. L., Boggs Waller, C., & Sheerer Penn, M. Learning more about what makes a good teacher through collaborative research in the classroom (1987). *Young Children, 42* (4), 34–39.

TRY IT
YOURSELF

1. Observe the children in your class and record (giving specific details) three different examples of children in the manipulative level of interaction. What is their level of social interaction based on your evidence?

2. Observe and record three different examples of children interacting at the mastery level, giving specific details; give evidence for their level of social interaction.

3. Record any children interacting at the meaning level, and try to capture on paper their conversations as well as their actions. What social levels of interaction do they display?

4. How would you respond to the children you have recorded in number 1, and why?

5. How can you serve as a learning model for the children recorded in number 2? Why?

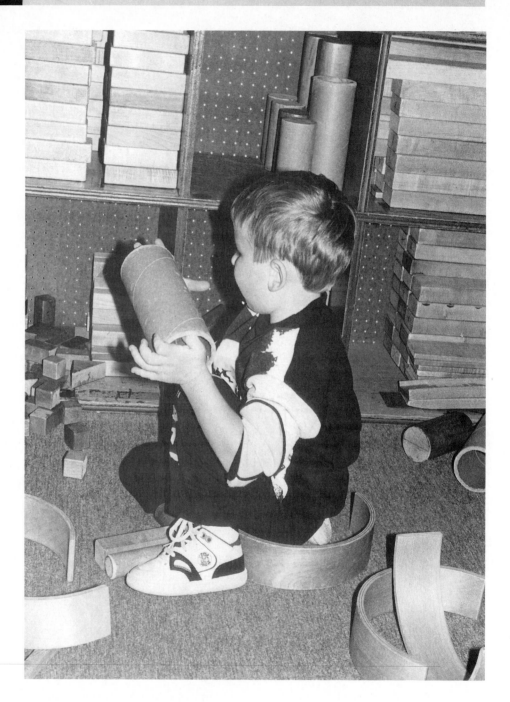

BLOCK CENTER

B L O C K S   *(Action chant)*

Towers and tunnels,	Some stack them gently,
Bridges and locks;	Others use knocks;
How do you build them?	Then down they tumble,
With blocks, blocks, blocks!	Those blocks, blocks, blocks!
A doll house, a farm house,	Pick them up quickly,
A road or a box;	No looking at clocks,
How can you make them?	When you are building
With blocks, blocks, blocks!	With blocks, blocks, blocks!

(March in circle for first three lines of each verse; stop and clap three times on last line of each verse)

• • • • • • • • • • • Curriculum Role of Blocks

Building with unit blocks has long been a favorite nursery school activity for both children and their teachers. Children love the feel of the smooth wood; they enjoy the clacking noise blocks make when you build with them; and they especially delight in the immensity of the buildings they can create all on their own. No teacher has to tell them what to do or how to do it. With blocks, there is no right or wrong.

Teachers, by the same token, like block-building activities because children enjoy them and because children can do them on their own without teacher help or interference. It is a classroom activity area that, once arranged, can be left on its own—or so it used to be.

Teachers using the Appropriate Practices Curriculum realize that there is more to unit block play than meets the eye. Not only can children play with blocks on their own—the key to the construction of their knowledge, as we have learned—but also the kinds of learning that children can accomplish in the Block Center touches on every facet of their growth and development in a way that few other learning activities do. Block building can contribute to children's development in physical, cognitive, language, social, emotional, and creative areas.

Children learn the physical skills of holding, stacking, and balancing blocks. They learn the social skills of sharing and cooperation. Their language is expanded through speaking and listening to others. Their creativity is enhanced by being able to build stupendous structures of their own design. All this activity promotes a positive feeling about themselves as worthy human beings. And their cognitive development? Almost every intellectual skill from categorizing, to counting, to problem solving is available for children's acquisition in a Block Center arranged with care by knowledgeable teachers.

Blocks are there to be used by children every day. But it is the creative teacher who arranges his or her Block Center and supplies the appropriate accessories that ensures that this important curriculum area serves the needs of every child most effectively. It is the sensitive teacher who observes what children are doing with blocks and saying about blocks, that knows how to rearrange and add to this curriculum area so that exciting learning will continue on a daily basis.

· · · · · · · · · · **The Block Play Story**

A long and fascinating history lies behind the blocks our children play with today. The history of block play, in fact, reflects the history of the early childhood movement in our country and in Europe. Started in Germany by the "father of the kindergarten," Frederick Froebel, block play became an integral part of his curriculum as early as the 1830s and 1840s. He believed that young children learned best through play, through self-expression, and through creativity with living things and movable objects. Thus, he developed a series of twenty "gifts" and "occupations" (i.e., educational materials and activities) for children to play with and learn from.

Several of his gifts were wooden cubes so split and divided that they became little table blocks with a 1-inch base and a height ranging from 1 to 12 inches (Provenzo & Brett, 1983). As children took them apart, reassembled them, and built with them, they learned differentiation, classification, and categorization skills, as well as numbers and counting. Thus began the use of blocks as an integral part of an early childhood curriculum wherever Froebel's ideas were adopted.

Following the Civil War in America, the Crandall family dominated the toy block industry, developing interlocking blocks and nesting blocks. Toy catalogs from that era show various types of alphabet blocks and construction blocks as well. German and later American companies also produced popular little cast-stone building bricks of various colors that parents bought for their children to play with during the last quarter of the nineteenth century and into the twentieth century (Provenzo & Brett, 1983).

Blocks for preschool educational purposes were also used by Italian physician-educator Maria Montessori in the early childhood program she developed at the turn of the century. One of her still-used block-building exercises consists of ten graduated wooden cubes called the "pink tower." However, *free play* with blocks was not advocated by any of the pioneer educators until the appearance of Carolyn Pratt from Fayetteville, New York, at the turn of the century (Koepke, 1989).

• • • • • • • • • •**Carolyn Pratt and Unit Blocks**

Pratt formulated her philosphy of early childhood education by observing children playing with materials. She saw one six-year-old boy so absorbed by his own creating with blocks that she never forgot it:

A child playing on his nursery floor, constructing an entire railroad system out of blocks and odd boxes he had salvaged from the wastepaper basket taught me that the play impulse in children is really a work impulse. Childhood's work is learning, and it is in his play . . . that the child works at his job. (Pratt, 1948, 10)

From then on, she was determined to develop a school for young children based on the free play impulse, using educational toys of her own design created to meet the needs of the children she observed.

While attending Teacher's College at Columbia University in 1892, Pratt noted that Patty Hill Smith, another pioneer early childhood educator, had developed large, slotted wooden blocks for the children in her laboratory kindergarten, with which the children could build child-sized houses in their free time. In her autobiography, *I Learn from Children,* Pratt reminisces:

Of all the materials I had seen offered to children . . . these blocks of Patty Hill's seemed to be best suited to children's purposes. A simple geometrical shape could become any number of things to a child. It could be a truck or a boat or the car of a train. He could build buildings with it from barns to skyscrapers. I could see the children of my yet unborn school constructing a complete community with blocks. (Pratt, 1948, 29)

With these ideas in mind, Pratt developed what we now call unit blocks, a unit being a block 5½ by 3¾ by 1⅜ inches. There were half units, double units, and quadruples, as well as curves, arches, ramps, triangles, pillars, cylinders, and switches. The blocks were of smooth, natural-finish hardwood—free from details or color. In addition, she designed unpainted wooden people, 6 inches tall, in the form of family members and community workers, to be used with the unit blocks. She omitted painted details on any of her toys because she wanted children to apply their own imaginations in their use of the materials.

She also designed large hollow blocks, ladders, walking planks, platform trucks, wooden interlocking floor trains, homemaking areas with child-size equipment, rhythm band instruments, and on, and on, and on. All these toys evolved directly from her work with children, especially those in her own Playschool, which eventually became New York's City and Country School (Caplan & Caplan, 1974). Today this equipment is such an accepted part of every preschool program that few people realize it all came from a young woman from upstate New York with a calling to teach and a vision about creating a school in which children would teach themselves through play.

Another pioneer educator and co-worker with Pratt, Harriet M. Johnson, validated Pratt's block-play ideas with her own careful observations of children's use of unit blocks in her nursery school during the 1920s and 1930s. She published the results in 1933 as "The Art of Blockbuilding," a classic observational study outlining universal stages of young children's block building as: repetition, bridging, enclosures, patterns, and representation (Johnson, 1974). Her ideas became an integral part of the Bank Street School she helped to found. Today we accept the block corner as an essential learning center in preschool classrooms everywhere.

· · · · · · · · · · **Setting Up the Block Center**

If your children are to choose blocks as an activity to engage in on their own, then the center needs to be arranged attractively and effectively. As with other centers in the classroom, children will choose to become involved with blocks if they can easily see what is available, if there are enough materials to make the activity viable, and if there is space enough to use the materials effectively.

With **unit blocks** it is essential that you **stock your shelves with enough
\+   of them.** Many nursery-school block sets are simply too small to allow effective building activities for more than one or two children at a time. Instead, it is important for you to order either large numbers of individual types of blocks to fit your own space and program needs or to order the full set of kindergarten blocks for twenty children.

Toy catalogs often list nursery-school sets as having 276 blocks in 11 shapes, whereas kindergarten sets have 644 blocks in 19 shapes. You will need the larger number of blocks if you expect children to build really large buildings that will teach them important skills in all the child development areas. On the other hand, it is not necessary to have 19 block shapes. Large numbers of blocks in a half-dozen of the basic shapes are a much more sensible purchase. Although unit blocks are expensive items, they are worth every penny spent when you consider the importance of their teaching/learning benefits.

Second to numbers of blocks is the **arrangement of the blocks length-
\+   wise on shelves at the children's height** for their easy access and return. Children should be able to see which blocks are available, need to be able to choose them easily, and then should be able to return them to their proper shelves when finished. The reason for such an arrangement is not merely a

housekeeping detail; instead, it is an essential learning arrangement for children in a self-directed environment.

For example, block activities are an effective method for teaching the cognitive concepts of shape and size. Therefore, children need to see clearly which sizes and shapes of blocks are available. Blocks also teach categorizing and matching skills. Therefore, children need to be able to return them to their proper places by matching their shapes against the cutout block labels you have mounted on every shelf or against the blocks remaining on the shelves.

For the same reasons, blocks should be stored lengthwise on shelves rather than in boxes, bins, or carts. Wooden carts and bins on toy catalog pages look neat and appealing; but in actual classroom use, they tend to be dumping grounds for mixed piles of blocks, after which the children cannot choose, find, or use the blocks easily. If we want real learning to take place in our activity areas, then we must arrange the materials so that they are usable. If we want children to use the materials with respect, then we must show our own respect by arranging and storing them carefully.

The **Block Center** itself should be **spacious in size with a carpet on the floor and its borders defined by block shelves.** Most classrooms carpet their block areas because the children sit on the floor to build, but too many classrooms do not separate this area from the rest of the classroom using shelf dividers. Instead, their block shelves stand against the wall, leaving the area open for all kinds of traffic: walkers, runners, and even riders of large wooden vehicles. To build in such an area, children take the chance that their buildings will be destroyed by accident or on purpose. "Oh well," you may respond, "don't children enjoy knocking down block buildings?" Yes, they do knock down their *own* buildings—often with relish and always with learning—but such tumbling down of the blocks should be of their own choice, not an outsider's.

Block Accessories

What should the Block Center contain other than blocks, you may wonder? The **materials** for this and every classroom activity area will **depend upon what you want to happen** in the area and **what you want children to learn.** Do you want children to build large and creative buildings in the Block Center? Then you will provide them will a good supply of unit blocks that they can choose and use easily. Do you want children to be able to build undisturbed? Then you will park large trucks and riding vehicles elsewhere. You will also store large, hollow blocks in the Large Motor Center since their use as a building material is entirely different from that of unit blocks. You will also store small table blocks and interlocking bricks in the Manipulative/Math Center for still a different use.

Do you want children to pretend and to use their imaginations as they build? Then you will want to stock the Block Center with all kinds of accessories to promote such creativity. Do you want children to represent in their building the field trips they have taken, the stories they have heard, or the visits from outside specialists they have had? Then you will want to stock the center with particular accessories to promote such pretending. Following are some of the little toys that children enjoy using with blocks currently available from toy catalogs and stores:

Sets of people such as:	*Sets of vehicles such as:*
Family members	Cars
Community helpers	Trucks
Children	Tractors
Construction workers	Construction vehicles
Hospital staff and patients	Emergency vehicles
Firefighters	Aircraft
Gardeners	Space vehicles
Westerners with horses	Boats
Clowns	
Airport crew	*Other accessories:*
Garbage squad	Doll-house furniture
Farm families	Miniature eating, drinking, and cooking utensils
Sets of animals such as:	Supermarket supplies
Farm animals	
Forest animals	
Zoo animals	
Dinosaurs	

These block accessories come in a profusion of sizes and materials. Some are of plain wood and have no details, much like Carolyn Pratt's originals. Others are highly detailed in wood, plastic, or die-cast metal. Most figures of people are multiethnic these days, showing skin colors and features of Caucasian, Hispanic, African-American, and Oriental people. Your selection will again be based on what you want to happen in the Block Center as well as on the particular skills and concepts you want children to learn. You need not have all your accessories available at all times for your children. When you visit a fire station, for instance, you will want to make available firefighting accessories. Specific suggestions for use of particular accessories can be found in the "Activities" section of this chapter. If your budget does not allow so many human and animal figures, then **cut them out of toy catalogs,** mount them on cardboard or foam backing, and laminate them with clear contact paper.

• • • • • • • • • • **Block Center Labels**

As noted in Chapter 1, learning centers should be identified by picture and word labels. The color-coded logo or picture you are using for the Block Center needs to be displayed prominently at the entrance to the center at the children's eye level. Use the name of the area often, and point to the sign when discussing with the children which activities are available. They will soon be reading the words. This same sign should appear in miniature on the pictorial Daily Schedule as well as on the pictorial floor plan. In addition, you should **mark every block and accessory shelf with a picture and word label** of what it contains. Trace around each block's shape on colored contruction paper, cut it out, and mount it on a white sign or directly onto the shelf itself. The name of the block should be labeled on the sign or on the shelf as well. Then, use the names frequently when you are talking about blocks, and soon the children will be discussing "ramps," "units," and "quadruples" as well. Do not assume that these words are too difficult for children to remember. If you use the words, the children will, too—and will be delighted with their use of such big words.

As for the accessories, if you are storing sets of little cars, trucks, and planes in separate trays or baskets on a shelf, then mount the labels directly

Block accessories can have picture labels made for their space on the shelf, just as you have done for the blocks.

onto each basket. You can trace around each kind of toy as you did each block shape, or you may want to make a photocopy of the item and then color it for a label. Three-dimensional items can be copied exactly the same as flat materials can. If you stand up your people or vehicles separately on shelves, mount each label at the toy's location. Again, include written names of each accessory. Every accessory item on the shelves should be labeled. Children need to see words as well as pictures of the items they are playing with and talking about.

• • • • • • • • • • • Activities to Promote Physical Development

Children's interactions with unit blocks promote both large and small motor development. Arms and hands are strengthened as children take blocks off the shelves and put them back. The small muscles of the fingers are strengthened as children pick up smaller items and stand them in place. Balancing the blocks in wall and tower construction promotes eye–hand coordination, as does placing little figures of people and equipment in precarious positions on buildings and towers. These are spontaneous activities that children often do on their own in the Block Center. Teachers can use other ways to involve children in activities that will promote physical development.

Although most block building is spontaneous on the part of the children, teachers may want to motivate or stimulate particular kinds of building through a teacher-directed activity. For children whom she knows are in the manipulative stage of block play, she could invite several into the Block

+ Center to **hear a story** she would read to them or tell them that would then

+ **motivate them to do the physical manipulative activities** with blocks so necessary before actual building can begin.

One such story is *The Gift* by John Prater (1985). A preschool girl and boy receive the gift of a little chair that comes in a cardboard box. Although the chair is nice, it is the box they like best. The story of what they find to do with the box is told in a series of wordless pictures that become more imaginative as the pair progresses in their box to adventures with trucks, trains, the underwater world, and finally, the jungle. The teacher can read the story or ask the children to make it up according to what they see in the pictures. At the conclusion of the story, the teacher can bring into the Block Center

+ one or more **cardboard boxes for the children to play blocks with**—not large enough for them to climb into, but big enough to use for the filling and dumping of blocks that children at the manipulative level enjoy doing. The teacher need not remain in the area to see what happens, but she can check back occasionally to lend her support.

The same story can be read another day to a different group of children already adept at block building. This time, at the conclusion of the story, the teacher can bring into the Block Center **a new basket of accessories: a collection of little empty boxes** of all kinds that she has assembled, from match boxes, to bandage boxes, to toothpaste-tube boxes. Let the children use their imaginations and eye–hand coordination to incorporate these boxes into their block play. If you do not want the wording on the boxes to affect the play, paint the boxes, or cover them with contact paper ahead of time. Be sure this collection is also labeled with a picture and word sign on its storage container.

Balancing is another physical skill that block builders need to acquire. A book that could motivate balancing in your Block Center is *The Balancing Girl* by Berniece Rabe with illustrations by Lillian Hoban (1981). The story describes Margaret, a girl in leg braces and a wheelchair, who nevertheless is adept at balancing things. She balances books, blocks, magic markers, and finally dominoes in an elaborate line. Although the story is a long one for preschoolers, it is full of enough excitement to command their attention. With the teacher's encouragement, it could motivate children to **line up the tall double-unit blocks on their ends,** like Margaret did with the dominoes, and then invite someone to start the chain reaction by pushing the last block. Obviously, you will need a large number of double units for this activity.

Block pickup games are other excellent activities for promoting physical skills. Want children to strengthen their hands and wrists? Have them **hold one block flat in their hand and pile up one or two other blocks on top for them to carry to the block shelf.** How many can they carry this way without dropping them? What other physical skills can you think of that could be promoted by using block pickup games?

The action chant "Blocks" at the beginning of the chapter is another small group activity to use in the Block Center for promoting physical development. As a teacher-led activity with a small group of children, it can be done at the end of block play, after pickup is completed. The movements children make as they chant can be changed every time. Maybe they would like to jump three times rather than clap when they say, "Blocks, blocks, blocks." Perhaps all the children would like to hold two blocks and clack them together three times on the last line. Ask your children about other motions they would like to make.

• • • • • • • • • • • Activities to Promote Social Development

Social skills children need to learn in the Block Center include: gaining access to ongoing play, becoming a leader or following a leader, taking turns, playing cooperatively, and the prosocial skill of helping.

Many of these skills children may learn on their own. The Block Center is an excellent site for spontaneous experimentation regarding social skills. Some children band together to build cooperatively. Others try to gain access to this group play but learn that the best way to be admitted is to play parallel to the group, building their own structure. Others try out the roles of leader and followers. Sometimes the followers become leaders because the group recognizes their good ideas!

The teacher may decide that certain children who have difficulty accepting another player or another point of view may want to consider other approaches. A **good book for block builders that speaks to the problem of different approaches to the same task** is *Hank and Frank Fix Up the House* by Joanna and Philip Cole (1988). Hank and Frank are the fix-up brothers who decorate people's houses. Hank is the fast one, and Frank is the other one. The book tells the hilarious story of a house they are hired to redecorate (the wrong house, it turns out), each doing things his own way. A good idea for a teacher is to have this book in reserve for the right time, when such a social problem presents itself. Then, you can read it to the builders in the Block Center who cannot agree with one another. Talk about the story afterward, but leave it to the players to arrive at their own solutions.

Working together cooperatively is a social task some children may need help with in the Block Center. A book that speaks to this topic is *Building a House* by Byron Barton (1981). A simple story told with full-page colorful illustrations and single lines of text, it describes the work of carpenters, bricklayers, plumbers, electricians, and painters as they build a house from the ground up. You may want to read the story to a small group of your block builders who are having trouble cooperating. At the same time, prepare round hook **name tags for the children to choose and wear with names of the various workers on them.** Be sure to have several duplicate name tags for each worker. If you cannot locate this particular book, **make up a simple story of your own about what carpenters, bricklayers, plumbers, electricians, and painters do** as they erect a building. Children wearing a tag may want to carry out the task their tag suggests as they build a house together.

If boys dominate your Block Center, you may decide to have a "Girls Day" for block building. Read this same story to a group of girls whom you have invited into the Block Center. Once they experience the fun of block building, they may choose to do it on their own.

• • • • • • • • • • Activities to Promote Emotional Development

Children can develop emotionally in the Block Center as well. Every success they experience in their building or playing with others here adds immeasurably to the good feelings they have about themselves: their positive self-images. In addition, they can learn to deal in a positive way with emotional situations if they have the experience to learn how and the support of the teacher in helping them cope. When things get out of hand during block play, the teacher may need to intervene with her three-part rule of helping children learn to care for themselves, care for others, and care for the materials.

To help children learn how others cope in emotional situations, the teacher can read the wordless picture book *Changes, Changes* by Pat Hutchins (1971), the story of the little wooden man and woman who respond with great enterprise to emergency situations by changing their buildings from a house that catches fire, to a fire engine that floods, to a boat that lands, to a truck that runs out of gas, to a train that runs out of track, and finally, back into their original house: and all with the same set of blocks! Then, **let the children tell how they might try to solve their own building problems.**

Another book to read that deals with emergency situations and people's problems is *A Chair for My Mother* by Vera B. Williams (1982). In this instance, a little girl, her mother, and her grandmother all save their money in a big jar to buy a beautiful chair to replace the one that burned in their apartment fire. Besides reading the book, you can contribute a similar beautiful chair to the Block Center by **covering one of the wooden dollhouse chairs with colorful wallpaper from a sample book.** Introduce your chair as a surprise after you read the book. If the children like the idea, they may want to help cut out and glue wallpaper to a whole set of dollhouse furniture for use in their block buildings.

• • • • • • • • • • **Activities to Promote Cognitive Development**

Play with unit blocks has long been associated with cognitive development in young children. In order to develop intellectually, children need to have experience with the concepts of size and shape, wholes and parts. They need to experiment with counting, sorting, matching, and categorizing. Block play gives them this opportunity. Unit blocks are especially well-suited because they have been carefully designed as fractions and multiples of a mathematical unit. Short blocks are half units. It takes two of them to make a unit. Blocks that are twice as long as a unit are called doubles. Blocks four times as long are called quads or quadruples. Children in your classroom will learn these names because they are on the shelf labels and because the children will hear you and the other teachers call the various blocks by their names. The children will eventually come to understand that a unit means one, a double means two, and a quadruple means four.

Another math concept promoted by block building is one-to-one correspondence. Young children at first learn to count by rote. Later, they learn the meaning of each number by using it with concrete, three-dimensional materials. Ask a child to bring you seven blocks. He may be able to count by rote to seven, but he may not understand what seven actual items are. When you are in the Block Center with children, talk to them by **using spe-**

+ **cific names for the blocks** and **specific numbers** they are using: "Andrew, can you bring Betty five half-unit blocks, please."

As children build on their own, they will be solving the perceptual problems that all young children experience: fitting the right block to the space. Somehow, it is difficult for youngsters to choose the right length of block to fit as a bridging block between two uprights. This problem can be solved either by finding a block long enough to reach the uprights or by moving the uprights close enough so that the child's block will fit. Children solve such perceptual challenges through trial and error in the Block Center. Through such activities they learn how to judge length and width, that building problems can be solved in more than one way, and that they can solve those problems successfully.

Teachers can lend their support to children's cognitive learning by leaving challenges in the Block Center for the builders to solve on their own. At the appropriate time, when the children are learning about circles or squares, the teacher can make **masking tape circles or squares on the floor**

+ **of the block center** for children to build around. Be sure to make your figures fit the size of the blocks. You can also make **contact paper cutouts of**

+ **various blocks** and **stick them to the floor of the Block Center** so that children can select the proper blocks and stack them up in a tower on top of the cutout.

Such activities should be done in conjunction with other activities promoting the concepts of circle or of square, rather than in isolation in the Block Center. Perhaps children are tracing around circles in the Writing Center, you are reading about circles in the Story Center, or children are singing circle songs in the Music Center. Take the tape off the floor when you are finished so that it does not restrict creative building.

Block pickup games help children learn sorting, categorizing, and matching skills. When you introduce a new pickup game, use the same game for at least a week, until the children really understand it. If you make block pickup into a game in which you also participate, it may become one of the favorite activities of the day. Children enjoy routines if we help them to have fun with the routines. Here are several block pickup games that promote cognitive skills:

Sorting: Sorting out all the unit blocks in one pile, the half units in another pile, and the doubles in a third pile. **Pretend that the long quad**

+ **blocks are bulldozers,** and push all the piles over to the shelves on which they belong. Then, put them on the shelves.

Matching: Find all the blocks that match the **cylinder block** cutout, **put**

them in the dump truck, and drive them over to the shelf. Then, match   +
the unit cutout, and put those blocks in a pile for the dump truck to carry.

Counting and identifying shapes: Put on a **hand puppet** (for example,
a dog) and **ask the children to feed the dog three curve block "bones."** The   +
dog will then hide his "bones" on the shelf. You can put them on the wrong
shelf and ask the children to find where the dog hid them and to put them
on the right shelf.

Parts and wholes: Put on another hand puppet (an alligator) and have it
pick up a double. Say to the children that the **alligator will help them pick
up** and put away each of the **double blocks if they can find two other
blocks that make a double,** which they will then put back on the shelf.   +

Make up your own similar pickup games. It is fun to use hand puppets or
stuffed animals. Do you **have a dinosaur who eats only quads?** Put him on   +
the block shelf and have the children feed him. What other games can you
or your children think of? Have a different game every week.

· · · · · · · · · · **Activities to Promote Language Development**

Language development occurs in the Block Center, whether you promote
it or not. When children build together, they tend to talk together. Listen to
what they are saying. You will learn something about their social roles of
leader or follower. You will learn something about their cognitive concepts
of size, shape, and number. And you will certainly learn how they are handling language. Do they speak in expanded sentences? Are they asking
questions with words in the right order? Are they using new vocabulary
words—"arch," "quad," "skyscraper"? Which children contribute to the
conversation? Which ones seem always to be the listeners?

If you tell them or read them stories about buildings, then you can ask
them to tell you stories about the structures they are building if they would
care to. You could ask a child to **dictate something about his building that
you would write down for him.** Or you might ask the child to **tell about his
building to the tape recorder,** and then listen to it later.   +

In order to motivate such stories by the children, you could read a book
about other people's houses such as those in *Shaker Lane* by Alice and Martin Provensen (1987), a wonderful story about the houses and the people
who lived in them on Shaker Lane from the beginning when it was mostly
farms, to the time when it was full of shanties and people who took things
easy, to fancy Reservoir Road when most of Shaker Lane was under water.

When children go on **field trips** involving buildings, you can encourage
them to **represent such buildings in the Block Center.** Put up pictures of   +
the post office, fire station, or farm they have visited. If you have no pictures, take photos of the children and buildings on the field trip. Mount

these pictures in the Block Center as a reminder of the trip and as a stimulus for representing the trip in blocks. **Mount the pictures or photos on the wall at children's eye level when they are sitting.** They will then be able to see the pictures when they are building. Many of your children may not be at the developmental level at which they can actually construct anything in art, stories, or block building. For them, it is the manipulative process that counts most of all.

If you have been to a construction site or viewed a new house being built or an old house being renovated, you might want to read your block builders the book *This Old New House* by Sheila McGraw (1989). It tells the tale of an old, run-down house that is being renovated, next door to little boy Graham's house. Although the story is long and difficult for most preschoolers, teachers can adapt it, reading the pictures where necessary. If children have experienced a house being renovated on a field trip, this book will reinforce their learning with many wonderful new vocabulary words they have probably encountered. Young children are proud to use long and unusual words if you do not overwhelm them. They are in the language-play period of their learning and love to roll different-sounding words off their tongues. Graham learns about *renovating, architect, blueprints, contractor, dumpster,* and *fiberglass insulation.*

Children enjoy talking about the field trips they have taken. The Block Center can extend their learning by providing pictures of trip sites and accessories for building in the days following a trip. The teacher can mention the new accessories in the center, or she can ask the children what new things they see in the Block Center. Children who choose to play with blocks may then want to build something from the trip. What they do, though, is up to them, not the teacher. She can interact verbally with them during their building as she observes, to see what is happening and help them clarify what they are doing. Here are some ideas for field trips and block-building accessories you can provide.

Field Trip	**Accessories**
1. Airport	Toy planes, people, cars
2. Beach	People, paper umbrellas, little boxes, boats
3. Circus	Zoo animals, horses, people, trucks
4. Construction site	Construction vehicles, workers, pipe cleaners
5. Drugstore	People, little boxes, plastic bottles
6. Farm	Farm animals, people
7. Fire station	Fire truck, people, plastic tubing for hoses
8. Gas station	Cars, trucks, plastic tubing
9. Hospital/clinic	People, emergency vehicles, little stretcher
10. Lake	People, boats, sticks for fishing poles, string
11. Museum	Dinosaurs, people

Field Trip	Accessories
12. Park	People, little trees, dollhouse tables
13. Pet store	Animals, people, little boxes
14. Supermarket	People, miniature food items, boxes, bottles
15. Restaurant	People, miniature food items, tables
16. Zoo	Zoo animals, people, train

• • • • • • • • • • • Activities to Promote Creative Development

Creativity in young children has to do with their imaginations and pretending. They take the information they have and use it in new and original ways. Children of the preschool age are at the perfect stage for creating new forms, new ideas, new words, new block structures, new anything—because they are not bogged down with the rules and regulations that make older children conform to what adults expect of them. Therefore, they are free to experiment and find out on their own—that is, if we let them.

The Block Center is a wonderful place for creative development to occur because the materials are unstructured and available for children to use in any way they want. Your most effective intervention strategy in the Block Center, in fact, is to keep out! Let the children build on their own. But what about all of the previously mentioned activities, you may wonder. Teacher-initiated activities should be used sparingly. Use the activities mentioned to follow up a field trip, for instance, or when other play breaks down, or especially for pickup time.

When nothing much is happening in the Block Center, the teacher may want to encourage some kind of pretending. Perhaps if the builders pretend they are someone else, they can use their blocks in imaginative ways. To **encourage pretending in the Block Center, the teacher can read a book** to a small group of builders in the area and then leave them afterward to do some pretending on their own.

If the book the teacher chooses is *Martin's Hats* by Joan W. Blos (1984), then she needs to plan ahead of time to have a collection of hats on hand. Martin spends his nighttime dreams joining a series of different people performing an array of activities in their special hats: explorer's hat, party hat, engineer's cap, conductor's cap, chef's hat, police officer's cap, mail carrier's cap, firefighter's helmet, welder's goggles, farmer's hat, cowboy's hat, and finally, nightcap. You should **have a selection of** similar **hats** in a sack to be drawn out one at a time as you read the story or **to be hung on a hat rack that you bring into the Block Center** for this particular activity. Where will you get the hats? Perhaps they can be donated or mayble found as plastic hats at a party or costume store. Such hats are definitely worth the investment for the wonderful pretending they motivate. After the story, children can put on a hat and pretend to be someone in particular as they create a farm or a fire truck with blocks.

The teacher could read the picture book *Block City* by Robert Louis Stevenson (1988), based on Stevenson's poem about a little boy who builds a block city and imagines it to be an old-time city with towers, palaces, and ships. The children can then try their own imaginations on their block creations. What stories can they tell about their buildings?

• • • • • • • • • • • The Teacher's Role in the Block Center

• Observing Developmental Levels

As in the other learning centers, the teacher's role is to set up the center as previously described so that children can choose to become involved with blocks on their own and so that interesting and exciting things will happen within the center. Then, the teacher steps back to observe individual children in this and every center of the classroom during the free-choice time period. As described in Chapter 2, the teacher first looks for children's developmental levels as they interact with blocks. The three levels of manipulative, mastery, and meaning play are usually highly visible in the Block Center.

Children at the manipulative level do almost everything with blocks except build with them. They take them off the shelves, carry them around, push them into piles, fill up boxes and trucks with them, dump them out, fill up containers again, and dump them out once more. These children are usually the youngest in the group or the ones with the least experience. Give them this manipulation time to get used to the blocks. The cardboard box activity previously described is for children at this level.

Children at the mastery level of building like to demonstrate the same building skill over and over. If they have learned to stack vertically in a tower-type structure, they will construct many, many towers. Lining up blocks horizontally in long rows or building walls or roads is another kind of mastery play. The mastery level of block play can become very elaborate as children teach themselves the skill of bridging—putting one block across the space between two other blocks. Soon they are repeating a pattern of bridging over and over in an elaborate wall or tower. The way children express their individuality with blocks is as different as individual adults' doodling with a pencil. The balancing and cognitive stacking activities previously described are especially appealing to children at the mastery level.

Children at the meaning level of block play apply the skills they have learned to building real buildings. They may give their buildings names at the outset or wait until they finish before they decide what the structures are. Because preschool children are still in the process stage of interacting with the things in their environment, it is the *doing* of the thing that is important to them rather than the final product. They soon come to realize, however, that adults seem more concerned with the final product: the building, the picture, the story. So they will usually give a name to their building if pressed, and they may even make up a story about it. Children at the meaning level of building are probably the only ones who will enjoy representing in blocks the structures seen on field trips. Even their structures will come from their own creative impulses rather than from the actual shape of a real building.

• Observing Social Levels

Children in the Block Center display obvious social interaction levels in their play. Some are onlookers. Others build blocks in a solitary manner. Some build structures parallel to other children, while others build in cooperation with a group. As the teacher observes in the Block Center, she or he can record the actions and words of all the children involved on the Child Interaction Form.

• Recording on the Child Interaction Form

One teacher observed two four-year-old boys (Rick and Edward) and two three-year-old boys (Jake and Robbie) in the Block Center. They were engaged as follows:

Edward was building near the block shelf making a square, log-cabin-like building with quadruples he got from the shelf one at a time. Rick was lining up unit blocks in a long line parallel to the block shelf. When he came to Edward's building, he started another line parallel to the first one. Rick said to Edward, "Look what I am doing!" and Edward replied, "Watch out for my building. This is a space station." Edward then got toy figures of people one at a time and stood them on top of his building. Jake entered the center and began pulling various blocks off a different shelf one by one, backing up a wooden dump truck, piling his blocks in it, then dumping them out, and loading it again. When Rick said, "Look what I am doing!" a second time, Jake repeated the same sentence, "Look what I am doing!" to no one in particular. Meanwhile, Robbie had followed Jake into the center and stood watching him and the others, but not playing.

The teacher recorded the incident on the Child Interaction Form as shown in Figure 3–1.

FIGURE 3–1	Child Interaction Form

Child _Edward, Rick, Jake, Robbie_   Observer _D. B._
Center _Blocks_   Date _4/15_

CHILD INTERACTION FORM
With Materials

Manipulation Level   Actions/Words
(Child moves materials around
without using them as intended.)
  Jake comes in center after other boys; takes various blocks off opposite shelf; fills & dumps dump truck.

Mastery Level   Actions/Words
(Child uses materials as
intended, over and over.)
  Rick makes long line of unit blocks parallel to shelf & up to Edward's bldg & then makes second line parallel to first; says to Edward 2x: "Look what I am doing!"

Meaning Level   Actions/Words
(Child uses materials in
new and creative ways.)
  Edward makes log-cabin-like bldg. with quads, 1 at a time off shelf; puts toy people on top; replies to Rick: "Watch out for my bldg. This is a space station."

With Other Children

Solitary Play   Actions/Words
(Child plays with
materials by self.)
  Jake plays by self, not near other boys. (Robbie looks on but doesn't play.)

Parallel Play   Actions/Words
(Child plays next to others with same
materials but not involved with them.)
  Rick & Jake play parallel, talking to one another, but not interacting with blocks.

Cooperative Play   Actions/Words
(Child plays together with
others and same materials.)

• Interpreting the Interactions

Before she left the area, the teacher jotted down on the back of the form her interpretation and suggestions. These would be noted by other staff members at the end of the day and incorporated into plans for individual children at the staff planning session. Her notes read as follows:

Accomplishments:
  Edward can do creative building.
  Rick is fine at mastery level.
  Jake still at manipulation level.

Needs:
  It would help Edward to be involved in building with others.
  Robbie needs to get involved with blocks.

Plans:
  Look for another child at meaning level who could build with Edward.
  Have a staff member try to involve Robbie with blocks; he is new and
    still unsure.

• Interacting with the Unsure Child

As the teacher comes to recognize individual children's developmental and social levels from her observations, she can make plans for such children. Most children handle block building well without adult intervention. For certain children who have not become involved, perhaps because they do not know how, the teacher may decide to intervene.

Stationing herself in the Block Center is an effective technique for enticing children into the area. Young children often choose to work in an area where the teacher is located because they want her attention. If they do not come, she can invite them. If they still refuse, the teacher should not pressure such children because they are probably not yet ready. Instead, she may read one of the building books previously mentioned to an individual child in the Story Center. The teacher eventually comes to realize which children need to be left entirely on their own in the beginning.

For those who do come into the center through a teacher's invitation, she can then begin to take blocks off the shelf for a building of her own. She may even start to build a simple structure. **Serving as a block-building role model** may be all that is necessary **to get a reluctant builder started.** On the other hand, a shy or unsure child may need a more direct approach. "Robbie, can you find another block like this on the shelf? That's the right one. It's called a unit block. Can you put it on this building? You choose where you think it should go. That's fine. Thanks. We'll need a few more unit blocks like that one." Once the child is involved on his own, the teacher can extract herself unobtrusively from the activity.

• Interacting with Disruptive Children

Before intervening with a disruptive child, the teacher should observe what is happening. If the disruption is occurring because the block play has disintegrated, the teacher may decide to **redirect the activity by asking for or giving specific suggestions for a new direction.** For example, she might say: "Brian and Tommy, I see that the two of you have finished building your race track. What else could you build near your track? Are people going to watch the race? Will you need a grandstand for them?"

If the disruption has more to do with emotions than blocks, the teacher may ask each child to tell her what is happening. **Putting emotions into**
+ **words often diffuses a tense situation.** On the other hand, if the children are really out of control, the teacher needs to intervene in a firm but matter-
+ of-fact manner. She needs to **reiterate the caring motto of the program:** "Brian and Tommy, in this classroom we *care* for one another. We do not hit each other. I can't let you do that. Show me that you can play without hitting."

If the disruption involves throwing blocks, the teacher's intervention needs to stress: "Brian and Tommy, in this classroom we *take care* of our materials. We do not throw the blocks. Show me how you can build with the blocks." Or she may use herself as a role model: "Boys, these blocks are for building, not throwing. I am going to build with them. If you would like to build, too, you can sit right here by me and help."

• Interacting with Builders

You will learn from your observations when and if you should interact with builders. Make it a point to interact on an individual basis with each child every day. This could occur when a child is building with blocks. Be sure it is not merely an interruption. On the other hand, if you see something you would like to comment on, this may very well be the appropriate time. As noted in Chapter 2, watch and listen carefully before making your comment. The comment itself can give the child support, encouragement, or direction in his or her building. It should be specific and nonjudgmental. You may be reflecting what you see the child doing with blocks; or you may be asking a question to clarify what you see. "You're using most of the blocks on the shelf in your building today, Jennifer. How did you ever get those three cylinders to balance?"

As you observe and respond to children in the Block Center, you will be learning more about 1) *the children* and their wonderful inventiveness when they have the freedom to work with unstructured materials; 2) *the blocks* and what valuable learning opportunities they add to your program; and 3) *yourself* and how else you can use blocks to make your program for children both effective and exciting.

IDEAS+
in CHAPTER 3

1. *Setting up the Block Center*

    a. Stock your shelves with *enough* unit blocks. (p. 44)

    b. Arrange the blocks lengthwise on shelves at the children's height. (p. 44)

    c. Have a spacious area with the floor carpeted and the area defined by shelves. (p. 45)

    d. Have accessories that support field trips and other learning center themes. (p. 45)

    e. Cut figures out of toy catalogs and mount them on cardboard. (p. 46)

    f. Mark block and accessory shelves with pictures and word labels. (p. 47)

2. *Using stories and activities to promote physical development*

    a. Read a story to motivate physical manipulative activities. (p. 48)

    b. Use cardboard boxes for children to play blocks with. (p. 48)

    c. Have a basket of little boxes as accessories. (p. 49)

    d. Line up tall double-unit blocks on ends for balancing. (p. 49)

    e. Hold one block flat, and pile up blocks on top for pickup. (p. 49)

3. *Using stories and activities to promote social development*

    a. Read a book about different approaches to the same task. (p. 50)

    b. Use workers' name tags for children in the Block Center. (p. 50)

    c. Read or make up a story about workers in the Block Center. (p. 50)

4. *Using stories and activities to promote emotional development*

    a. Read and then let children tell how they might solve their own building problems. (p. 51)

    b. Cover dollhouse chair with wallpaper and read the "chair" book. (p. 51)

5. *Using stories and activities to promote cognitive development*

    a. Use specific names for blocks and specific numbers for amounts. (p. 52)

    b. Tape circles and squares on the floor with masking tape. (p. 52)

    c. Stick to the floor contact paper cutouts of blocks. (p. 52)

6. *Using block pickup games*

    a. Pretend quad blocks are bulldozers. (p. 52)

    b. Match blocks to a sign and carry them in a dump truck. (pp. 52–53)

    c. Feed "bone" blocks to a hand-puppet dog. (p. 53)

    d. Bring two blocks to a puppet to make a double. (p. 53)

    e. Feed quad blocks to a dinosaur. (p. 53)

7. *Using activities to promote language development*

    a. Write down a dictated story about a child's building. (p. 53)

    b. Have a child tape record a story about his building. (p. 53)

    c. Represent field trip buildings in the Block Center. (p. 53)

    d. Mount pictures or photos at children's eye level when sitting in the Block Center. (p. 54)

8. *Using activities to promote creative development*

    a. Read a book on pretending in the Block Center. (p. 54)

    b. Bring in hats of all kinds for a Block Center hat rack. (p. 54)

9. *Interacting with children in the Block Center*

    a. Serve as a block-building role model for a reluctant child. (p. 59)

    b. Redirect a disintegrating activity with specific suggestions. (p. 59)

    c. Help disruptive children put their emotions into words. (p. 60)

    d. Reiterate the caring motto of the program. (p. 60)

REFERENCES CITED

Caplan, F., & Caplan, T. (1974). *The power of play.* Garden City, NY: Anchor Press/Doubleday.

Johnson, H. (1974). The art of blockbuilding. In E. S. Hirsch (Ed.), *The Block Book* (pp. 9–24). Washington, DC: National Association for the Education of Young Children.

Koepke, M. (1989). Learning by the blocks. *Teacher Magazine, 1* (3), 52–60.

Pratt, C. (1948). *I learn from children.* New York: Simon and Schuster.

Provenzo, Jr., E. F., & Brett, A. (1983). *The complete block book.* Syracuse, NY: Syracuse University Press.

OTHER SOURCES

Beaty, J. J. (1990). *Observing development of the young child.* Columbus, OH: Merrill Publishing Company.

Beaty, J. J. (1992). *Skills for preschool teachers.* Columbus, OH: Merrill Publishing Company.

Cartwright, S. (1988). Play can be the building blocks of learning. *Young Children, 43* (5), 44–47.

Kuschner, D. (1989). Put your name on your painting, but . . . the blocks go back on the shelves. *Young Children, 45* (1), 49–56.

NAEYC. (1988). *Classroom with blocks* (video #821). Washington, DC: National Association for the Education of Young Children.

Tudge, J. & Caruso, D. (1988). Cooperative problem solving in the classroom: Enhancing young children's cognitive development. *Young Children, 44* (1), 46–52.

CHILDREN'S BOOKS

Barton, B. (1981). *Building a house.* New York: Viking Penguin.

Blos, J. W. (1984). *Martin's hats.* New York: William Morrow and Company.

Cole, J., & Cole, P. (1988). *Hank and Frank fix up the house.* New York: Scholastic.

Hutchins, P. (1971). *Changes, changes.* New York: Collier Books.

McGraw, S. (1989). *This old new house.* Toronto, Canada: Annick Press Ltd.

Prater, J. (1985). *The gift.* New York: Viking Penguin.

Provensen, A., & Provensen, M. (1987). *Shaker Lane.* New York: Viking Kestrel.

Rabe, B. (1981). *The balancing girl.* New York: E. P. Dutton.

Stevenson, R. L. (1988). *Block City.* New York: E. P. Dutton.

Williams, V. B. (1982). *A chair for my mother.* New York: Greenwillow books.

TRY IT
YOURSELF

1. Label each type of block and each accessory with picture and word signs in your Block Center.

2. Observe and record the behaviors, interactions, and talk of three different children in the Block Center for three days. Make comments on their developmental levels, social play levels, and how you were able to determine these.

3. Go on a field trip to a building or a construction site with some or all of the children. Do a follow-up activity in the Block Center by bringing in new accessories to support your trip; by mounting pictures of the building in the Block Center; by reading a picture book about buildings or construction to a small group. Record what happens with blocks.

4. When cognitive concepts such as circle, square, rectangle, and triangle are being presented, put masking tape on the floor in the Block Center for children to build those shapes.

5. Make up a new block pickup game or use one suggested in this chapter. Use it for a week and record the results.

4

COMPUTER CENTER

COMPUTER *(Action chant)*

Disk in the disk drive,	(Push hands forward and back)
Shut down the door;	(Bend and touch toes)
Turn on the monitor,	(Move right hand up and down)
Feet on the floor;	(Stamp each foot)
Boot up the program,	(Move left hand up and down)
What will we see?	(Shade eyes with hand and turn head)
Program is ready:	(Hands on hips)
"Press any key."	(Move right hand forward and back)

• • • • • • • • • • • Role of the Computer in an Early Childhood Classroom

"You don't mean to say you're going to teach those little three-, four-, and five-year-old children to use a computer, do you?" is the comment heard most frequently by teachers who have set up a Computer Center in their classrooms. The answer, of course, is: "No. We are not going to teach young children how to use a computer. They are going to teach themselves!"

Teachers who understand classroom computers realize that not only are these amazing machines powerful teaching/learning tools for everyone but that they lend themselves especially well to the self-discovery learning style of young children. Teachers who understand preschool children realize that computers do not intimidate them as they often do adults, but that on the contrary, the youngsters are ready and willing to play around with the computer in order to discover how it works. Just as play with unit blocks touches every aspect of a child's development, so the computer, too, can make a similar contribution when set up with care and used with sensitivity.

There are many reasons why an early childhood classroom should consider including a Computer Center. Here are a few:

1. *The computer's style of interaction favors young children.*

Young children learn best through exploratory play. They do not know what to expect from things in their environment, so they try them out playfully and keep on trying them out until they finally get the thing to work. We could say they learn from their mistakes, except that for young children, there are no "mistakes," only different kinds of responses.

Computer programs work in the same way. The user keeps trying until he gets the program to respond in the way it is supposed to. He is rewarded for his effort when the sought-after response appears on the monitor screen. Now he knows what do to in order to proceed. This is how young children learn, constructing their own knowledge by interacting playfully with things in their environment. Because the child sees computer programs as games, he is even more highly motivated to continue this exploratory play because it is fun.

In addition, computer programs are well-suited to the three levels of interaction experienced by young children in their play: manipulation, mastery, and meaning. Children can manipulate keys on the keyboard as long as necessary until they finally extract the cause and effect sequence that will get the program to work. Then, they can proceed through the mastery stage of repeating a sequence over and over. Programs will repeat responses as long as the operator wants them to. Finally, children are able to apply their own meanings, that is, to make up their own games and express their own creativity once they have mastered the workings of a program. This is how young children learn, and this is exactly how computer programs work.

2. *The computer's combination of visual and verbal learning is especially helpful to young children.*

Computer programs respond to their users through a combination of animated visual graphics (pictures), sound, and written words on a monitor screen. Young children are in the visual stage of thinking until about age seven, when they make a transition to verbal thinking after they have learned to read and write. Thus, they respond well to the visual images they have caused to appear on the screen. The words on the screen that they see (and sometimes hear) help make their transition to verbal thinking easier as they eventually learn to read and write.

This powerful combination of pictures, words, and sometimes voice has even made it possible for certain children to teach themselves to read. Although learning to read is not a goal in most preschool programs, children's prereading skills are nevertheless enhanced whenever carefully selected computer programs are available for the youngsters to choose and use.

3. *The computer makes it easier to individualize learning.*

As Barnard Banet puts it in his article on "Computers and Early Learning": "Rather than prescribe a child's learning experience, the computer can present an inviting menu from which the child can choose, freeing him or her from adults' limited ability to prescribe optimal educational experiences" (Banet, 1978).

We already understand that the entire self-directed learning environment is set up in order for children to make choices and become deeply involved in their own learning. Now here is a learning tool designed for exactly the same purpose: to allow its users to choose from a range of activities at different levels. If they choose a program that is too difficult, they can try an easier one. When they are ready for more advanced activities, they can proceed. The children themselves decide.

Teachers realize how difficult it is to match learning activities with individual children's levels of abilities. They frequently underestimate or overestimate a youngster's abilities. Computer programs, on the other hand, present a variety of levels of activities, and children themselves find the level best suited to their own individual capacities through trial and error.

4. *The computer serves as an equalizer for children from different backgrounds.*

The computer seems to have a universal appeal to children. Thus, a classroom computer can serve children of every socioeconomic level, of both genders, of every racial or ethnic group, of every ability, and even of those with disabilities. While home computers seem more in evidence among middle-class families, a computer in the classroom is available for every child, no matter what his background. The so-called "learning gap" between rich and poor, black and white, and gifted and impaired children can be reduced and perhaps even overcome through use of a classroom computer.

Many families cannot afford their own home computers. For those who can, their children sometimes have a learning advantage over others. A computer in the classroom available for everyone helps to equalize such learning opportunities. Learning-impaired children can use computer programs at their own levels in the same way as gifted children do at their levels, since computer programs work at a variety of speeds and with unlimited patience. Studies have shown that bilingual children, handicapped children, and children from low-income families often learn from computer programs what they had difficulty learning in regular classrooms (Lee, 1983).

Gender discrimination among elementary-age computer users can be reduced and even eliminated if early childhood programs include this valuable tool as an intregal part of their curriculum. Judith Lipinski and her colleagues' 1984 study showed concern over male dominance of computer use in elementary and secondary schools. One respondent stated that "among children ages 8, 9, 11, and 12, girls were never identified as computer experts" (Lipinski, Nida, Shade, & Watson, 1984, 5).

Happily, this is not the case in early childhood programs. Studies of gender differences in preschool computer use do not show young boys dominating the computer or becoming more expert than girls. Lipinski's own early childhood program, in fact, showed young girls spending more time than boys at the computer. The author's study found that both preschool boys and girls demonstrated equal interest, and both became competent users. We concluded that early childhood educators should definitely consider introducing the computer to all young children before any sort of gender stereotyping can take place (Beaty & Tucker, 1987).

5. *The computer is an effective promoter of young children's positive self-image.*

To feel good about themselves, young children need to be involved in experiences in which they are successful, and especially in those activities in which they are in charge. A classroom computer lends itself especially well to the development of such positive feelings. If teachers have set up the Computer Center so that children can choose and use it on their own, and if teachers have selected the software programs with care, then children can proceed at their own speed toward success.

As the author discovered in her study of young children and computers in two nursery schools and a kindergarten:

> Good programs reinforce the correct responses from children. When children make mistakes, such programs ignore errors and do not respond. Thus, the young computer operators learn how to work the program as it should be done. In addition to gaining competence, they gain confidence in their ability to handle not only this adult-type tool, but also other learning activities. Success breeds success. Shy children who may have held back in other classroom activities are often the ones who gain such competence and, therefore, confidence from the computer. (Beaty & Tucker, 1987, 13)

• • • • • • • • • • • Setting Up the Computer Center

The Computer Center in an early childhood classroom should be treated the same as any of the other activity areas. That is, it should occupy a special space sectioned off from the other learning centers, exactly as the Block Center does. In elementary schools, computers are often relegated to a computer lab separate from the regular classroom. This is not recommended for young children. The computer needs to be available in the classroom for children to choose during their free-choice periods.

The center itself can contain a low table for the computer, two chairs in front of the machine for a team of users, low shelves for the software, and a table for books and activities related to the computer programs, as well as a tape recorder to record children's stories or conversations. Shelves should be pulled away from the walls to section off the area. Wall space can contain a rules chart, pictures that often accompany computer programs, photos of children engaged in computer activities, or book jackets featuring the books currently available in the Computer Center. Ideas for other items to be located in the Computer Center are discussed in the activities section of this chapter.

You may decide to include a second table and chairs in the center for a typewriter—a real one, not a child's toy typewriter. From this machine, children gain not only the experience of using a keyboard similar to the computer keyboard, but they learn that it is necessary to press one key at a time in order to print a letter. "Piano-playing" the keyboard of a typewriter will only jam the keys. This skill can be transferred to the computer, where it is also necessary to press one key at a time in order to operate the programs.

On the other hand, some teachers prefer to locate a typewriter in the classroom Writing Center instead (see Chapter 7, "Writing Center"). As children become adept at printing letters with writing tools, they enjoy practicing their newly acquired skill with all sorts of writing implements, including a typewriter. However, if you are fortunate enough to own a printer in addition to a computer, you may decide that the typewriter does belong in the Computer Center with the other printing machines.

• • • • • • • • • • • Number of Computers

How many computers should you have in your Computer Center? Because of the high cost of computers, one machine per classroom is usually all a program can afford and all it really needs. With the numerous other activities available during the free-choice period, one computer used by two children at a time, with two or three other children watching, serves the intended purpose. Each of your learning centers is set up to accommodate a small group of children, say four to six, depending on the activity and the space. A well-arranged Computer Center can handle this number of children comfortably with only one computer.

Should you have more than one computer, be sure they are the same and not different brands of machines. Although all computers use the standard typewriter keyboard, different machines may have subtle variations in their operation that will confuse young children. Additionally, the software you own may not be compatible among different computers.

• • • • • • • • • • Kind of Computer

What kind of computer should you purchase? This is an extremely important consideration to which you should give careful thought. A computer includes three principal parts: the computer with keyboard, the monitor, and the device for loading the program (e.g., the disk drive). On some machines, these three parts may be separate. On others, the parts are all in one unit. Either type of computer can be used with ease by young children.

The computer is operated by a keyboard similar to a standard typewriter keyboard, although it also contains special function keys. If the computer uses disks for its programs, it will have one or two disk drives, either built in or in separate boxes. When a program disk is inserted into the disk drive and the machine is turned on, the program will appear on a television-like

screen called a monitor. Because all the programs are in color, **it is essential**
+ **that a color monitor be used** in order to gain the most benefit for the children. Not all computers come with color monitors. Be sure to check on
whether the monitor is a color one before you make your purchase.

Other external devices are required by certain software and by certain
computers in order to operate their programs. While most computer programs are operated by the keys on the keyboard, some programs also use an
external joystick, mouse, touch pad, touch screen, or separate set of keys.
Young children can learn (or be taught) to use such devices, but it has been
our experience that the keyboard itself is the best way for preschoolers to
control a program. The entire keyboard needs to be available to the children
in order for them to make optimal use of learning opportunities. No keyboard overlay or any kind of coding of the keys is necessary, even for the
younger children.

An additional piece of equipment that you may consider is a printer. A
printer is a machine somewhat like an electric typewriter without keys that
types on paper the material that the computer operator has put on the
computer screen and saved on a disk. Such material can be words, designs,
drawings, or even scribbling. More and more early childhood software allows the user to save and print his work. While printed material like this
benefits young children by allowing them to save their work and share it
with others, it is not absolutely essential to have a printer unless the children are doing early writing activities and using word processing programs.

With so many considerations, how can you decide which computer to
purchase? The **most important consideration in the purchase of a**
computer for an early childhood program is the number and kind of soft-
+ **ware** programs **available for the particular brand of machine.** Software is
not interchangeable among different machines, for the most part. Apple
software, for instance, will work only on an Apple computer (or an Apple-
compatible computer). Furthermore, appropriate early childhood educational software is not available in significant numbers for every kind of
computer. Currently, the largest number of appropriate early childhood
computer programs are those designed for Apple computers. Many of the
same programs also have an IBM version available. Our suggestion is to
purchase one of the Apple or IBM computers (or compatible machines).
Commodore and Atari computers can also be used with their own appropriate software. The Apple Macintosh computer is beginning to develop a wider
range of early childhood software than was originally available.

New, more exotic, and more expensive versions of all the computers come
on the market every year. It is not necessary to have the most advanced
model in an early childhood classroom. Young children can gain as much
(and maybe more) from one of the earlier, more basic machines as they do
from the most advanced computer.

• • • • • • • • • • Choosing Appropriate Early Childhood Software

Once you have chosen your computer, the next extremely important task is to choose appropriate software programs for children of ages three, four, and five. A great many programs are available from a wide range of sources. Some of these programs are excellent. Others are incredibly poor. In order to choose programs suitable to your children and the goals of your program, it is necessary either to **try the software yourself (and preferably, with your children) or** to **read reviews of early childhood software that you can depend on.** Manufacturers' descriptions of their own software do not always give you the information you need in order to make a wise choice.

One of the best review sources we have found is High/Scope's *Survey of Early Childhood Software* by Warren Buckleitner (1989). This book reviews 355 computer programs for children of ages three to six years on the basis of user friendliness, educational value, and instructional design. The software reviewed is primarily for Apple, IBM, Commodore, Macintosh, and Atari computers. Two especially valuable comments on individual software are whether reading is necessary and whether the youngest children will have difficulty operating the program.

Many of the latest programs feature voice-synthesized speaking. Because voice technology is still in its beginning stages, not every program has sound that is clear enough to be understood easily. Fortunately, Buckleitner's software reviews also comment on whether the voice is understandable. Because such programs are more expensive than non-talking software, it is important to know whether the voice feature adds enough to the program to be worth the extra expense. Another consideration is the fact that an older computer may require the purchase of additional equipment in order to use voice-activated software.

Many talking programs seem to emphasize the voice rather than the content or design of the program. Software that uses a voice to give directions or make evaluative comments has about the same appeal as a car instrument panel that speaks to the driver. Many users turn off the sound. Our present feeling is that a voice is not necessary. Instead, the best software for preschoolers should contain:

1. Nonverbal directions
2. Ease of operation by children
3. Control by children
4. High-resolution graphics, sound, and animation
5. Content that can be integrated into the curriculum

These criteria are an ideal not attained by every piece of software you will purchase. Your own judgment and the goals of your program will help you to choose software that meets as many as possible of these criteria.

· · · · · · · · · ·**Children Choosing and Using the Computer Center**

+   **Three-, four-, and five-year-olds should use the computer in pairs,** not
alone. Social skills, language skills, peer teaching, and even creativity will
blossom when more than one young child uses the computer at the same
time. This statement is contrary to adult assumptions. Adults see the
computer as they do a typewriter, as a tool for a single person to use.

In an early childhood classroom, however, the computer is not a tool for a
single child. It is an *activity* for a team, that is, for two children to explore,
to talk about, and to take turns using. The goal for computer use in an early
childhood classroom is different from the goal of computer use by an adult.
For adults, the computer is a *working* tool that performs a particular task.
For young children, the computer is a *learning* tool that helps them develop
certain skills.

Early childhood programs include computers in their learning centers to
allow this powerful interactive learning device to promote children's development in the social, emotional, physical, cognitive, language, and creative areas. Whether children learn to use the machine itself in an efficient
manner is irrelevant. What is important is that young children improve

*In early
childhood
classrooms the
computer is not
a tool for a
single child, but
an activity for a
team of
operators with
onlookers.*

their social skills, their language skills, their cognitive skills, and so on. If the computer can help them to accomplish these goals effectively, then it is worth having in the classroom.

To choose to use the computer during the free-choice period, a child should be able to go to the Computer Center and select one of the two computer necklaces hanging at the entrance or any other self-regulating devices you have arranged. If both necklaces have been taken already, then the child should be able to sign up for the computer or take some kind of numbered ticket that will give him or her a turn.

The Computer Center is often one of the more popular learning centers in your classroom. Be prepared to have a sign-up sheet or other device for children who want to take a turn. **Preliterate children can sign up by printing their names in conventional script or scribbling their names in a personal script on the sign-up sheet** at the entrance to the Computer Center. (see   +
Chapter 7, "Writing Center"). If they do not get a turn on the day they sign up, they will be first in line for the next day if they are still interested.

At the beginning of the year, you or one of your assistants should show small groups of children (say, four or five at a time) how the computer works. Take the children into the center and sit down yourself at one of the two chairs in front of the computer. Invite a child to sit in the second chair. Then point out to this child and the onlookers the three parts of the computer: the computer itself with its keyboard, the monitor that looks like a television but isn't, and the disk drive where the program disk goes.

Show the children what a program disk looks like. Take it carefully out of its envelope. Show them how to hold the disk so that it will not be damaged. Demonstrate to them how to insert the program disk into the disk drive, how to close the disk drive, how to turn on the monitor, and how to turn on the computer. Then, turn off all the components and give your partner in the chair next to you a chance to try inserting the disk and turning on the system. The other three or four children will be watching.

· · · · · · · · · · **Rules for Using the Computer**

One at a time, the other children can take a turn inserting the disk, turning on the monitor, and turning on the computer. Be sure to point out to them **the illustrated rules chart mounted nearby.** It should contain not   +
more than three rules stating that: 1) Hands should be clean (sticky fingers may gum up the keys); 2) no liquids are allowed in the area (spilling liquids on the computer is perhaps the only damage children might do); and 3) two children at a time should use the computer.

Computers are remarkably sturdy machines. About the only potential hazards in an early childhood classroom are sticky fingers and spilled liquids. Obviously, you would not allow pounding on the keys or other destructive actions. By the time children come to use the computer, they should be well aware of the three-part classroom rule: We care for ourselves; we care for one another; and we care for our classroom and the materials in it.

· · · · · · · · · · **Initial Computer Program**

+   **In the beginning, use only one program for a week or so,** or until all the children have a chance to use the program as long as they want. It should be a simple piece of software that will introduce the computer through all its keys. Choose a nonverbal program that uses most or all of the keys. Show the children your pointer finger. Have them hold up their own pointer finger. This is their "computer finger." **They should use it to press one key of**
+   **the computer at a time.** They should then wait to see what happens on the screen before pressing another key. You will want to stay in the Computer Center to see how they get along with the program. You may have to answer a few questions at first, but let the children try to figure out their own answers as much as they can by trying out the program and playing around with it.

Be sure you have previewed the program yourself. If there are any written directions, you may have to point out the meanings of the words. Many computer programs start out with the direction "Press any key" at the beginning. Here are several simple programs you might choose to start with:

1. *Jeepers Creatures* (1983)

This is a colorful mix-and-match animal game showing a picture of one animal divided horizontally into three parts: its head at the top of the screen; its body in the middle; and its feet at the bottom. This animal is typically scrambled with a head joined to the wrong body and the wrong feet. The point of the game is to reassemble one whole, correct animal. The top row of letter keys controls the head (i.e., a different head appears for each different top key pressed); the middle row of letters controls the body of the animal (i.e., a different animal body appears for each different middle key pressed); and the bottom row of letter keys controls the feet of the animal (i.e., a different pair of feet appears for each different bottom key pressed).

Children learn the rules of this game by trial and error. Do not tell them what they are supposed to do or how to do it. Let them find out on their own. That is the point of the self-directed environment. Sooner or later, the children will discover how to work the game: that a vertical row of three letters makes a whole animal. Then they will tell one another or be the leader and demonstrate to their partner. In the meantime, they will learn how a computer works.

Try to **integrate every computer program you use into the rest of the curriculum.** In what ways can the content of this particular program be   + used in other activity areas? Or what materials from other areas can be brought into the Computer Center while this program is being used? For instance, **children's picture books can be found that correspond to the content of computer programs.** Whenever *Jeepers Creatures* is being used,   + you can plan to have the following books available. Be sure to read them to individuals or a small group of children who have used *Jeepers Creatures*. Then you can discuss the idea of mixing up animal parts. Perhaps they would also like to **make their own mixed-up animal puzzles** from cut-up   + pictures of animals.

A Funny Fish Story by Joanne and David Wylie (1984) is a simple, colorful book showing the strange-looking fish that a girl has caught. A line of text at the bottom of each page asks whether the fish looks like the animal pictured on the page. The following page shows a fish looking like that animal (e.g., a dog and a dogfish).

In Leo Lionni's book *Fish is Fish* (1970), a fish in a pond watches his tadpole friend turn into a frog who later comes back to the pond to describe the strange land creatures he has seen. They all turn out to have a decidedly fishy cast to them as the fish's mind pictures wonderful bird-fish, cow-fish, and people-fish. Have your listeners talk about the strange creatures they, too, have created with *Jeepers Creatures*. Would they like to **make some out of play dough or clay?** Could they **raise tadpoles** from a pond and watch   + them turn into frogs?

Children can actually create their own animals in flip-books such as *Croc-gu-phant* by Sara Ball (1985), which is divided horizontally into three parts like the computer program.

2. *Stickybear ABC* (1982)

This is another colorful program simply controlled by the letter keys of the computer keyboard. Pressing any letter key brings up an animated graphic scene with sound featuring an object or animal whose name begins with the letter pressed. A brief animation then occurs to the accompaniment of an interesting sound or tune. For example, pressing the letter *D* brings up a scene with a duck that quacks and swims around. Each letter key controls two graphics illustrating the same letter. When *D* is pressed a second time, the graphic shows a door, has a knocking sound, and then shows the door opening and closing with sound effects.

When *Stickybear ABC* is being used in the Computer Center, be sure to have another activity available that will integrate it into the curriculum. Have an alphabet book and some alphabet blocks in the area, for instance.

3. *Toybox* (1986)

Pressing each key puts a different shape, color, or special effect on the screen. These occur in random locations and will accumulate one by one until the screen is filled. The composition created by the pair of computer users can then be saved on the disk.

To integrate this program into the curriculum, perhaps the children
+ would like to **make their own toybox** for their little toy cars. Bring in an appropriately sized cardboard box, and have the children paint it and paste pictures of cars on it.

Ron Maris has written two books that illustrate wonderfully the toys in a child's room. In *My Book* (1983), the double-spread illustrations have a half-page in between that opens a door into the child's house, his bedroom, his toy cupboard, and so on. It is a wordless book for an individual child or small group to use in naming the many objects they see. In *Are You There, Bear?* (1984), a child investigates the same room at night with a flashlight that lights up the objects under the bed, in the toy cupboard, in a box, and in a toy basket, bringing them all to life. How could you use this book in conjunction with the program *Toybox?*

• • • • • • • • • • Activities to Promote Social Development

The development of social skills in an early childhood classroom involves the young child in learning to get along with the other children. This means that he or she needs to learn to share equipment and materials, to take turns using favorite toys and activities, and to work and play in cooperation with others. Such behavior is not all that easy for an egocentric young three-year-old, four-year-old, or five-year-old to accomplish. After all, they are at the age and stage of thinking that everything revolves around them. Your classroom may be their first group experience outside the home.

How are they to deal with the idea that not every piece of equipment is theirs to use when they want it? How can they resolve the problem of not being first every time? And what should they do when they must share a favorite toy or activity with another child?

The Computer Center is a wonderful practice area for social skills to be worked out by the children themselves. That is why it is essential to set up the computer for two children to use at a time. Because the computer often becomes one of the favorite pieces of equipment in the classroom, there is a strong motivation on the children's part to work out the sharing and turn taking necessary for them to use it.

• Turn Taking

Your self-regulating devices at the entrance to the Computer Center can begin the process. A child who wants to use the computer must choose one of the two computer necklaces. If they are already taken, then he or she can sign up for a turn or **take a numbered ticket for a turn.** In the meantime, if   + a child has a ticket, then she can stand behind the computer users and watch while she waits for her turn. When it is her turn, she can put on the computer necklace and return her ticket to the ticket envelope at the entrance to the Computer Center for the next child.

Once the two children are seated in front of the computer, other social tasks await them. Who chooses the program disk? Who gets to put in the disk and turn on the machine? Who gets to press the first key? How many keys can one child press before the second child gets a turn?

The computer programs you will be using are educational programs appropriate for young children. They are not arcade-type games. They are not games in which the child wins or loses, nor do they require two children at the keyboard in order for them to work. We suggest having two children use a program as partners in order for them to learn and practice the social skills necessary for cooperative use as well as to promote peer teaching.

At the outset, one of the classroom adults may need to assist the children to get them going. She can suggest that Sondra put in the disk and turn on the computer while Betty takes the first turn pressing the keys. The number of times each partner gets to press a key per turn can depend upon the computer program. If children are using *Jeepers Creatures*, they might press three keys each time they take a turn. In that program, it takes three different keys to make a whole animal. In the program *Stickybear ABC*, each letter key controls two different picture graphics. Thus, children might get to press two keys per turn.

On the other hand, the children themselves may want to work out their own turn taking or have each child alternate key presses. If one child takes too long or presses too many keys when it is her turn, the other child will soon complain or step in. We were impressed with how youngsters were able to work out turn taking in one nursery school. At first, certain children seemed to dominate. We observed one girl who completely dominated her partner during her first computer experience. Even when she was waiting a turn, she would reach over a seated child's shoulder and press a key to see what would happen. Imagine our surprise on the second day, after she had insisted on playing the computer game first, when she finally turned around, noticed how many children were waiting for turns, and remarked, "Well, I've been playing long enough. Let me let somebody else take a turn" (Beaty & Tucker, 1987, 41).

Sometimes **books about turn taking help children internalize ideas.**   +

Dorothy Corey's book *Everybody Takes Turn* (1980) shows two pictures of the same activity with first one child and then another taking turns. The teacher can read the book to individuals or a small group in the Computer Center and then discuss with them how they plan to take turns using computer programs.

• • • • • • • • • • Activities to Promote Physical Development

Although we seldom think about computers as promoters of a child's physical development, there are two areas of such development where appropriate computer programs can contribute: eye-hand coordination and visual discrimination.

• Eye-Hand Coordination

This small motor manipulation skill is an important one for young children to develop. They must learn to control fine movements of hands and fingers according to visual clues their eyes detect. Such coordination will lead them into handling writing implements and eventually into reading.

A number of computer programs promote eye-hand coordination and can be integrated into the self-directed curriculum described here. Some of the simplest ones are coloring programs that move the cursor (the electronic marker on the monitor) via an external mouse or joystick or with the keyboard arrow keys.

A mouse is a small box which, when rolled on a flat surface, moves the cursor on the screen. Pressing a clicker on the mouse also gives commands to the computer. A joystick is another external device in a small box with a rod or stick extending from it. Moving the rod causes the cursor to move. Young children with their small hands and pudgy fingers often have difficulty with external devices. They seem to be more successful in controlling movements of the cursor by pressing the arrow keys on the keyboard. Nevertheless, **using any of these devices to move the cursor gives youngsters practice in eye-hand coordination**.

Polarware, Inc. offers several simple coloring programs that even very young children can operate successfully by moving the cursor with a mouse, joystick, or arrow keys to fill in sections of the pictures with color. In this case, use of a mouse is recommended. The programs print the pictures in color if you have a printer:

Dinosaurs Are Forever (1988, Polarware, Inc.) has twenty-six blank dinosaur pictures to be filled in. A delightful picture book that can be enjoyed at the same time is *If the Dinosaurs Came Back* by Bernard Most (1978). It, too, has simple pictures of dinosaurs, each a different color, and each doing an activity to help people, from rescuing kites stuck in tall trees to building skyscrapers. Children may be motivated to **tell their own stories about dinosaurs,** or they may want to **do an art project** about these fascinating beasts. +

Fun on the Farm (1986) has thirty blank farm scenes to be colored in. **A basket of farm animals from the Block Center** along with a set of table blocks can be kept in the Computer Center to promote a different kind of eye-hand coordination when this program is in use. +

Another good program using a joystick is *Pals Around Town* (1985). The operators explore and add objects to Sesame Street scenes. The five scenes include Bert and Ernie's house, Sesame Street itself, a playground, a schoolroom, and downtown. Before or after using this program, you may want to take the children for **a walk in which they see how many different objects they can find in the park or on a street.** +

Puzzles are another excellent activity to promote eye-hand coordination. **Move several puzzles from the Manipulative/Math Center to the Computer Center when you feature computer programs** such as the following: +

Peanuts Picture Puzzlers (1984) shows a "Peanuts" picture on the screen and then divides the picture into sections and scrambles them up. The computer users must then put the picture back together, at which time it becomes animated.

With *Puzzle Master* (1984), the operators use either a joystick or the arrow keys to select a picture, scramble it up, and then put it back together again.

Another way to use a joystick for eye-hand coordination is by moving a computer figure through a maze. One of three games in *Early Learning Friends* (1985) moves Alf through maze-like caves.

In *Peanuts Maze Marathon* (1984), when the users complete their move through a simple maze, the "Peanuts" cartoons included in the maze become animated. This program can be used with the keyboard, but seems to work best with a joystick. After using maze programs, **children may want to build a maze out of blocks and drive their little cars through it.** +

• Visual Discrimination

Discriminating shape, size, and color through sight can be both a physical skill as well as a cognitive ability. Many computer programs are designed to help children discriminate visually. Here, we look at computer programs that ask children to **find a certain object hidden within a scene.** Can you + play a hidden object game in your classroom? A good computer program to promote this skill is *Stickybear Shapes* (1983), in which two of the games ask users to identify objects in scenes in the shape of a circle, square, rectangle, triangle, or diamond. Interesting animations and sounds reward the operators when they find the shape that is missing, for instance, a tire on Stickybear's car.

Another good program is *Inside Outside Shapes* (1986), with eighteen scenes in which a star, a square, a diamond, or a rectangle is hidden. A correct response animates the scene with motion and music.

In the program *Easy Street* (1988), children use arrow keys, joystick, or mouse to move a boy down the street in search of certain objects. This program also features speech synthesis as an option.

Books featuring hidden objects can be kept in the Computer Center when programs such as these are being used. In *Have You Seen My Duckling?* by Nancy Tafuri (1986), a mother duck swims around a pond with her brood of seven, looking for her eighth duckling who is seen on every page almost out of sight behind some object. It is a wordless book with lovely full-page illustrations that need to be read at close range for individuals to be able to find the duckling.

The book *If At First You Do Not See* by Ruth Brown (1982) goes better with the *Stickybear* computer games in which children must find a shape within an object. This story shows a caterpillar encountering a variety of growing things that turn out to be quite different from what they seem. Readers must rotate the book until it is upside-down to get the full effect of the transformations. In the end, the caterpillar itself is transformed into a butterfly.

• • • • • • • • • • Activities to Promote Cognitive Development

There are perhaps more computer programs designed to promote cognitive skills than any other kind. Children find such software an appealing approach to learning shapes, sizes, colors, opposites, matching, classifying, counting, measuring, estimating, sequencing, problem solving, and memory skills. Here we consider only opposites, matching, and memory programs. Math computer programs are discussed in Chapter 5, "Manipulative/Math Center."

• Opposites

The cognitive concept of opposites also involves language for young children who must learn not only the idea of two things being at polar extremes but also the names of the things. Computer programs featuring opposites are among the simplest, often using only two arrow keys to animate the graphics.

Stickybear Opposites (1983) contains twenty-five colorful scenes, each with a pair of opposites that can be animated by pressing the opposite arrow keys. Pressing the space bar changes the scene. One of our children's favorites was Stickybear on a seesaw. Pressing one arrow key brought up the word *HIGH* and made the seesaw go up. Pressing the opposite arrow key brought up the word *LOW* and made the seesaw go down. Children pressed their favorites over and over without changing the scene.

The book *Yes and No, A Book of Opposites* by Richard Hefter (1975) accompanies the program, showing cartoon pictures of several opposites in the program. The teacher should play some opposite games with the children when this program is in use. Children seem to know the words by rote but do not always understand their meanings. Doing **body movements with a small group of children in the Computer Center helps.** Have them stretch high and squat low; look up and look down; stand in front and stand behind; clap their hands loudly and softly. If you have guinea pigs in your Science Center, another good book to look at together is *Guinea Pigs Far and Near* by Kate Duke (1984).

Inside Outside Opposites (1986) works in the same manner with twenty pairs of antonyms. Still another program, *City Country Opposites* (1986), alternates city and country scenes using arrow keys.

• Matching

Many matching programs are included on disks, featuring counting, the alphabet, and other learning games. Following are some computer programs that specialize in matching.

Patterns and Sequences (1984) contains four games at different skill levels in which large objects need to be matched. *Comparison Kitchen* (1985) has six games for children to match food objects as to shape, color, and size. *Dinosaurs* (1984) contains five games in which six kinds of dinosaurs need to be matched to similar outlines as well as be classified according to what they eat and where they live. You will want dinosaur books in the Computer Center when this disk is being used.

Be sure to have lotto games in the Computer Center when computer matching games are on tap. Matching lotto cards with one another or with similar designs on a lotto board are favorite activities for many children. **Make your own lotto cards** by cutting out sets of similar pictures and mounting them on cardboard cards. Duplicate catalogs from toy stores, department stores, and car dealers are good sources for lotto game pictures.

• Memory

Animal Hotel (1985) is a memory game at two levels of difficulty. At the easy level, three animals are shown and then hidden behind a different door on the screen. Children select the animal they think is behind the door by pressing a number key. The more difficult level shows six animals that hide. Have **a set of animal figures** in the Computer Center for children to play

+   with while waiting their turn for this game. **A set of little boxes the animals can hide in** might motivate the youngsters to play their own memory game.

Memory Master (1985) contains three games, two of which are matching object with object and word with object; one is a picture Concentration game to promote memory ability. *Rainy Day Games* (1985) allows up to three players to play against the computer in three different card games: Old Maid, Concentration, and Go Fish. Children can use a mouse, joystick, arrow keys, or touch pad to move the cards in the games. **Before they play on the computer, familiarize your children with these games by playing**

+   **them with real cards.** Then, leave decks of the card games in the Computer Center to play when this program is being used.

Those who feel that card games are not appropriate in an early childhood classroom should remember that young children learn best through playful interaction with materials in their environment. Card games give them practice with the fine motor skill of picking up and handling the cards, matching cards through visual discrimination, and memory practice with these particular games.

• • • • • • • • • • • Activities to Promote Language Development

When pairs of children operate the computer together, every program they use promotes language development. We tape-recorded children's conversations as they played together with computer programs and were impressed with the many functions they served:

1. Giving information
2. Giving directions
3. Asking questions
4. Answering questions
5. Setting turn-taking rules
6. Telling the partner what the operator plans to do next
7. Critiquing the partner's work
8. Making comments about the program
9. Making up games
10. Making exclamations

(Beaty & Tucker, 1987, 146)

On the other hand, particular programs do promote certain kinds of language skills. In this chapter, we focus on computer software that promotes stories.

An adult needs to work with the children at the computer when the programs *Flodd, the Bad Guy* (1988) and *Jack and the Beanstalk* (1988) are being used. The adult reads the story along with the children, who press any key to change the screen. After five or six pages the children must make a choice in order to proceed. Clever graphics and sounds assist children throughout both programs. *Jack and the Beanstalk* is a space-age version of the traditional tale. The choice that children must make here is whether or not to continue climbing the beanstalk.

D. C. Heath Company offers several programs in their Explore-a-Story Series for children of ages five through ten. Younger children can use a mouse, touch pad, joystick, or arrow keys to select and move objects, backgrounds, and characters, although they may not have reached the stage of adding their own words in creating the story. The programs include:

Just Around the Block (1988)
Not Too Messy, Not Too Neat (1988)
The Sleepy Brown Cow (1988)
What Makes a Dinosaur Sore? (1988)
Where Did My Toothbrush Go? (1988)

Whatever story program you use, be sure to integrate it into the entire curriculum. Put up pictures and posters of dinosaurs, for instance. Play games and sing songs about these beasts. Have art projects that depict them and construction activities that build them a place. Then be sure to **tape record the children's own stories** or **write them down through dictation** on experience charts or in personal books for them to share with others.

• • • • • • • • • • Activities to Promote Creative Development

Can computer programs really be creative? We were at first surprised to find that young children are able to use even the most uncreative computer programs in imaginative ways. But then we realized that this is exactly what youngsters do with every material or piece of equipment they come across: treat it playfully as they experiment to figure out what it can do, and then use it in all sorts of new and unexpected ways. That is what creativity is all about: making use of ordinary things in extraordinary ways. In the hands of young children, every computer program becomes creative. They learn how it works; they master its intricacies; and then they go on to add their own unique meanings. We watched children make up their own games, in fact, for every program they mastered.

On the other hand, certain pieces of software are designed specifically to promote creativity. These include many of the art programs, a few of the music programs, and some of the story programs already discussed.

• Drawing Programs

Early Games (1984) contains nine simple games involving letters, names, numbers, counting, and drawing. Its "Draw" game uses the cursor as a crayon to make colored lines in sixteen different colors. The game starts with a pink dot in the middle of the screen. Tell children that this dot is an electronic crayon. They then need to find out on their own how to draw with this computer crayon. Soon they discover that pressing any of the keys once makes a color dot that becomes a line if they continue pressing the same key. Then they find that certain keys make their color line go up, down, across, back, and even diagonally. Through experimentation, they eventually discover that it is the position of the keys on the keyboard that controls the cursor: keys on the top row move the cursor up; keys on the bottom row move it down; keys in the right middle rows move it right; keys in the left middle rows, left; and corner keys control diagonal movement. Pressing the space bar changes the color. Children's drawings can be saved on the disk.

Even before they internalize these rules, they are off and running, making colorful designs in a sort of geometric scribble wherever the cursor takes them. Soon they are naming their drawings and making up stories about them. One child told us that what she had made was a house, the stairs, and "a way out in case there is a fire" (Beaty & Tucker, 1987, 116).

Can children draw as well on the computer as they do with paper and crayons? The answer to this question is really irrelevant because with children's art, it is the process and not the product that counts. Yes, they can master this process on the computer as well as they do any other.

Although children ordinarily do paper and crayon drawing as individuals, we found that with computer art programs, partners work better than single users. The geometric designs children drew reminded us of drawings made on an **Etch-A-Sketch,** so we **added one of these toys to the Computer Center. Paper and Crayons** should also be available when computer drawing programs are in use.

Another good drawing program is on the *Kindercomp* (1982) disk that includes five other games, or its more recent version, *Kindercomp Golden Edition* (1986), with seven other activities. *Magic Crayon* (1983) also offers simple drawing at three difficulty levels.

Rainbow Painter (1984) is an electronic coloring book in which colors are chosen by the children and outlines of animals are then filled in. The disk also includes a free drawing option. Although coloring books are not always accepted in early childhood programs because of their stilted and uncreative nature, computer coloring book programs have the same advantages of every computer program: promoting manipulation skills in using the keys, social skills in taking turns, language skills in conversing with a partner, creative skills in finding new ways to use the program, and emotional development in boosting a child's self-image because he can use an adult instrument.

• Painting Programs

In order to paint with a computer "brush," the operators need to be free of the keys and their geometric patterns. Painting programs, therefore, use either a mouse, a joystick, or a touch pad of some sort. *Learning with Leeper* (1983) uses a joystick to select with a brush one of four colors from pots at each corner of the screen. Children can then swish them around as they do paints at an easel.

Koala Pad Graphics Exhibitor (1983) is the computer program that accompanies the Koala Pad touch tablet. Children paint by moving a finger or pointer across the pad. **When painting programs are in use, have easel painting available** in the center or nearby.

• Construction Programs

Just as children delight in constructing things with scissors, paste, and paper, they also enjoy doing art projects on the computer. The various programs for creating faces are among the most advanced that your children will use. With a minimum of help on your part, they can get started and then teach one another to use them. **Have some "Mr. Potato Head" Dolls available or make your own when you use these programs:**

Facemaker (1982). The faces that the children make can be programmed to wink, cry, frown, stick out their tongues, or wiggle their ears. Although this program was discontinued in 1986, it is often available in software libraries.

Facemaker Golden Edition (1986) is similar, but it has more complete color graphics than the original program. In addition to moving, this face can also be printed.

Mr. and Mrs. Potato Head (1985) uses a joystick or the arrow keys to animate an existing character. In addition, children can also build their own animated potato person.

In *Creature Creator* (1983), children use the space bar to select parts of a monster and can then make it dance.

In *Mask Parade* (1984), children can design their own masks by choosing the features of a face. They then can save their masks on the disk or print them. This is a good program to be used at Halloween time.

• Music Programs

Most of the educational music software currently available is for children older than preschoolers. A program geared for children of ages three through seven, however, is *Peter and the Wolf Music* (1985), containing six musical games and an exploratory activity. Children use the joystick or arrow keys to practice distinguishing tones and recreating simple melodies.

•••••••••• Activities to Promote Emotional Development

Being able to use the computer independently—this wonderful and complicated adult instrument—gives the young child a bigger ego boost than any one computer program could hope to do. When child users find that computers are not merely passive television-screen-type machines but interactive instruments with keys they can use to control what happens, marvelous things do happen! Learning-impaired children actually learn. Shy children blossom. And all the others have the same opportunity to work independently and to be successful in an activity of their own choosing.

Thus, the teacher need not concern her- or himself with particular activities or software to promote the child's self-image. Instead, she should set up the Computer Center for self-directed learning to take place. The rest is up to the children.

•••••••••• The Teacher's Role in the Computer Center

• Observing Developmental Levels

One of the great advantages of having a computer in an early childhood classroom is the ease of observation it affords the adults. When children are engrossed in operating a computer program, they are frequently oblivious to everything around them. There they are, sitting still and undisturbed by events often swirling around them. Teachers and assistants can make wonderful and unobtrusive observations at almost any time and for as long as necessary. Furthermore, if the adult knows what to look for, a great deal of information on children's developmental levels can be gained.

Teachers can note whether a child is still at the *manipulation* level in the operation of a program. If he or she is still playing around with the keys—"piano playing," we call it—it is obvious that she is still trying things out. She may also overgeneralize from one program to another at this level. That is, she may apply the rules she learned in the previous program to this new program. For instance, the previous program may have used arrow keys and the return key to control the graphics. This one may use all the keys and the spacebar. Children play around at the *manipulation* level of operation until they learn how.

At the *mastery* level, children have learned how the program works, and now they put their knowledge to use—over and over. In *Stickybear Oppo-*

sites, they make the bear climb up the ladder for TOP and climb back down for BOTTOM again and again. They will laugh and point and do it still again. In *Stickybear ABC*, they will press one letter again and again. But quickly they learn that each letter controls two different graphics, so that the same letter pressed twice does not bring up the same picture—not until the third press. One or the other of the partners usually points this out. For instance, pressing *E* brings up elephants moving their trunks to the tune of "Baby Elephant Walk." Pressing *E* a second time brings up an egg that bounces and then breaks. This is an intriguing discovery. They try out a few more letters. Then they go back to the first graphic.

After they have finally mastered the rules for this program by pressing the letter keys over and over, they begin playing their own games with favorite graphics. They have arrived at the *meaning* level of interaction. We watched children in four different classrooms in three different schools invent and play the same type of meaning level game with *Stickybear ABC*. They called it "I Caught You" or "I Stopped You." A child would press the letter either once or twice to bring up the wanted graphic (they always knew how many presses to make); and then one or the other would try to press the space bar to stop the animation before something happened. For instance, they would watch the egg bounce but try to stop it from breaking. The one who was successful would call out, "I caught you!" and laugh. They also tried to stop the cloud in "I" for "island" from reaching the palm tree on the island; to stop the grass in "G" from growing to the top of the screen; and to stop Mama and Papa Stickybear in "K" from kissing (Beaty & Tucker, 1987).

It is possible to observe these levels quite clearly in all the computer programs the children use. Placing a tape recorder on the table next to the computer makes it possible to record children's remarks as well. New words and the creative use of old words is often apparent. Not every child will reach the meaning level with every program. Some may not reach this level with any program. But the number of children who progress through all three levels with remarkable speed is astounding.

• Recording on the Child Interaction Form

The observer in the Computer Center can record the actions and words of each pair of children using the computer on the same Child Interaction Form. The teacher can then use this developmental information to plan activities for individual children and small groups both in the Computer Center and the classroom at large.

For example, one teacher observed Maria and Rhonda playing with computer programs for about ten minutes as follows:

Maria and Rhonda came into the center with the two computer necklaces around their necks, the self-regulating method that gives children a turn in this center. Maria took the *Stickybear ABC* program off the shelf and inserted it into the disk drive. Both girls sat down in front of the computer, but it was Maria who turned on the computer. They began pressing keys one at a time and waiting for a graphic to appear on the monitor screen. Maria took charge, taking the first turn. She searched the keyboard and finally pressed *M*. A graphic showing a mountain with a floating cloud appeared. "That's me!" she said, and laughed. Rhonda pressed several keys without looking at the keyboard. Maria said, "No, you have to press one." The graphic of an octopus doing a dance came on the screen. Both girls laughed, and Maria started bouncing around in her seat doing a sort of dance like the octopus. "It's an octopus," laughed Maria.

Rhonda started to press another key, but Maria held her off, saying, "It's my turn. It's my turn." She searched the keyboard for some time, finally pressing *V*. A graphic showing vegetables on a table appeared, but before any action could occur, Maria pressed *V* again, and the graphic appeared showing a volcano with a bubbling top and a cloud floating across the screen. Maria laughed and said, "That's me. That's me blowing my top!" Rhonda tried to press a key, but Maria reached over and pressed one without looking, saying, "I stopped it!" (possibly meaning that she stopped the cloud from reaching the volcano).

The two girls continued pressing keys, with Maria searching for the letter key she wanted and making comments on the graphics. Rhonda pressed keys without looking or commenting. Whenever she got the chance, Maria pressed a key to stop the action of the graphic, saying, "I stopped it again!" They finally changed programs to *Stickybear Numbers*, but neither girl could make it work. They were not pressing the number keys. Rachel and Kurt came into the Computer Center to watch. Rachel said, "I know how to do it," and "It's our turn now," so the first two gave up the seats and their computer necklaces.

The teacher recorded on the Child Interaction Form as shown in Figure 4–1.

On the back of the Child Interaction Form the teacher recorded the following interpretation of her observation, as well as suggested plans for these two children as follows:

Accomplishments:
Maria knows how to insert a disk and turn on the computer.
Maria understands one-key-pressing and cause-and-effect.
Maria can control the graphics on *Stickybear ABC* and plays a game with them.
Maria and Rhonda both take turns.

Needs:
Rhonda needs more time playing with one program.
Maria is ready to apply her skills to other programs.

FIGURE 4–1	Child Interaction Form

Child _Maria, Rhonda_   Observer _D. B._

Center _Computer_   Date _10/21_

CHILD INTERACTION FORM
With Materials

Manipulation Level   Actions/Words
(Child moves materials around
without using them as intended.)
Rhonda presses various keys for "Stickybear ABC" & "Numbers" without looking.
Maria presses 1 key at a time for "Numbers" but not a number key.

Mastery Level   Actions/Words
(Child uses materials as
intended, over and over.)
Maria has mastered "Stickybear ABC" & knows the letters A, C, D, M, O, V

Meaning Level   Actions/Words
(Child uses materials in
new and creative ways.)
Maria brings up graphics she wants by pressing proper key; then plays
"I stopped it" by pressing key to stop action. She calls M her letter &
identifies self as a mountain ("That's me.") & a volcanoe (That's me blowing my top!").

With Other Children

Solitary Play   Actions/Words
(Child plays with
materials by self.)

Parallel Play   Actions/Words
(Child plays next to others with same
materials but not involved with them.)
Rhonda plays next to Maria but not with her or helping her.

Cooperative Play   Actions/Words
(Child plays together with
others and same materials.)
Maria tries to involve Rhonda in her game; she also comments
on Rhonda's graphics ("It's an octopus").

Plans:
 Encourage both girls to continue playing together as well as with
  others on the computer.
 Encourage Rhonda also to pair with another child whom you have
  identified at the manipulative level (perhaps Jean?).

• Interacting with Computer Users

The teacher should introduce a new computer program to a small group of children at a time in the Computer Center. Talk with the children about its subject or content. Let teams of children try it out. Point out the books or activities that support the new software. Let this group of children continue working with the computer for the first day. On the next day, have another group of children learn to use this program. Continue day by day, until everyone who wants to has had a chance to use the program.

When introducing a new program, it is usually best to have only this program available in the Computer Center for the first week. The observant teacher can learn to tell when it is time to introduce a new program appropriate for current curriculum activities and children's computer abilities. Because some programs are more complicated to use than others, it is im-
+ portant to **begin with simple ones first.**

How long at a time should a child use the computer? It is **better that two children have a long enough time** on the computer to understand what
+ they are doing **than that everyone has equal turns** of, say, five minutes each. We have found that in classes where teachers regulate turn taking, giving everyone equal but short amounts of time, it takes the children a great deal longer to learn how programs work. Children who have plenty of time at one sitting progress more quickly and come away with a real understanding of the programs.

One adult on the classroom team should be identified as the computer
+ **expert.** He or she can then supervise this activity area, not necessarily closely, but with an eye to assuring that all is going well. Some computer programs do not work as well as they should. Sometimes children have difficulty changing programs. The Computer Center teacher can come to the rescue when she deems it necessary.

Children understand that computers are complex and expensive machines. They are excited and pleased to be allowed to use one in the classroom. But to be secure in the use of the computer, children should feel that they can turn to one of the adults when they need help. Both they and the other classroom staff can thus be assured that good things are happening with children in this new and dynamic classroom learning center as a part of the Appropriate Practices Curriculum.

....

IDEAS +
in CHAPTER 4

1. *Purchasing hardware and software*
   a. Buy a color monitor. (p. 70)
   b. Purchase a computer for which appropriate software is available in ample supply. (p. 70)

   c. Try out the software yourself or with children if possible before purchasing. (p. 71)

2. *Using the computer*
   a. Set up center so that pairs of children use computer. (p. 72)
   b. Have children "sign up" for turns to use computer. (p. 73)
   c. Have children take ticket for a turn. (p. 77)
   d. Read books about turn taking. (p. 77)
   e. Have illustrated rules chart in the area. (p. 73)
   f. Use only one computer program a week or so at first. (p. 74)
   g. Begin with simple programs first. (p. 74)
   h. Have children use their computer finger to press one key at a time. (p. 74)
   i. Give children as much time as necessary rather than equal time for each program. (p. 74)
   j. Designate one adult as the computer expert. (p. 74)

3. *Integrating computer programs into the curriculum*
   a. Have off-computer activities for every program. (p. 75)
   b. Find children's books that correspond with every program. (p. 75)
   c. Have children make their own mixed-up animal puzzles. (p. 75)
   d. Have children make strange animals out of clay. (p. 75)
   e. Have them watch tadpoles turn into frogs. (p. 75)
   f. Have them make a toybox to go along with the *Toybox* program. (p. 76)
   g. Have them tell stories and do art project about dinosaurs. (p. 79)
   h. Have a basket of farm animals and table blocks to accompany the farm program. (p. 79)
   i. Go for an "object walk." (p. 79)
   j. Help children build a maze with blocks. (p. 79)
   k. Play games about finding a hidden object. (p. 79)
   l. Do body movements to illustrate opposites. (p. 81)
   m. Make your own lotto cards. (p. 81)
   n. Bring in a set of animal figures and little boxes. (p. 82)
   o. Play children's games with playing cards. (p. 82)
   p. Tape record or write down children's stories. (p. 83)
   q. Bring in an Etch-A-Sketch. (p. 84)
   r. Have an easel in the computer area when art programs are used. (p. 85)
   s. Bring in a Mr. Potato Head doll or make your own. (p. 85)

REFERENCES

Banet, B. (1978, Sept.–Oct.). Computers and early learning. *Creative Computing*, pp. 90–94.

Beaty, J. J., & Tucker, W. H. (1987). *The computer as a paintbrush*. Columbus, OH: Merrill Publishing Company.

Buckleitner, W. (1989). *Survey of early childhood software.* Ypsilanti, MI: The High/Scope Press.

Lee, M. W. (1983). *Early childhood education and microcomputers.* Urbana, IL: ERIC Clearinghouse on Elementary and Early Childhood Education. (ERIC Document Reproduction Service No. ED 231 503).

Lipinski, J. M., Nida, R. E., Shade, D. D., & Watson, J. A. (1984). *Competence, gender and preschooler's free play choices when a microcomputer is present in the classroom.* Urbana, IL: ERIC Clearinghouse on Elementary and Early Childhood Education. (ERIC Document Reproduction Service No. ED 243 609).

OTHER SOURCES

Beaty, J. J., Tucker, W. H. (1986). *Becoming partners with a computer: Preschoolers learn how* (video). Elmira, NY: Three-to-five.

Campbell, P. F., & Fein, G. G. (1986). *Young children and microcomputers.* Englewood Cliffs, NJ: Prentice-Hall.

Clements, D. H. (1987). Computers and young children: A review of research. *Young Children, 43* (1), 34—44.

Clements, D. H. (1985). *Computers in early and primary education.* Englewood Cliffs, NJ: Prentice-Hall.

Haugland, S. W., & Shade, D. D. (1988). Developmentally appropriate software for young children. *Young Children, 43* (4), 37—43.

Hoot, J. L. (1986). *Computers in early childhood education: Issues and practices.* Englewood Cliffs, NJ: Prentice-Hall.

Olson, K., & Buckleitner, W. (1989). Kids at the keyboard. *Child Care Information Exchange,* 66, 3—6.

Papert, S. (1980). *Mindstorms: Children, computers, and powerful ideas.* New York: Basic Books.

CHILDREN'S BOOKS

Ball, S. (1985). *Croc-gu-phant.* West Germany, ars edition.

Corey, D. (1980). *Everybody takes turn.* Chicago: Albert Whitman & Company.

Duke, K. (1984). *Guinea pigs far and near.* New York: E. P. Dutton.

Lionni, L. (1970). *Fish is fish.* New York: Pantheon Books.

Hefter, R. (1975) *Yes and no, a book of opposites.* New York: Weekly Reader Books.

Maris, R. (1984). *Are you there, bear?* New York: Viking Penguin.

Maris, R. (1983). *My book.* New York: Viking Penguin.

Most, B. (1978). *If the dinosaurs came back.* San Diego: Harcourt Brace Jovanovich.

Wylie, J., & Wylie, D. (1984). *A funny fish story.* Children's Press.

CHILDREN'S COMPUTER PROGRAMS (by publisher)

Advanced Ideas, Inc.
2550 Ninth Street
Berkeley, CA 94710
  Dinosaurs 1984 (Apple, IBM, C64)

Baudville
5380 52nd Street
Grand Rapids, MI 49508
Rainy Day Games 1985 (Apple, C64, Atari, Mac)

CBS Software
One Fawcett Place
Greenwich, Conn. 06836
Pals Around Town 1985 (C64, IBM, Apple)

C & C Software
5713 Kentford Circle
Wichita, KS 67220
Magic Crayon 1983 (Apple)

D. C. Heath & Company
125 Spring Street
Lexington, MA 02173
Just Around the Block 1988 (Apple)
Not Too Messy Not Too Neat 1988 (Apple)
The Sleepy Brown Cow 1988 (Apple)
What Makes a Dinosaur Sore? 1988 (Apple)
Where Did My Toothbrush Go? 1988 (Apple)

DLM
One DLM Park
Allen, TX 75002
Comparison Kitchen 1985 (Apple, IBM)

Designware, Inc.
185 Berry Street
San Francisco, CA 94107
Creature Creator 1983 (Apple, IBM, Atari)

Hartley Courseware, Inc.
Box 419
Dimondale, MI 48821
Patterns and Sequences 1984 (Apple)

Kangaroo, Inc.
110 S. Michigan Ave
Chicago, IL 60605
Jeepers Creatures 1983 (Apple, Atari); discontinued by publisher;
found in software libraries

Learning Technologies, Inc.
Suite 131
4255 LBJ Freeway
Dallas, TX 75244
Animal Hotel 1985 (Apple, C64)

Mindplay
100 Conifer Hill Drive
Danvers, MA 01923
Easy Street 1988 (Apple, IBM, Mac, IIGS)

Polarware, Inc.
P.O. Box 311
2600 Kesinger Road
Geneva, IL 60134
   Dinosaurs Are Forever 1988 (Apple, IBM, C64)
   Fun on the Farm 1986 (Apple, IBM, C64)

PTI/Koala Industries
269 Mount Herman Road
Scotts Valley, CA 95066
   Koala Pad Graphics Exhibitor 1983 (Apple, IBM)

Random House Software
400 Hahn Road
Westminster, MD 21157
   City Country Opposites 1986 (Apple)
   Inside Outside Opposites 1986 (Apple)
   Inside Outside Shapes 1986 (Apple)
   Mr. and Mrs. Potato Head 1985 (Apple)
   Peanuts Maze Marathon 1984 (Apple, IBM, C64)
   Peanuts Picture Puzzlers 1984 (Apple, IBM, C64)

S.D.L.
Dale Moss
2715 Cabrillo #105
San Francisco, CA 94121
   Toybox 1986 (Apple, IBM, C64)

Sierra On-Line
Coarsegold, CA 93614
   Learning with Leeper 1983 (Apple, C64, Atari)

Spinnaker Software Corp.
One Kendall Square
Cambridge, MA 02139
   Early Learning Friends 1985 (C64)
   Facemaker 1982 (Apple, IBM, C64, Atari) Discontinued
   Facemaker Golden Edition 1986 (Apple, IBM, Amiga)
   Kindercomp 1982 (Apple, IBM, C64, Atari)
   Kindercomp Golden Edition 1986 (Apple, IBM)
   Peter and the Wolf Music 1985 (Apple, C64)

Springboard
7808 Creekridge Circle
Minneapolis, MN 55435
   Early Games 1984 (Apple, IBM, C64, Atari)
   Mask Parade 1984 (Apple, IBM, C64)
   Puzzle Master 1984 (Apple, IBM, C64
   Rainbow Painter 1984 (Apple, C64)

Stone and Associates
Suite 319
7910 Ivanhoe Avenue
La Jolla, CA 92037
   Memory Master 1985 (IBM, Atari, ST)

Tom Synder Productions, Inc.
90 Sherman Street
Cambridge, MA 02140
   Flodd, the Bad Guy 1988 (Apple, IBM, Mac)
   Jack and the Beanstalk 1988 (Apple, IBM, Mac)

Weekly Reader Software
Middletown, CT 06457
   Stickybear ABC 1982 (Apple, Atari)
   Stickybear Opposites 1983 (Apple, Atari)
   Stickybear Shapes 1983 (Apple, Atari)

TRY IT
YOURSELF

1. Set up your Computer Center with interesting pictures and activities to support your latest piece of software.
2. Observe and record children using your computer games to see which developmental levels they have attained. How can you tell?
3. Use a tape recorder to record children's language at the computer. Which new words or ideas are they expressing?
4. Introduce a new computer program and help children get started.
5. Read one of the suggested books to accompany a new computer program the children are using, and then set up a followup activity to integrate this program into another activity area.

5

MANIPULATIVE/MATH CENTER

N U M B E R S   *(Finger play)*

One, one,	Six, six
See me run!	Watch my tricks!
Two, two,	Seven, seven,
You come too!	Here comes Kevin!
Three, three,	Eight, eight,
Up a tree!	Don't be late!
Four, four,	Nine, nine,
Down once more!	Just on time!
Five, five,	Ten, ten,
See me dive!	Home again!

• • • • • • • • • • Math in Preschool Programs

"Surely preschool children do not have to learn such a difficult subject as mathematics until they are in first grade!" you may hear certain adults exclaim when you talk about your preschool math activities. "Why, I would put it off as long as I could!"

People who express such sentiments may not be familiar with what math encompasses for young children. They may not realize how excited preschool children can become over numbers, and they may not know that for young children at this stage of their learning, math is manipulative.

Math in preschool programs involves interacting with interesting collections of objects: sets of little toy cars and trucks; a bucketful of seashells; a basket of buttons; a box of empty plastic bottles of all kinds and the bottle tops to screw on them; a set of used-up colored markers and the colored caps that match them; a board full of bolts of all sizes and a box of nuts to fit them; a pail of smooth beach pebbles; a bunch of keys and locks, a bag of acorns, buckeyes, and hickory nuts; a set of colored golf tees; a pan of uncooked pasta in many shapes; a set of miniature prehistoric animals.

Math in preschool programs also involves playing with some fascinating games: picture dominoes, lotto cards, puzzles, color bingo, and tic-tac-toe. It involves manipulating stacking blocks, nesting cubes, shape blocks, color bricks, snap blocks, bristle blocks, parquetry blocks, slotted wheels, pegboards, geoboards, an abacus, lacing dolls, dressing frames, cylinder boards, Cuisenaire rods, and giant dice. It involves reading books, using computer games, and playing with the toy cash register.

If such activities do not stimulate your children's interest in math—if such materials do not pique your own interest—then you need to learn something more about the importance of math in all of our lives, how crucial it is that young children get a good start in the basic pre-math skills, and how critical it is that young children do not start out with negative attitudes toward math.

· · · · · · · · · · ## Attitudes about Math

How do you feel about math yourself? It is important to ask yourself that question—and to answer it honestly. Too many of us have to admit a strong negative feeling about mathematics. Why is that? Is it because of unfortunate school experiences we have encountered with math? Is it because we were bored with math in school, or did poorly in math classes, or even failed? If that is the case, then we need to be sure that such attitudes are not passed on to our children. Our children should come to love math and be successful with it. They should **feel free to explore math just as they do**

+   **blocks.** They should learn **to have fun with numbers.**

"Fun with numbers?" you may respond. "How can anyone have fun with numbers?" Use your imagination. At the preschool level, children can eat them, sing them, dance them, and build with them! They can count numbers, sort numbers, draw numbers, clap hands to numbers, finger play with numbers, paint numbers, weigh numbers, dissolve numbers, and pile up numbers into miniature mountains! If you provide such activities for your children, they should learn to love and not to fear mathematics. If you make math meaningful for your youngsters, they should develop a math mania, not a math anxiety.

We desperately need young people who have grown up comfortable with math. Both the world of today and the world of the future depend upon young people who have math ability to understand the high-tech society we have created. Our country needs young people who have math skills equivalent to those young people in other countries. Give your children that opportunity. Make math magical for them!

· · · · · · · · · · ## Preschool Child Development

Swiss psychologist Jean Piaget spent his life observing and interviewing children to determine how they acquired knowledge. His theories have been accepted by most early childhood specialists and refined by cognitive psychologists and modern scientists specializing in information-processing skills. Piaget describes two kinds of knowledge: *physical knowledge* that young children build when they interact externally through their five senses with concrete objects in their environment, and *logico-mathematical knowledge* that children build internally when they interpret their physical knowledge and extract relationships about the objects they have acted upon.

For example, young children find out physically about rubber balls by chewing on them, squeezing them, smelling them, dropping them, rolling them, hitting them, and throwing them. They process this information mentally and apply it to other round objects and other kinds of balls, making mental comparisons and noting likenesses and differences. The knowledge they have thus acquired is stored in their brains to be drawn upon when needed or refined when new facts are added.

Neither physical knowledge nor logico-math knowledge can really be separated in a child. They develop together and depend upon each other. Both kinds of knowledge depend upon manipulation. A child needs to manipulate the objects in his or her environment in order to provide the brain with the sensory stimuli necessary to form logical thought (Williams & Kamii, 1986). That is why the promotion of math skills in your classroom needs to be manipulative. Your Manipulative/Math Center will also be helping children develop good small motor coordination. As children handle the materials and activities you provide, they will be strengthening their finger muscles and developing eye-hand coordination along with the logico-mathematical knowledge they acquire.

• • • • • • • • • • Math for Preschool Children

The particular skills that preschool children need to learn involve four areas:

1. *Classification:* the ability to group objects that have common characteristics
2. *One-to-one correspondence:* the ability to match objects one with another because they belong together
3. *Seriation:* the ability to order objects by size, texture, taste, color, sound, and so on, in ascending or descending order
4. *Counting:* the ability to name numbers in a fixed sequence and apply this to an object at a time, arriving at a total

• Classification

The skill of classification is one of the first that the human brain acquires: the ability to sort out one thing from another on the basis of its characteristics. Classification involves visual perception. The child needs to discriminate visually among various shapes, sizes, and colors. Then, the child needs to compare one object with another. He or she learns that some things are alike and that others are different. What makes them this way? The child's brain extracts this information from her handling and interacting and looking at the things in her environment. Oh, yes, these pets are the same because they all have this fuzzy stuff called fur all over them. And this pet is different because it is covered with things called feathers. It moves differently, too. The other pets run around the floor on feet. This one flies through the air with wings. The child does not need to express such observations verbally. Her brain processes these facts. The more experiences of this nature the child has, the more information her brain will process.

Next, the child learns to group together all the things that seem to belong together because they are similar. At first, young children overgeneralize about things. For instance, toddlers frequently discover a particular category of things and then put all those things together in their minds. They might learn to distinguish a category of pets that they call "doggie," for example, because of their size, body covering, and actions. These are little animals that have fur, four legs, and walk close to the ground. Soon, the toddlers may be calling all similar animals "doggie," even toy teddy bears and real kittens. Later, they learn to discriminate even further, and their categories become more refined. Doggies, they eventually realize, are in a different class from teddy bears and kittens.

To help young children develop this ability to classify, you need to **provide them with playful opportunities to practice identifying and naming, sizes, shapes, and colors.** Start with one concept at a time, for instance, shapes—a circle, then a square, then a rectangle, and finally, a triangle. Then, go on to the next concept, size, and finally, color—one at a time. Later, as children develop the ability to classify, they can try applying their knowledge to sorting out items that have more than one attribute alike, for instance, all the objects that are brown in color and at the same time are square in shape. These activities, you understand, are not lessons but play activities that you set up in the Manipulative/Math Center and that children choose to do on their own.

How long should they spend on one concept? As long as it takes the children in your classroom to absorb it. Surely, spend at least a week at a time and maybe more for one simple concept. Some children will grasp the concept of a circle immediately. Perhaps they have already learned it at home. Others wil take longer, according to their level of development. Give them all time. There is no need to hurry. Even those who understand the concept can have the fun of practicing and applying it over and over. Remember, mastery takes time and repetition.

• One-to-One Correspondence

In order to be successful in the math skill of correspondence, the young child needs the ability to match one thing with another because they belong together. The yellow cap goes on the yellow marker; the brown cap goes on the brown marker. The napkin on the table goes with the plate. If there are four plates, there should be four napkins. In counting, the child says "one" while pointing to one object and "two" while pointing to two objects or to the second of a series of objects. Children need the ability to compare one thing with another in order to decide whether they go together. This is a step up from the simple sorting of things that look alike. These things go together because they have a correspondence one with the other. A hat goes on a head, a car goes in a garage, a spoon goes with a cereal bowl because they belong together.

Children need to be familiar with many things, according to information-processing experts, in order to be successful with such one-to-one correspondence tasks. For example, in order to match up different-colored lunch buckets to children wearing raincoats of matching colors, they need to be familiar with lunch buckets and raincoats. With young children, merely **looking at a picture is not enough.** They **need to have a hands-on encounter** with a lunch bucket and a raincoat.

Counting objects also involves the math skill of one-to-one correspondence, but it is more abstract. When children are asked to apply numbers to things, they are not simply putting a hat on someone's head. In counting objects, children need, first of all, to be familiar with the names of the numbers, then with the order of the numbers when counting, and also with what the objects are. Having a Manipulative/Math Center **full of interesting, concrete objects for counting** gives children this experience. Workbooks and worksheets are not appropriate materials. Children need hands-on experiences with concrete objects to develop these important math skills.

• Seriation

The third math skill, seriation, involves arranging objects in an order according to a certain characteristic, say, height, sound, or color, and then to place these objects in a series from first to last, tallest to shortest, loudest to softest, or darkest to lightest. This is a much more complicated math skill than the previous two. Young children need a great deal more knowledge and experience in order to accomplish such a task successfully. They need to be able to discriminate between objects on the basis of the special characteristic, say height. That is, they need to recognize that among the four toy family figures in the Block Center, they are all different in height.

How do they know this? Partly through *perception.* They can see visually and thus understand that the father figure is different in height from the mother, the son, and the daughter; that the mother is different in height from the others; and that the same is true with the son and the daughter. Some children need to line up the figures beside one another to make this determination. Other children seem to recognize this difference so quickly that they are probably using *intuition* as well, the ability of a person to know something is so without even thinking about it. Young children do not differentiate objects in the same way as older children or adults do, that is, on the basis of logical reasoning. They have not yet reached such an abstract stage in their cognitive development (Schultz, Colarusso, & Strawderman, 1989).

Language also plays a part in a young child's ability to differentiate sizes. He needs to know and understand the vocabulary involved: tall, short, big, small, tallest, shortest, and so on. The concrete materials and activities you provide help children to understand physically the cognitive concept of size differences and opposites through manipulation of objects. When you talk with them about what they are doing, or when they hear other children talking, they begin to acquire the words to go with their actions. As these activities are repeated, children process this information internally as logico-mathematical knowledge.

To complete the task of arranging four figures in a series from the tallest to the shortest, the child next must recognize that not only are all the figures of different heights, but that one is the tallest of all, a second figure is taller than two others, a third figure is taller than one other, and a fourth figure is not taller than any of the others, but shortest. Not all children of preschool age are able to arrange objects in a series such as this with accuracy. They may be able to identify the tallest figure and the shortest one, but not the ones in the middle. This is normal for preschoolers. They will eventually acquire this skill as their cognition develops and through the practice of interacting with materials.

• Counting

The counting skill requires children to do two different things: 1) say the number names by rote in the proper order, and 2) apply the number names in order to objects to find out how many there are. To perform the skill, rote counting, children need to know the names and order of the numbers. They quickly learn this by heart almost as a one-word litany, "onetwothreefourfivesixseveneightnineten," and will rattle it off on any occasion. The youngest children do not realize that they are saying ten separate number names in order. They love to count, nevertheless, and many four-year-olds enjoy counting to twenty and beyond—although they often omit a number here and there.

Counting objects, the second skill, is something altogether different. Here, children need to know the names of the numbers and the order of the numbers, as before. But then, they need to be able to apply one number to one object when they count (one-to-one correspondence). This is more difficult for preschoolers than simply rattling off a series of numbers. Counting the number of objects is based on the concept that each successive number is one more than the previous number and that the final number they say represents the total number of objects.

Because preschool children frequently omit a number when they count above ten, their totals are often not accurate. Even when they touch or point to each object that they are counting, somehow, they often skip one. There is no need to correct them. Let them try again. They will experience more success in this kind of counting if they are also **familiar with the objects being counted.** Counting the children in one of the learning centers gives them the kind of practice that appeals to them. In addition, they need all kinds of practice with one-to-one correspondence activities.

Setting Up the Manipulative/Math Center

It makes sense to locate an activity area such as this as close as possible to an area promoting similar skills. Children using the Manipulative/Math Center are most likely to practice their skills on the computer, or vice versa. Children using computer programs featuring opposites, matching, and memory will also want to play the matching games in the Math Center. Furthermore, they will soon be deeply involved in all sorts of activities with numbers, supported by appropriate computer programs. The self-regulating method you have put in operation throughout your program will help children to select manipulative and math activities during the free-choice period.

The center itself should be large enough to accomodate four or five children comfortably. A table with four or five chairs and floor space for children who prefer to sit on the floor while they work should be sectioned off with material shelves or room dividers.

Manipulative and math materials are almost unlimited. Your shelves should feature many of the items listed in Table 5–1, including a section filled with collections for sorting and matching; containers of counting objects such as Cuisenaire rods; a shelf of table blocks or building sets; several sets of puzzles; a number of board games and counting games; materials for teaching particular concepts such as shapes and colors; eye-hand coordination activities such as stringing beads and buttoning boards; card games, lotto games, and dominoes; and all kinds of counting books, as well as size, shape, and other concept books.

Be sure to label your shelves with illustrated and lettered signs for all your materials. Not only will children become familiar with such symbolization, but they will also be able to see what is available and later return materials to their places with greater ease. Change some of the materials from time to time as interest wanes or as new concepts are being featured throughout the program. Be sure, however, that particular materials are available for a

TABLE 5–1	Manipulative/Math Materials

Toy cars	Keys and locks	Picture dominoes
Seashells	Golf tees	Lotto cards
Buttons	Uncooked pasta	Color bingo
Bottle tops	Slotted wheels	Tic-tac-toe
Pebbles	Giant dice	Stacking blocks
Seeds	Shape blocks	Nesting cubes
Nuts	Color bricks	Snap blocks
Toy planes	Geoboards	Parquetry blocks
Toy animals	Pegboards	Bristle blocks
Abacus	Game boards	Cylinder boards
Lacing dolls	Computer games	Cuisenaire rods
Play money	Colored chips	Toy cash register
Boxes	Sectioned boxes	Egg cartons
Cards	Paper punches	Markers and caps
Rulers	Yardstick	Carpenter's rule
Balance	Stopwatch	Kitchen timer
Hourglass	Postage meter	Balance
Puzzles	Zipping/buttoning frames	

long enough time for most of your children to become deeply involved. Also have a bulletin board or an attractive wall space to display your children's math activities.

• • • • • • • • • • Activities to Promote Physical Development

The physical development promoted within the Manipulative/Math Center is small motor coordination. This is principally concerned with strengthening finger and wrist muscles: picking up, inserting, fastening, unfastening, zipping, buttoning, lacing, turning, and screwing.

In addition to the commercial buttoning and lacing boards, pegboards, and blocks, you should consider many excellent homemade materials and activities. **To strengthen muscles as well as providing a wonderful**
+   **counter, bring in several paper punches.** It may take two hands at first for your children to punch a hole in a 3-by-5 card. This activity is such an intriguing challenge to young children that they will eventually become experts with one hand. Let them practice on cards of different sizes, shapes, and colors in the beginning.

Then, use the paper punches to count things in the classroom. **Paste a**
+   **picture or draw an outline** of a cup, a dish, an animal figure, a doll, a dress-

up dress, a dinosaur figure, and so on **on each card.** Let children choose a   +
card, go to the part of the room where the item is located, and punch the
picture card for each item they count. Accuracy in counting is not the point.
Young children are only at the beginning in developing the skill of one-to-
one correspondence, that is, that there should be one hole punched for each
item. Any effort they make is acceptable. Later, as they develop both small
motor and counting skills, they will become more accurate. Children can
sign their names on each of the cards they punch. These **cards can then be
displayed on a "punch board" in the area,** and later either pasted in a   +
child's personal scrapbook or taken home.

Next, **have picture punching field trips** with small groups of children,   +
each carrying a paper punch and a picture card. You can prepare the cards
ahead of time with pictures cut from magazines and catalogs. The field trips
can be short ones to an area near your building. If you are near a busy
street, have a picture of a car or truck or bus on each card. Let children
make one punch for each vehicle that passes by. If you are near a park, have
tree, bush, or flower pictures on each card. Use school supply catalogs to cut
out pictures of playground equipment for your cards. What other items can
you think of?

Finally, **print a number on each of the cards, and let the children punch
that many holes in the card.** This is the most abstract activity of all. Save   +
it for the time when you are introducing number symbols and using other
number symbol activities such as computer programs, magnetic numbers,
and counting books.

Other small motor activities involving real objects or real tasks include
shucking peas and beans, which will later be cooked for eating. Your children can learn to **open pea pods and bean pods and** then extract the peas
and beans. Can they **count them**? If you cooperate with them in this activ-   +
ity, you will eventually have enough to be cooked. If there are not enough individual vegetables for everybody, how about putting the vegetables in a
soup or a stew? Kernels of corn on the ears also provide an interesting
counting activity for children. Have children help husk the corn. Then the
kernels can be cut off, counted, and put in a dish. If you have ears of pop
corn, the kernels can be popped.

Obviously, preschool children cannot be expected to count all the kernels
on an ear of corn, but with your help, they might **count the kernels in one
row and then a second row, and then compare the numbers in each row.**   +
Were they the same? Can they guess how many kernels will be in a third
row? Use empty margarine containers to collect the results of your children's vegetable counting tasks.

Children also need opportunities to pick up between their fingers objects
that are larger or heavier than peas and corn. Be sure to **have some kinds
of knobbed materials on your manipulative shelves.** Puzzles with knobs   +

on one side give children that practice. Montessori cylinder boards with knobs on the tops of graduated cylinders promote such small motor coordination as well as seriation skills. These can be ordered through school supply catalogs.

\+   If you want to **make your own finger strengthening materials that will also promote color and shape concepts, make geoboards and pegboards** for the children. Make a geoboard from a 1-foot-square board with headless nails pounded in rows 1 inch equidistant from one another. A set of colored rubber bands allow children to make all sorts of designs by stretching the rubber bands over the nails. Once they master this activity, you can **make**

\+   **simple patterns on graph paper** cut to the size of the board with colored pencils in the same colors as the rubber bands. Make only one or two patterns on each sheet, for example, a red square, a blue triangle, and so on. Let children put the graph patterns next to their geoboard and try to copy them using rubber bands.

\+   Do the same with **homemade pegboards.** Ask a lumber dealer for end-pieces or scraps of pegboard. Cut them into individual boards, sand them

\+   down, and **bring in sets of colored golf tees** to fit in the holes. Later, make simple colored patterns on paper cut the same size as the boards. Can the children copy your patterns with golf tees on their pegboards?

Although the physical development promoted within the Manipulative/ Math Center is small motor coordination, outside of the center you should also consider movement activities that will promote large motor skills. During creative movement sessions, **have children put on number necklaces**

\+   **or number vests from the math area and become those numbers.** If they are "number three," for instance, they can twirl three times or jump three times when the action calls for it. Ask them to show you how "number five" can dance to music with a beat.

· · · · · · · · · · **Activities to Promote Cognitive Development**

· **Number Games**

Of the several cognitive concepts previously mentioned, numbers and counting are discussed here. Make numbers personal, and you will make numbers a hit in your program. Children already associate personally with numbers. They are a certain age: three, four, or five. They can hold up the proper number of fingers to prove it. That is them—a certain number. If

\+   you **start with personal numbers** (just like their names), you will quickly have the attention of your children.

Have sets of three-dimensional numbers in plastic, wood, or metal for them to handle. A parent with a jigsaw might be willing to cut out wooden numbers 0 through 9 for you. Be sure that at least five copies of each number are made (or as many as the number of children allowed in the center). To introduce these particular numbers, you can **trace around each number on a sheet of posterboard.** Let children try to **match the wooden numbers** with their shape outlines. Another day, have small groups of children in the Manipulative/Math Center **find their own personal number,** their age. Have them choose a colored marker and trace around their own number on a paper. They can color the number with crayons if they want. Let them make as many number tracings as they want. The first ones may not be very accurate. One of these papers can be signed by the child, displayed in the Manipulative/Math Center, and later taken home.

Although number symbols are abstract, just as letters are, young children can learn their personal number name and number symbol just as they learn the letter names and letter symbols of their own names. Keep numbers personal like this, and children will want to be involved with them. When they are able to sign their papers with the letters of their name, **they can also sign their age number.**

Another personal number for a child is his or her house or apartment number. Does he know it? You can print it on a card for him. Can he find the numbers from the set of three-dimensional numbers in the area? Maybe two children together can find their house numbers. When they have found them, you can **give them similar peel-off numbers to be stuck on their cubbies or wherever they choose.** Another personal number is the child's **telephone number.** You may want to **print it on a 3-by-5 card to be put on a ring** with others and hung in the Dramatic Play Center **for pretend play with the telephones.**

• Counting Games

Before children experience actual counting, let them **play number counting games, songs, chants, and fingerplays.** From such games, young children learn the names of numbers and their sequence, rather than how to count. Books full of children's chants abound. A good one is *One Potato, Two Potato, Three Potato, Four! 165 Chants for Children* compiled by Mary Lou Colgin (1982). Or make up your own number chants, such as the one at the beginning of this chapter. **Let children help make number chants.** They can substitute their own rhyming words for the words of the number chant.

Keep counting books in the Manipulative/Math Center. Children will read them there and make the connection. When you are in the area, read a counting book to the children who are interested. Start with counting rhyme books, such as *Dancing in the Moon* by Fritz Eichenberg (1983), which counts in rhyme from one to twenty with a full-page cartoon-like drawing and a rhyming line of print at the bottom. Children love the zany pictures and rhymes and are soon making up their own.

The book *Count-a-Saurus* by Nancy Blumenthal (1989) counts in rhyme from one to ten with a different species of dinosaur on every double-spread page. **Have the container of little dinosaur figures** from the Block Center
+ on **hand when this book is being used.** Children's great interest in dinosaurs may carry them over to the Computer Center to operate the coloring program *Dinosaurs Are Forever* (1988) or the matching program *Dinosaurs* (1984). This may be the time to **expand the concept of dinosaurs into the**
+ **entire program with art activities and songs** about dinosaurs, as well.

One bear two bears, the strawberry number book by Richard Hefter, (1980) accompanies the computer program *Stickybear Numbers* (1982). The book contains full-color pages of multiple Stickybears in waiters' uniforms and jogging suits as it counts from one to ten and back down again in two-line rhymes. It is a clever and enjoyable introduction to the computer program.

The computer program itself is controlled by number keys and the space bar. Can your children find the number keys? Even children who can count often have trouble finding the number keys on the computer keyboard. Preschool children do not seem to recognize numbers as they do letters, perhaps because they have had less experience with them. Your children might do better because they have played with three-dimensional numbers in the Manipulative/Math Center. You may need to point out that the computer
+ number keys are on the top row or **play a find-the-numbers game.** Can they name any of the numbers? When they press a number, a full-color graphic scene appears with animated objects appearing one by one according to the number key pressed. Pressing the space bar either adds or subtracts an object from the scene every time it is pressed. Let children play with *Stickybear Numbers* as long as they want.

Another computer counting program is *Charlie Brown's 1-2-3's* (1985), in which the computer users select a number and then use the space bar or the number keys to count out that number. A correct response animates one of sixteen different Peanuts scenes.

In *Number Farm* (1984), six good counting games challenge the computer users, including one in which the children count sounds. In *Numbers Count* (1987), children color in number scenes using a mouse, joystick, or arrow keys. Their picture can be printed in color.

Once children have become familiar with rote counting to ten, they may
+ be ready to **count objects.** Such counting should always **begin with concrete objects** at first, before children use the computer or have counting
+ stories read to them. Again, **make counting personal,** and the children will not only enjoy it, but also begin to understand it. Can they count the fingers on one hand? On two hands? Let them count their hands themselves and their feet. How many shoes are they wearing? Give them a peel-off number sticker to put on each one: the numbers *1* and *2*. They can also wear these numbers on the backs of their hands.

What else can they count in the classroom? Perhaps the number of fish in the aquarium, guinea pigs in the cage, plants on the windowsill, puzzles in the puzzle rack (that's a hard one!). This is the time to **introduce number symbols at the entrance to each learning center.** Until now, you may have been using hooks, tickets, or necklaces as self-regulating devices for children to control how many can work in each center. Now, you can also post the number symbol next to the hooks in each area. Have the children help you.

This is also the time to read books about counting adventures. *So Many Cats!* by Beatrice Schenk de Regniers (1985) is the story of how a family came to end up with a dozen cats. The illustrations are cleverly done from a cat's point of view, with only the legs and feet of humans showing. *The Bears' Counting Book* by Robin and Jocelyn Wild (1978) is a wonderfully wild take-off on the traditional "Three Bears" story with counting from one to ten and then twenty, thirty, forty, and fifty.

Another way to count is to tally, to put down one mark for one object or one time. **Children enjoy tallying on the same kinds of picture cards** you made for picture punching. Let them choose a card and then tally the cars, trucks, trees, or people they see. Counting by fives is still beyond most preschoolers, so it is not important at this time for them to learn to tally in fives.

• • • • • • • • • • Activities to Promote Language Development

Children love to roll around big words on their tongues. **Let them have the chance to use big number words.** Wanda Gag's classic picture book *Millions of Cats* (1928) repeats a verse about huge numbers of cats, using the words *millions, billions,* and *trillions.* Those big rhyming words sound wonderful to children, and they will be joining in on the verse before you are finished reading.

But how much is a million? David M. Schwartz's book *How Much is a Million?* (1985) tells us this answer and so much more with Steven Kellogg's expressive illustrations. He makes numbers personal as children count from one to a million, to a billion, to a trillion, and then take a balloon ride through 100,000 stars.

• • • • • • • • • • Activities to Promote Social Development

Children can continue their exploration of number words as they operate the computer in pairs. They can learn that a pair is two things together. They can look for other pairs in the room. **Put all the shoes from your dress-up area in a sack for children to dump out and sort into pairs.** What else makes a pair in your classroom? A knife and fork, a cup and saucer, two mittens, two boots.

Do people come in pairs? What makes them a pair? How should the individual people in a pair act toward each other? A pair of children can also be called partners. What do partners do together? Can they take turns? Can they share with each other? Can they walk down the hall or down the street with each other? This is a good time to talk about caring and cooperation.

• • • • • • • • • • Activities to Promote Creative Development

Young children love to pretend. They take on the roles of the people they know or the people they have met as they play in the Dramatic Play Center. These activities, in turn, stimulate their creative imaginations as they make up situations about the people around them. How do such activities involve mathematics? The dramatic play that children perform after a field trip can include many number activities.

If children have taken a field trip to the post office, the teacher should put out props in the Dramatic Play Center that will stimulate post-office play, such as stamps, envelopes, a postage meter, letter-carrier caps, a mailbag,
+ and so on. Children can **pretend to weigh the letters on the meter** that you provide. Which numbers do the stamps have on them? What do these numbers mean? Which numbers are in the address on the letters? What do these numbers mean? If children are pretending about their trip to the post office, they will like to hear you read *The Post Office Book: Mail and How It Works* by Gail Gibbons (1982), as well as the simple, colorful book *The Postman* by Rosalinda Kightley (1987).

After the children have visited a health clinic, they may want to pretend to be doctor and nurse in the Dramatic Play Center. In addition to the props you provide, such as stethoscope, white coat, and other doctor parapherna-
+ lia, you can **bring in a real scale and also a tape measure or yard stick.** Let them weigh and measure one another. You can record the results on a chart. These are other personal numbers children will want to know about. Why is it important to be weighed and measured? What do the numbers mean? Discuss such concepts with the children.

The children may want to continue this clinic pretend play in the Block
+ Center. Put **the postage meter there as a scale for weighing the toy people.** You can make a chart to record these weights as well. The heights of the block people can be measured with a tape measure or ruler and recorded on another chart. What else can children weigh and measure in your classroom? They may want to weigh their dolls and the guinea pig, or they may want to measure how tall their bean plants have grown.

Keep an eye open for the pretending that goes on in various areas of your classroom. There may be other opportunities for you to contribute math activities to dramatic play where appropriate. Are the children pretending to have races with the little cars in the Block Center? You can **bring in a stop watch to time the races.** Children love to handle and operate such devices. An excellent book that is sure to stimulate their interest in measuring this very abstract concept of time in a more concrete, hands-on manner is David Lloyd and Penny Dale's *The Stopwatch* (1986). If the children express further interest in measuring time, bring in a three-minute hourglass egg timer, or put a toy clock with wooden hands in the Dramatic Play Center for hands-on exploration.

+

• • • • • • • • • • • The Teacher's Role in the Manipulative/Math Center

• Observing Developmental Levels

Teachers will need to keep careful track of individual children in this center in order to determine their developmental levels. What should a teacher look for at the *manipulation* level, for instance? Children at this level will be playing around with the materials but not making or doing anything constructive with them. For example, they may dump out all the blocks from a plastic container but not build with them. They may put them back into the container and then dump them out again. They may get out puzzle pieces and scatter them around. The bag of hickory nuts and acorns you have collected for sorting into plastic cups may be poured out on the floor or dumped into another container and carried away.

The teacher who sees this realizes that this is the child's first level of interaction with materials, the manipulation level. He or she needs such exploratory activities in order to discover what use can be made of materials. The teacher records such actions on the Child Interaction Form and writes suggestions on the back of the form for helping such children progress to more mature levels of interaction.

Children who put together the snapping blocks, who string the beads, who make the puzzles, who pile up the stacking blocks, or who line up the dominoes—are most likely to be at the mastery level in their exploratory play. You may want to observe them closely to be sure. Are they using the materials in the ordinary way, or have they created their own games with them? Are they repeating the activity again and again? Most of your children will be playing at mastering the materials like this, but a few may have progressed beyond mastery to meaning, the level at which children apply their own creative ideas using the materials in new and unusual ways.

Whatever their levels, give them time to use the materials you have provided. An expert at puzzle making may not have mastered bristle blocks at all.

Children who string beads over and over are most likely to be at the mastery level in their exploratory play.

• Recording on the Child Interaction Form

Children playing in the Manipulative/Math Center may be at the same or different levels of development as they interact with the materials. Careful observation and recording of children in the center can help teachers support children needing assistance, as well as help in planning for individuals who are ready for more challenging activities. An example of such recording shows Lisa and Beth at work in the Center one morning.

Lisa takes from the shelf a container of large, colored counting beads with holes in their centers and dumps them out on a nearby table. She sits down at the table and moves the beads around with both hands, almost as if she is fingerpainting. She begins stacking them up, but the stacks fall over, so she mixes them around on the table again with both hands. Beth comes into the center, watches Lisa, and then gets a board with stacking rods off the shelf. "This is how you do it," she declares. She sits down and begins to stack beads on each rod according to their color. Lisa tries to put

FIGURE 5–1	Child Interaction Form

Child __Lisa, Beth__   Observer___D. B.___

Center __Manipulative / Math___   Date_____9/25_____

CHILD INTERACTION FORM
With Materials

Manipulation Level   Actions/Words
(Child moves materials around
without using them as intended.)

Lisa moves counting beads around on table. Tries to stack them (without rods) but they fall. She mixes them around with both hands.

Mastery Level   Actions/Words
(Child uses materials as
intended, over and over.)

Beth gets board with rods; begins stacking beads by color; says, "This is how you do it." Dumps beads & stacks them several times.

Meaning Level   Actions/Words
(Child uses materials in
new and creative ways.)

With Other Children

Solitary Play   Actions/Words
(Child plays with
materials by self.) *Lisa plays with beads by herself (as usual). Beth comes in & begins stacking beads on rods. She takes over & does not let Lisa play. (Beth usually plays alone like this.)*

Parallel Play   Actions/Words
(Child plays next to others with same
materials but not involved with them.)

Cooperative Play   Actions/Words
(Child plays together with
others and same materials.)

Lisa tries to put beads on rods that Beth is using but not by color; Beth dumps them off.

beads on the rods, but not according to their color. Beth dumps all the beads off the rods and begins again. This time she refuses to let Lisa help. When she is finished, she dumps the beads off the rods and begins to stack them again. Beth gets up and leaves. A nearby observer records the actions as shown in Figure 5–1. On the reverse side of the Child Interaction Form the observer records her interpretation of this incident and suggests plans for the girls. This form will be collected at the end of the day, along with any other observation forms, and used in the daily and weekly classroom planning. The observer writes the following:

Accomplishments:
Lisa made the first move I've seen to play with another child by trying to stack blocks on Beth's rods.
Beth is at the mastery level of stacking-block play.

Needs:
Beth seems to need more practice playing at this level.
Beth also needs to become involved playing with others.
Lisa needs to get involved with others, maybe be more assertive.

Plans:
Bring out more stacking materials and colored counters (nesting cubes, stacking blocks, colored chips).
Encourage Lisa to play with another child with these materials; maybe someone else at the manipulative level (observe to see who).
Ask Beth to show another child how to stack.

• Interacting with Children in the Manipulative/Math Center

Children often play with these materials on their own or parallel to other children seated at the same table. Your daily observations will help you to know when and how to interact with the children. If Tammy is still filling and dumping the parquetry blocks as she did when the program began, you may want to sit beside her and ask what else she can do with the blocks. It may take a question like this to get her thinking or to get her started doing something else. Stay beside her for awhile if it seems appropriate. You could play with a few of the blocks parallel to her. Try sorting out all the red ones, or stack up one of the shapes in a pile, or make a simple design from them. If she is ready to try something different, she may enter your play or start something similar parallel to yours. If not, you can continue to observe. Your presence delivers an important nonverbal message to Tammy: that the teacher cares enough about me to spend time watching what I do.

You may want to comment on what some of the other children are doing in the area in order to learn more about their thinking or the concepts they are dealing with. Rather than a direct question, it is often more appropriate to make a statement about their work: "Rodney, you are lining up many of the Cuisenaire rods of the same color." Rodney may respond in a totally unexpected way: "These yellow ones are carrot sticks, and I'm going to feed them to my rabbit." From this, you realize that Rodney has gone beyond merely sorting or counting to the meaning level of exploratory play with the Cuisenaire rods. Another day, you may want to bring Rodney several Cuisenaire pattern sheets to build with: a more complex skill than many pre-schoolers can handle, but it may be a stimulating challenge to Rodney.

• Introducing a New Activity

Some manipulative/math activities are best introduced by the center it-self, with the children finding them on the shelves and figuring out how they work on their own. Others are better introduced by one of the teachers. If you know that your children have become really interested in a particular topic and want to go further with it, you may decide to introduce the new ac-tivity to a small group of children in this center. Later in the day or on the following days, other children can come into the center and be introduced to the new activity either by you or by the children who already know some-thing about it.

For example, the children in one class became interested in measuring things because of a carpenter who had been working outside in the hall. They had watched him measuring the dimensions for a new door for the caf-eteria. The teacher overheard some of them playing carpenter in the Block Center, building a structure that needed a new door.

She decided to introduce some measuring tools in the Manipulative/Math Center. After five children had entered the area, she followed with a small metal box and a book. The children were used to having the teachers bring surprising new things into the various centers like this, so they gathered around her at the table with great anticipation. First she **read them the book,** *Tool Book* by Gail Gibbons (1982). It showed simple pictures of all   + kinds of tools that help people build things.

Then she told them that the metal box contained some of the tools pic-tured in the book. They, of course, wanted to know which ones. She asked them to guess. Some children said "hammer" or "screwdriver," but Tony asked to pick up the box so he could feel it. He rattled it around. Everyone watched and waited while he made his guess. Tony said, "It's not very heavy. Maybe it's a ruler." He was partly right. The box contained a flat ruler, a folding ruler, and a metal tape measure. The children were delighted because they knew they were going to get to use these tools. The teacher was delighted because of the way Tony had made his guess. He had really used a scientific method of inquiry rather than making a stab in the dark, so to speak. Afterward, the children got to measure the door of their own class-room using each of the tools. Other children who watched the Manipu-lative/Math Center group do the measuring knew that their turn would come later that day or the next. The teacher added her box of tools to the manipulative shelf and put a label on it illustrating measuring tools.

In this way, the children in this classroom and in your classroom, too, can become excited about numbers: how to recognize them, what to do with them, and how they help us get along in our world.

IDEAS +

in CHAPTER 5

1. *Promoting positive attitudes about math*

   a. Have children explore math as they work with blocks and have fun with numbers. (p. 98)

2. *Teaching math concepts*

   a. Give children playful opportunities to practice identifying shapes, sizes, and colors one concept at a time. (p. 100)

   b. Give them real experiences. Looking at pictures is not enough. (p. 101)

   c. Have the center full of interesting, concrete objects for counting. (p. 101)

   d. Use familiar objects for counting. (p. 103)

3. *Promoting small motor development*

   a. Strengthen finger muscles and provide counting practice by bringing in several paper punches. (p. 104)

   b. Make picture punching cards with a picture or outline on each. (pp. 104–105)

   c. Display cards on punch board in the area. (p. 105)

   d. Have picture punching field trips. (p. 105)

   e. Have small motor and counting practice from opening pea pods. (p. 105)

   f. Count kernels in two rows of corn and compare. (p. 105)

   g. Have knobbed materials on manipulative shelves. (p. 105)

   h. Make homemade finger-strengthening materials such as geoboards and pegboards. (p. 106)

4. *Promoting number concepts through personalizing*

   a. Have children put on a number necklace or vest and become that number. (p. 106)

   b. Start with personal numbers such as age. (pp. 106–107)

   c. Match three-dimensional numbers to their outlines. (p. 106)

   d. Have children sign their age. (p. 107)

   e. Use peel-off personal numbers on cubbies. (p. 107)

5. *Promoting counting concepts*

   a. Play number counting games, songs, chants, and fingerplays. (p. 107)

   b. Keep counting books in the Manipulative Center. (p. 107)

   c. Have a collection of dinosaur figures, dinosaur counting books, and dinosaur computer programs. (p. 108)

   d. Play find-the-numbers game with the computer keys. (p. 108)

   e. Make counting personal with peel-off numbers on hands and shoes. (p. 108)

   f. Put a number symbol on the entrance to every activity area when children begin learning number symbols. (p. 109)

   g. Do tallying activity on picture cards. (p. 109)

6. *Promoting math language concepts*

   a. Use big number words such as *millions*. (p. 109)

   b. Let children collect a dozen in egg cartons. (p. 109)

7. *Promoting social development*
   a. Learn the meaning of pairs/partners from shoe activity. (p. 109)

8. *Promoting creative development through dramatic play*
   a. Bring in a postage meter and weigh letters. (p. 110)
   b. Have a scale, tape measure, and yard stick to weigh and measure children. (p. 110)
   c. Use a postage meter to weigh toy people in the Block Center. (p. 110)
   d. Let children weigh dolls or guinea pig and measure plant growth. (p. 110)
   e. Bring in a stopwatch or egg timer to time little car races. (p. 111)

9. *Introducing a new activity*
   a. Introduce a carpenter's measuring tools with a book. (p. 115)

REFERENCES CITED

Schultz, K. A., Colarusso, R. P., & Strawderman, V. W. (1989). *Mathematics for every young child.* Columbus, OH: Merrill Publishing Company.

Williams, C. K., & Kamii, C. (1986). How do children learn by handling objects? *Young Children, 42* (1), 23–26.

OTHER SOURCES

Bauch, J. P., & Huei-hsin, J. H. (1988). Montessori: Right or wrong about number concepts? *Arithmetic Teacher,* 8–11.

Beaty, J. J., & Tucker, W. H. (1987). *The computer as a paintbrush.* Columbus, OH: Merrill Publishing Company.

Buckleitner, W. (1989). *Survey of early childhood software.* Ypsilanti, MI: The High/Scope Press.

Colgin, M. L. (1982). *One potato, two potato, three potato, four! 165 chants for children.* Mt. Rainier, MD: Gryphon House.

Harsh, A. (1987). Teach mathematics with children's literature. *Young Children, 42* (6), 24–29.

Price, G. G. (1989). Mathematics in early childhood. *Young Children, 44* (4), 53–58.

Richardson, L. I., Goodman, K. L., Hartman, N. N., & LePique, H. C. (1980). *A mathematics activity curriculum for early childhood and special education.* New York: Macmillan.

Stone, J. I. (1987). Early childhood math: Make it manipulative. *Young Children, 42* (6), 16–23.

CHILDREN'S BOOKS

Blumenthal, N. (1989). *Count-a-saurus.* New York: Four Winds Press.

Cleary, B. (1987). *The growing-up feet,* New York: William Morrow and Company.

De Regniers, B. S. (1985). *So many cats.* New York: Clarion Books.

Eichenberg, F. (1983). *Dancing in the moon.* San Diego, CA: Harcourt Brace Jovanovich.

Gag, W. (1928). *Millions of cats.* New York: Putnam Publishing Group.

Gibbons, G. (1982). *The post office book: Mail and how it moves.* New York: Harper & Row.

Gibbons, G. (1982). *Tool book.* New York: Holiday House.

Hefter, R. (1980). *One bear, two bears, the strawberry number book.* New York: Weekly Reader Books.

Kightley, R. (1987). *The postman.* New York: Macmillan.

Lloyd, D., & Dale, P. (1986). *The stopwatch.* New York: Harper & Row.

Schwartz, D. M. (1985). *How much is a million?* New York: Lothrup, Lee and Shepard Books.

Wild, R., & Wild, J. (1978). *The bears' counting book.* New York: Harper & Row.

Winthrop, E. (1986). *Shoes.* New York: Harper & Row.

CHILDREN'S COMPUTER PROGRAMS (by publisher)

Advanced Ideas, Inc.
2550 Ninth Street
Berkeley, CA 94710
   Dinosaurs 1984 (Apple, IBM, C64)

DLM
One DLM Park
Allen, TX 75002
   Fish Scales 1985 (Apple)
   Number Farm 1984 (Apple, IBM, C64)

Polarware, Inc.
P.O. Box 311
2600 Kesinger Road
Geneva, IL 60134
   Dinosaurs Are Forever 1988 (Apple, IBM, C64)
   Numbers Count 1987 (Apple, IBM, C64)

Random House Software
400 Hahn Road
Westminster, MD 21157
   Charlie Brown's 1-2-3s 1985 (Apple)

Weekly Reader Software
Middletown, CT 06457
   Stickybear Numbers 1982 (Apple, IBM, C64, Atari)

TRY IT *YOURSELF*

1. Set up your Manipulative/Math Center attractively with several activities each to promote the skills of sorting, matching, one-to-one correspondence, seriation, numbers, counting, weighing, and measuring. In addition to the shelf materials, include books, computer games, and a bulletin board.

2. Do a counting activity based on a theme (animals, acorns, etc.) with a small group of children. Include hands-on materials they can explore with, an appropriate book, and an activity in some other center of the room, for example, Art or Dramatic Play.

3. Do a counting or tallying field trip with children using picture cards of objects to be counted or tallied.

4. Do a weighing or measuring activity with children using real tools and recording the results.

5. Introduce a new math concept to a small group of children, bringing in a new activity or material for them to use.

6

STORY CENTER

B O O K S   *(Action chant)*

"Come in, come in!"	(Motion with hand)
Said the library door;	
I opened it wide	(Fling arms apart)
And saw books galore!	
Tall skinny books	(Raise arms straight up)
Up high on the shelves;	
Little fat books	(Arms down and swinging)
That stood by themselves.	
I opened one up	(Squat down)
And sat down to look;	
The pictures told stories!	(Jump up)
What a wonderful book!	

• • • • • • • • • • Books and Stories in the Early Childhood Classroom

Your classroom should be filled with wonderful, warm, happy, exciting, and inviting books. Each of the learning centers needs a book nook where children's picture books about the experiences happening in that area can be featured: books about buildings in the Block Center, books about concepts in the Computer Center, books about counting in the Manipulative/ Math Center, books about letters in the Writing Center, books about colors in the Art Center, books about songs in the Music Center, books about pets and plants in the Science Center, books about people doing things in the Dramatic Play Center, and books about running and jumping in the Large Motor Center. This text has offered suggestions in every chapter about specific books to use in each center in order to support or extend the activities in progress.

Most important of all, however, your classroom should contain a wonderful, warm, happy, exciting, and inviting Story Center where individuals or small groups of children can gather and snuggle in for their favorite stories—to be read by them or told by you. The Story Center should be one of the most attractive learning centers in your classroom. A colorful shag rug with puffy pillows and a bean bag chair or bolster can invite your youngsters to come on in and relax with a book.

"Can three-, four-, and five-year-old children actually read?" you may ask. That is not the point. The idea of locating books throughout the classroom and integrating them into every facet of the curriculum is to bring together children and books in wonderful ways. Children need to have good feelings about books. They can learn how important books are in the functioning of the classroom. They can experience how enjoyable books are when they are sat down with and read from. They can see how beautiful books become when they are opened up and looked at.

Bringing together young children and picture books may be one of the most important services you perform for your youngsters. As almost every current study on children's learning points out: "The power of reading to children is also reflected in their success in school. Research has shown that children who have listened to stories and poems from an early age experience the most success in school" (Friedberg & Strong, 1989, 46). We can add that the *more* you read to young children or tell stories from books, the more children will want to be associated with books, and the more they will want to learn to read on their own.

Finally, both you and the children will find the book experience one of the most delightful activities you can do together. Snuggling up close to the teacher with a lovely book is a warm and wonderful way for both of you to express caring. By her actions, the teacher is saying to the child: "I am taking time out of a busy day to share something nice with you because I care about you." The child's actions say to the teacher: "I enjoy being close to you like this because I care for you, too."

• • • • • • • • • • Emergent Literacy and Reading Readiness

Current research about how children learn to read and why some do not learn very well has made us change our minds about so-called "reading readiness." We used to believe that children were not ready to learn to read until a certain age, say six, or until various developmental processes, say eye-hand coordination, had been completed. The best we could do for them was to give them reading readiness activities such as ditto sheets and workbooks that had children matching letters and sounds or circling which picture was the same or which was different.

Today, we know that children are ready to learn to read at birth. Yes, that's right—at birth! We have discovered that learning to read was not at all what we thought it was. Instead of learning a rigidly sequenced set of skills, children need to learn print awareness, that is, they need to encounter print very early in life and have all kinds of interactive experiences with it (McKenzie & Pinnell, 1989).

They need to see and interact with environmental print: the signs and symbols in everyday life such as television ads, fast-food signs, supermarket products, gas station signs, and video cassette covers. They need to be exposed to books, reading, and storytelling as soon as they are old enough to be held on their mother's or father's lap. They need to see the adults around them reading books, magazines, and newspapers and writing letters, shopping lists, and notes to one another. They themselves need to be involved with sending a card to Grandma, or writing a letter to Santa Claus, or telling Uncle Al the story about where the new kitten came from, or typing their name in a computer game.

What has this to do with learning to read? Through current research, we have discovered that learning to read and to write are, in fact, developmental processes that emerge naturally in youngsters given the proper conditions and encouragement.

Just as children acquire language naturally, they can also acquire literacy. In the case of language acquisition, children need to be exposed to people speaking the language. They, in turn, need to use language themselves in a developmental sequence over time until they have refined it. So, too, with reading and writing. Given the proper conditions, many children can also acquire reading and writing naturally over time. Some children's acquisition of literacy may not be terribly refined before age seven, but other children as young as four have taught themselves to read.

Kindergarten teachers are acknowledging the fact that every year a child or two enters their classes already knowing how to read. In checking with parents, they sometimes find that this fact is a complete surprise to them, as well. Not only did the parents not teach their youngster to read, they did not even know he could read. How, then, did it happen? Their child was evidently exposed to a print-rich environment through which he picked up the necessary knowledge and skills to crack the reading code on his own. Perhaps there were older siblings whose reading motivated him to learn how. Seeing ads on television, going to fast-food restaurants with signs he knew the meaning of, seeing familiar print on boxes of breakfast cereal, looking at magazine pictures with simple captions he could understand, being read to from familiar picture books, playing games on the computer—all these print activities assisted his literacy to emerge naturally.

Yet emergent literacy is no new phenomenon. In every era in which books and print have been accessible and encouraged, children have taught themselves to read. Samuel Clemens (Mark Twain) made these notes about his two daughters in 1880:

> Bay and Susy *taught themselves to read English, and without knowing the alphabet,* or making any attempt to *spell* the words or divide them into syllables. . . . Bay (who has never been allowed to meddle with English alphabets or books lest she would neglect her German) collared an English juvenile-poem book sent her from London . . . and *now,* 10 or 12 days later . . . she reads abstruse English works with astounding facility! Nobody has given her an instant's assistance. . . . They both read fluently, now, but they make no attempts at spelling; neither of them knows more than half the letters of the alphabet. They read wholly by the *look* of the word. (Salsbury, 1965, 128)

• • • • • • • • • • Reading in the Preschool Classroom

What do these findings mean for the preschool teacher? Should you, in fact, begin teaching your children to read? No. Emergent literacy does not happen through formal teaching. It occurs in environments that are filled with print: signs, lists, records, charts, graphs, pictures, books, labels, stories, magazines, newspapers, computer programs, and food containers. It happens where books are read by teachers to individuals and small groups, where books are available for children to look at on their own, where stories are told orally for children to listen to and respond to, and where children make up their own stories that are tape recorded or written down.

What you should be providing for your children includes three important items:

1. A print-rich environment as described above.
2. The freedom for children to choose books and activities.
3. The time to become deeply involved so that books and activities become meaningful.

Children are marvelous meaning extractors. They come equipped with the curiosity to find out about their world and with five senses with which to explore their world. The sensory input they receive from their explorations is then processed in their brains, where its meaning is extracted. Some children are better explorers than others. Some children are better meaning extractors than others. Literacy may thus emerge naturally in some children sooner than in others, but we know that in order to support this self-directed process of learning, teachers must allow children the freedom to choose books and activities that interest them. They must then allow children time enough to become deeply involved with the books. From such activities, children should be able to extract the following information:

1. How a book works.
2. How a story goes.
3. When to turn the pages.
4. How print conveys messages.
5. How illustrations help make sense of print.
   (Friedberg & Strong, 1989, 43)

Children also seem to learn on their own such details as:

1. Stories are written in horizontal lines of print.
2. Lines of print are read from left to right.
3. Stories start at the top of the page and work down.

• • • • • • • • • • Reading at Home

The above information, we now realize, is necessary for young children to make sense of the reading process. If children have been read to at home, they have already begun the process. If they have not, you will want to involve parents in reading to their children as well. **Have a duplicate collection of lending books for children to borrow at the end of the day** and + return in the morning. **Invite parents to the Story Center to listen** with the + children to your reading, **and then let parents take a turn at reading** them- + selves. Send home a **newsletter with the names of the books** that their chil- + dren are involved with, and **give directions for making** some of the **book extension puppets, puzzles, and games** in the Story Center. **Have a "book bee" for the parents** to attend to become familiar with good children's + books and to make book games to take home for their children. Ask parents to send in the **titles of books that their children have read at home** so that + you can **keep track on the "My Favorite Books" chart**. What other parent- + involvement book activities can you think of? How about a **field trip to the public library** with parents to help? Library cards can be issued to those + families that do not have them.

• • • • • • • • • • Setting Up the Story Center

As already mentioned, *make this area inviting*! Do whatever necessary to make it attractive so that children cannot wait to become involved with books. **Use bright colors** wherever you can: on rugs, on pillows, on furni- + ture, on the walls, and on the shelves. Put up **book posters** on the walls. Col- + orful posters by favorite picture-book artists are now available in children's book stores or from the Children's Book Council, Inc., 350 Scotland Rd., Orange, NJ 07050; or use dust jackets from some of the books on your shelves. Have book **puppets, book puzzles, and book games** displayed. Have a **flan-** + **nelboard** on the wall at the children's height or on a low easel. Have **child-size bookshelves that display the fronts** of your books. Also include a **tape recorder and tapes you have made from reading aloud some of the books on your shelf**. +

Make this area comfortable. Some children like to lie on the floor to read. Provide soft, colorful rugs and pillows. Some children like to lounge on a **window seat** when they read. Put in a wooden bench, box, or ledge under a + window; pad it with foam, and cover it with colorful upholstery material and pillows. Some children like to sit in chairs or rockers to read. Make room for child-size chairs and rockers, or perhaps a bean-bag chair or two. **Inflated chairs,** low wooden **benches, sit-on foam animals, giant foam blocks,** and +

Make your Book Center inviting and comfortable by using colorful pillows and a soft rug.

+ upholstered **junior couches** are other popular seating devices. One teacher we observed made her Story Center the most popular place in the room by putting in **an old bathtub** that she **painted, decorated with stick-ons, and**
+ **filled with pillows**.

You may want a small, round table with chairs in the area for displaying magazines and book-related games or puzzles, but if your area is a small one, it is often better to make room for comfortable floor reading space with cushions rather than by taking up the space with a table.

What about the adult readers? Make the area comfortable for yourself, too, and other adult readers. An adult-size rocking chair is not really safe for children whose feet or fingers often end up under the rockers. You may be able to arrange, instead, for a donated couch or daybed. Be creative. Be different. Be daring with your Story Center.

What about the display of books? Be sure to have a good number and selection of picture books of all kinds as suggested in the remainder of the chapter. Display them on vertical shelves with the covers visible for easy selection by the children. Be sure the books are in good condition. Nothing is more discouraging to potential readers than books with torn pages and covers missing. The condition of such books makes a nonverbal statement you should not be making: that you do not take care of books. Remove such books and either repair them or remove them for use in some of the suggested games to follow.

It is not necessary to display all the books you have at one time; but **have a core of favorites that is always on the shelves**. Children should be able to read a favorite book over and over. Adding new books from time to time adds a new dimension and new interest to the area.

Other innovative ways to display books may attract children to this and other areas. One method is to fasten a clothesline or rod against the wall of the classroom from one end of the room to the other. **From this horizontal device, hang several colored ribbons for books** in each of the learning centers. The colors of the ribbons can match the color code of the center. Tie one end of each ribbon to the rod or line, and fasten a clipboard-type clip to the other end of each ribbon at children's eye level. Then, clip the books you are using in each area to the ribbons, where they can be displayed in an attractive, yet space-saving manner against the wall. Children enjoy clipping and unclipping the books if you show them how—another good small motor task. Can they also choose which books can be clipped to the ribbons every week?

• • • • • • • • • • Books to Promote Language Development

"Don't all books promote language development?" you may wonder. Of course they do. All children's books use language in ways that children may never have heard before. The books to be discussed in this section, however, are the ones that support the theme of the Appropriate Practices Curriculum—that children develop various skills through three levels of interaction: manipulation, mastery, and meaning.

It is not difficult to understand how children learn to build with blocks first through manipulating them, then through the repetition necessary for mastery, and finally by applying their own meanings. It is easy to see how children can interact at these three levels with materials such as puzzles, pegboards, or even computer programs, but it seems strange, indeed, that language development also occurs through this same interaction process. Nevertheless, it is true.

Children learn language by playing around (interacting) with vocal sounds and words at the same three levels. From infancy, through toddlerhood, and into the preschool years, youngsters first of all play with the *sounds* of language. The sound play of young children equates with the manipulation level of interaction with three-dimensional objects. Then, the youngsters repeat the sounds or words they especially like in interesting or funny *patterns* over and over. This pattern play equates with the mastery level of interaction. Finally, youngsters apply their own *meanings* to words by using them in original ways. This meaning play is the most advanced and mature interaction of children with words, and not every preschool child reaches this level.

Children's books can support these three important levels of interaction in youngsters' development of language skills. The books listed here have attracted children's attention and interaction at these three levels. Many other similar books can offer the same opportunities for your own children's language development. Keep such language interaction levels in mind when you select books to promote your children's language development.

• Sound Play

Young children play with words just as they play with blocks. Is this hard for you to believe? Then listen to your toddlers or preschoolers when they are lying down waiting to fall asleep. They often talk to themselves, murmuring sounds or words over and over. When they are awake, they often play around with similar sounds or sound words. If they stumble upon a funny one, they will repeat it again and again or make up similar words of their own to go along with it. If they hear you read a book with a word in it that tickles their funnybone, they will break up with laughter and leave you wondering what was so funny. Some children mutter to themselves constantly just under their breath as they play. If you could turn up the volume, you might hear a sound chant or a word being played around with.

With this knowledge in mind, you will want to **have books available that**
+   **feature interesting words or funny sounds**. One such classic picture book is Margaret Wise Brown's *Goodnight Moon* (1947). It is a simple story of a little bunny who says goodnight to all the things in his room as it grows progressively darker. The story contains one word that often sends children off into gails of laughter. Among the items the bunny says "goodnight" to are "a comb and a brush and a bowl full of *mush*." It is the sound of the word *mush* that children respond to so hilariously. If this is a favorite book for your youngsters, you will undoubtedly have to read it many times, just for them to hear the word *mush*.

This might make a good nap book in your program if you read it after the curtains are drawn and the lights are turned off. **Read it in a whispery**
+   **voice to lull the children to sleep**. You can extend the whispery, singsong
+   repetition if you also **say goodnight to the things in your own classroom** one by one. Perhaps the children will all be asleep before you finish.

Another classic with wonderful sounding words is *Caps for Sale* by Esphyr Slobodkina (1968). A tree full of monkeys who steal the peddler's caps make the fascinating sound "tsz, tsz, tsz" every time the peddler shakes his finger at them. Your children will love to hear you say it and love to repeat it themselves every time it occurs in the story. Here is a story **they**

may want to dramatize if it is a favorite. **Bring in some caps of various colors,** use them yourself in telling (not reading) the story to a small group, and then leave the caps in the Story Center for the children to use in their own versions of the story. +

A third classic story with sounds that children enjoy hearing and repeating is Robert McCloskey's *Blueberries for Sal* (1948). Little Sal and Little Bear go off with their respective mothers to pick blueberries on Blueberry Hill, where they all get mixed up with one another before the day is over. The sound of "kuplink, kuplank, kuplunk" as Sal drops berries into her little tin pail is another favorite of children. **Bring in a little tin pail and let your children take turns dropping various items into it**. Ask the children what the items sound like. +

Children like books about animals and their sounds as well. In Tana Hoban's *A Children's Zoo* (1985), colored photos of the animals stand out against totally black pages. The simple text in large, white print says three things about each animal on the opposite page. Some are action words, but most are sound words as "growls," "roars," and "squawks." This makes the last page all the more effective about the giraffe who is: "tall . . spotted . . silent." Children respond well to this last word, a new word for them, and want the book repeated over and over so they can hear it.

• Pattern Play

Once children have learned what to do with words, they begin playing with them at the next level of interaction by putting them into brief, repeated patterns. Such word play is almost like a chant, with one word repeated and another word rhymed, much like jump-rope rhymes. Children say things such as, "Hamburger, ram-burger, lam-burger, sam-burger," to themselves over and over. Researcher Judith Schwartz has found this to be the most frequent kind of language play she observed (Schwartz, 1981). It is almost a self-imposed language drill or practice of words and phrases, but again, it is done playfully and spontaneously by the children, who often burst into laughter over the funny sounds of the words.

You can support this type of language interaction in your program with a delightful selection of **books that feature repeated rhyming words or phases**. Bruce Degen's *Jamberry* (1985) takes a boy and a bear through a wild romp with all kinds of berries raining down on them, from blueberry and strawberry to "Raspberry, jazzberry, razzamatazzberry." Can your children **follow up by going out and picking berries**? If not, perhaps they can visit an outdoor market on a **field trip** and **buy some berries** for their lunch or snack. +

Another pattern play book that children can't get enough of is a wonderfully wild, modern version of the classic jump-rope rhyme, *The Lady with the Alligator Purse,* adapted by Nadine Bernard Westcott (1988). The pattern here is the repeated phrase *in came the*:

> *In came the doctor,*
> *In came the nurse,*
> *In came the lady with the alligator purse.*

If you read it to your children, be prepared for all of them to want pizza for lunch the same as "the lady with the alligator purse" provides for everyone in the story. You might, in fact, **consider making pizza with the children as**
+ **a followup** to this book. **Bring in some big purses** as well, and leave them in
+ the Story Center **for the opportunity of acting out this funny story**. Children tend to memorize such rhymes spontaneously after they have heard them repeated enough. Memory practice like this is another boost for emergent literacy.

A simple, silly rhyming book with another funny pattern play is *Sheep in a Jeep* by Nancy Shaw (1986). Five sheep jump in a jeep and take it for a rocky ride that will have your children making sheep and jeep rhymes after they finish laughing. If sheep are among the farm animals in the Block Center, you could **bring them into the story center along with one of your toy**
+ **vehicles** for followup play after you read this book.

On the other hand, this book also lends itself to being **converted for**
+ **flannelboard use** because of its large, colorful illustrations. Children enjoy doing followup activities with the books they like. If paperback copies are available, as they are with this book, you can buy duplicate books and cut them up to make flannelboard characters, puzzles, and other activities. Do your cutting, of course, out of the children's sight.

To make flannelboard characters, simply cut out a picture of the jeep, the five sheep, the pigs, and the tree. Glue them each to cardboard and sandpaper backing, and store them in a large, labeled envelope next to the flannelboard. Keep a second copy of the book in the envelope to be looked at when the children play with the flannelboard characters. They may want to act out the original story on the flannelboard or make up their own version. To make your own flannelboard, glue a square of felt onto cardboard backing. This, in turn, can be mounted on an easel, the wall, or a cardboard box cut into an easel for children to use with their flannelboard book characters. Children also like small, personal flannelboards big enough for a single child.

When children play with flannelboard characters, they often like to hear the book being read. They can do this independently if you **tape record your**
+ **reading of the book** for playback on the cassette tape recorder located in the Story Center. As you record the story, remember to include a sound cue every time you turn a page so that the children will be able to turn the pages

at the proper time when they use the tape and book independently. Tapping a glass with a spoon makes a good page-turning cue.

• Meaning Play

Meaning play is the most sophisticated form of word play. Children who have truly mastered the rules for using words in the normal ways sometimes go on to applying their own meanings, that is, they try out new and funny ways of using words. They try fooling around with the meanings of words, using puns, mixing up words in sentences, and using synonyms and homonyms, or words with double meanings. Schwartz found only ten samples of meaning play in her study of young children playing with language, all but one of these examples from children more than five years old (Schwartz, 1981).

More and more publishers of children's picture books recognize these abilities in young children and provide the kinds of books that will stimulate such play. Children who have not reached this interaction level with language may still enjoy the books because they are funny, although they may not really understand the joke.

In Pat Hutchin's *The Surprise Party* (1969), Rabbit whispers to Owl that he is having a party and that it's a surprise. Owl passes the message along, and it goes from one animal friend to another, but in a totally garbled fashion, so that when Rabbit finally has his party, it is a real surprise. Children love to laugh at the mixed-up words. They may also enjoy **playing the game of "Whisper" or "Gossip,"** where a simple bit of information is passed from one to another by whispering in another child's ear. Because some children do not know how to whisper, you may want to use **bathroom tissue tubes** for talking softly through. Keep them in the Story Center for children to use on their own.

Rugs Have Naps (But Never Take Them) by Charles Klasky (1984) is a book of words with double meanings that most young children can understand because of its illustrations for each line of text. A hen sitting on a pile of bricks and knitting illustrates the line, "Bricks are laid, but never hatch," for example.

Fred Gwynne's *The Sixteen Hand Horse* (1980) is a bit more sophisticated, with some double meanings your youngsters may not understand. Yet the large print and simple but humorous full-page illustrations help to make the point. The line, "Mommy says her nose is running," showing a little girl watching a nose on legs run down the hall, is the easiest one for a preschooler.

All three of these meaning-play books are in paperback. If your children enjoy them, you may want to **obtain duplicate copies, glue pages to cardboard, and cut them into simple puzzles** for the children to play with when they use the books. Make your puzzles with only three or four pieces each for easy assembly by the children. Keep each puzzle in a separate envelope with the text line on the outside to identify it—another use of print for children to see in their environment, whether or not they can read it. Some children will match the puzzle inside the envelope with the picture in the book. Others will match the print.

Books to Promote Social Development

Social development for young children involves the skills of getting along with others. This includes making friends, joining a play group, playing together in harmony, sharing toys, taking turns, and caring for one another. Books are an excellent means of reinforcing the caring theme of your program, that: 1) we care for ourselves, 2) we care for one another, and 3) we care for the things in our classroom.

A number of friendship books have appeared over the years because the making and keeping of friends occupies such an important place in early childhood relationships. Two of Miriam Cohen's books about Jim and his friends have become classics of their kind. In *Will I Have a Friend?* (1967), Pa takes Jim to nursery school for the first time. Jim is so worried about finding a friend that he spends the whole day looking for one. A tiny truck that Paul has brought from home finally brings Jim and Paul together as friends by the end of the day.

The story of Jim and Paul's friendship continues in Cohen's *Best Friends* (1971); but then, they have a falling out over who is really their "best friend." The problem is resolved realistically when together, they save the class's incubator eggs. Both these books are in paperback and are illustrated with Lillian Hoban's simple, sensitive drawings of preschoolers, which can be **cut out and backed with sandpaper** to be used **as flannel-board characters**. Be sure to tape record the stories for the children's independent use.

In *We Are Best Friends* by Aliki Brandenberg (1982), Robert's best friend, Peter, moves away, and Robert has difficulty dealing with his loss as well as finally accepting a new friend who moves in. Robert and Peter write letters to each other in children's print, which your youngsters may want to compare with the book print. The illustrations are large and colorful, just right for making into flannelboard characters. As a followup for this book, you might **help the children write a letter to a friend.**

In *Sharing* by Taro Gomi (1981), two little girls who look identical share everything equally by dividing it in two—candy, an apple, colored paper, a ribbon, blocks—and finally, together they share the love for their cat by putting that love together. The concept of sharing things by dividing them up can be experienced by your children by bringing in some items to be divided up among the small group who has heard the book. Food items such as **apples, oranges, bananas, melons, carrots, or celery can be sliced** and passed around so that everyone has an equal share for snack time. Have other small groups come into the Story Center and participate in the book and food-sharing experience until the entire class has had a turn.

· · · · · · · · · · **Books to Promote Emotional Development**

Emotional development in the preschool classroom often involves children learning to control negative emotions, such as anger caused by not getting their own way or being blamed for something they did not do; distress caused by becoming lost or being injured; anxiety caused by being away from home or being separated from a loved one. There are many ways to help children overcome strong emotional feelings, such as helping them express their feelings in words, redirecting their aggressive actions, or helping them play with soothing materials such as fingerpaints, dough, or water.

Reading certain books also ranks high as a technique in diffusing a tense situation or overcoming an emotional experience. Edna Mitchell Preston's *The Temper Tantrum Book* (1969) has seven different animals rebelling against an adult animal who is doing things such as combing their tangled hair, getting soap in their eyes, or making them stop playing before they are ready. Obviously, the teacher does not read the book to a child in the midst of his or her emotional outburst. Later, however, when things have calmed down, this is a book that can cause children to think about their actions.

It is especially effective if followup activities with a flannelboard or puppets are used. **Make flannelboard figures from a spare paperback copy,** and in addition, **make "smiley faces" and "frowny faces" on peel-off circles** to be stuck on the animals when they are upset and when they are finally happy. Children need to decide for themselves how the various animals can overcome their temper tantrums and smile again. Then, they can award their animal a smiley face.

A similar activity can be carried out with animal **hand** puppets. **Hot pad holders that come in the shapes of jungle animal mittens can be used.** Find them in specialty shops or museum gift shops. The children in your small group can each choose a lion, elephant, tiger, hippo, or some other animal puppet to put on. When it is their turn on the particular page of the book, ask them what kind of noise their animal might make because it feels so bad. Then, let them suggest what the animal can do to overcome its bad feelings.

A humorous book that may diffuse feelings about taking the blame for

something is *It Wasn't My Fault* by Helen Lester (1985). In this comical tale about Murdley Gurdson, who is always at fault for the unfortunate things that happen to him, a bird's egg lands on his head. When he goes off to see whose fault this is, he meets a cumulative group of silly animals who eventually put the blame where it belongs and end up at Murdley's house to cook scrambled eggs. A fine **followup activity** for this story is **for the children to**
+ **help cook scrambled eggs**. Do you have an electric frying pan?

In Anna Grossnickle Hines's book *Don't Worry, I'll Find You* (1986), Mama and Sarah go on a shopping trip to the mall, where Sarah loses her doll, Abigail, and Mama loses Sarah. Both eventually find each other by following the rule of staying put. **This is a good book to read before going on**
+ **a field trip.** And this is the time to make children aware of any field-trip rules they should follow.

• • • • • • • • • • The Teacher's Role in the Story Center

It is up to the teacher to see that this important classroom area lives up to its promise in a self-directed curriculum. Four crucial tasks are involved:

1. Providing a good selection of picture books appropriate to the children's developmental levels.
2. Reading books to individuals and small groups daily.
3. Providing interesting followup book activities that children can become involved with on their own.
4. Telling stories to children from books in the Story Center.

• Providing a Good Selection of Appropriate Books

How do you make selections of books for preschoolers from the wide range of books available? **It is important that you have hands-on experi-**
+ **ence with the books you plan to order.** Choosing them from catalogs is not enough. Many fine picture books are simply too sophisticated or too long for preschoolers. It is best to look at books in bookstores or try them out ahead of time if you can. Borrow books from the library and read them to your children. If the children respond well, you can consider purchasing them. Choose books that can be integrated into the curriculum, just as you do with computer programs. Here are some book selection tips. Choose books that have:

1. Simple illustrations in bright, primary colors.
2. Brief text, easily read, so that the pages can be turned quickly.
3. Possibilities for converting duplicate copies into puzzles, flannelboard characters, or other fun extension activities.
4. Topics that are part of your curriculum.
5. A story line that lends itself to storytelling.

The Child Interaction Form does not really lend itself to observing and recording children's interactions with books as well as it does with play materials. To involve children with books at the manipulation, mastery, and meaning interaction levels, it is instead suggested that teachers provide books that are suitable for children's sound play, pattern play, and meaning play, as previously described.

• Reading Books to Individuals and Small Groups Daily

A most important task on the part of every team member of your classroom staff is to read books to children. As you move around the room during free-choice time, be sure to stop in at the Story Center. There is sure to be a single child or small group who would like to hear a story. Often, the choice of book is theirs, but, sometimes, it is the teacher's, who has a new book in mind to be introduced to the children.

Story reading traditionally has been done for the total group of children. The Appropriate Practices Curriculum suggests that **story *reading* in particular should be done principally with individuals and small groups of children**. It has proven more effective for each child to be as close as possible to the book and to the reader. The book illustrations and the teacher's interactions with individuals can then really make a difference.   +

Plan on reading to individuals and small groups *at least once a day*. If you yourself are sometimes too occupied with children in the myriad of other activities going on simultaneously, then plan for other staff members to read on that day. Reading and storytelling with young children may be one of the most important activities that any of you do with them.   +

How do you do it? First of all, **become acquainted with the book you are going to read**. Read it through, out loud if possible. You may want to tape   + record your reading of a book ahead of time so that the tape will be available afterward in the center for the children to use on their own. Also ahead of time, **decide how you will introduce the book to get the children's attention**. It is no use beginning to read if the children are not listening. Showing   + them the cover of the book and asking what they think it is about is one technique. The cover of *It Wasn't My Fault* shows Murdley Gurdson with a cracked egg on his head, a bird in the air above him, and three animals beside him looking guilty. You can tell the children the title of the book and then ask them what they think it will be about.

Reading to an individual or small group gives everyone a chance to respond. This makes book reading interactive rather than only a passive, listening experience. It also makes books much more personal. Using a book film or video is such a passive and abstract experience for young children that it is not recommended. Children need to be close to the book and close to the teacher to gain the most from stories. Films and videos are really an entertainment medium for children and have little place in the preschool curriculum, where the goal is learning, not entertainment.

Another book introduction technique is to show the children the book, state what it is about, and then ask them how they think the main character is going to handle the situation. For example, the cover of the book *Sharing* shows two identical little girls with their arms linked. You can read the title and explain what this means. Then, you might ask the children how they think the girls are going to share things and which kinds of things they are going to share. Let everyone make a guess, and then read the book to find out.

+ **The reading itself should be done with expression.** If the story is funny, make your voice sound light-hearted. If it is spooky, make your voice low or whispery. Can you read each character's words with a different expression? Make your voice high for one character, low for another, loud for a third. Tape record your reading, and play it back privately to learn what you sound like. Practice more than once until you get it the way you want it. Reading aloud should be a fun activity for both you and the children. You will know you have been successful when the children ask you to "Read it again, teacher."

+ **Read the same stories over and over** if your children like them. This is how emergent literacy develops. This is what they themselves do at the mastery level of their interaction. (Now you know why children are always asking for the same story over and over!) This is how children begin to understand the reading process, by relating words and print to the story they have become familiar with and the pictures they have seen. To become really familiar with a book, children need to have it read again and again.

• Providing Interesting Followup Book Activities that Children Can Become Involved with on Their Own

Throughout this text, children's book followup activities are included wherever possible. Use such suggestions as model activities that you yourself can design with your own particular books. In this way, you can adapt children's books to your own classroom and curriculum needs. Just as homemade games and materials are more useful than commercial games, so homemade book activities will serve you better than any commercial language kits you can buy.

As you select books for your Story Center, try to choose them on the basis of possible followup activities. **Are paperback copies available for you to cut up and use for puzzles, flannelboard characters, board games, paper**
+ **dolls, stick puppets, and counting games?** Can the books themselves be used as followup activities with computer programs, science projects, art activities, cooking, or block building? Be creative in your use of books. How

can they be used in addition to reading or storytelling? When we realize that children create their own knowledge through interaction with materials in their environment, then we want books to be an active, not passive, agent in children's learning.

• Telling Stories to Children from Books in the Center

Storytelling is not the same as story reading. The storyteller knows the story by heart and does not depend upon a book. She or he can focus on the audience in front and does not have to look at a book or turn the pages. **The teller can adapt the story to the audience's responses,** sometimes speed- +
ing it up, and sometimes slowing it down. The teller can also add to the story or even omit certain parts, depending on the audience. In fact, **the storyteller can actually become the various characters in the story,** speak- +
ing in their voices like an actor would; or she can be a straight narrator and tell about the characters as something different from her.

Two big differences between story reading and storytelling are:

1. Story reading depends upon a book, while storytelling depends upon the audience.
2. With story reading, the pictures are in the book, while with storytelling, the pictures are imagined in the listener's mind.

Both story reading and storytelling are important in the preschool curriculum. If we want to bring together children and books, we will want to employ both these techniques. We should be especially mindful, however, of the value of storytelling in this day and age, for children do not have enough opportunities to use their imaginations. Marvelous imagery is projected for them in television programs, computer graphics, book illustrations, and film special effects. Children desperately need **the opportunity to make their own pictures in their mind's eye**. This is where creativity originates. +
Storytelling gives children this opportunity. You owe it to the children in your classroom to give them this possibility. The following outline provides a brief overview of ideas to get you started in storytelling:

STORYTELLING
....

1. *Choosing the story*
   a. Choose a book from your Story Center.
   b. Choose a simple folk tale or formula story.
   c. Choose a story with repetitive lines.
   d. Choose a story you really like.
   e. Choose a book for which you have a puppet.

2. *Learning the story*

    a. Read it silently, ahead of time.

    b. Read it orally, ahead of time.

    c. Convert the written story to an oral story.

    d. Practice, ahead of time.

3. *Delivering the story*

    a. Get audience attention.

    b. Use your voice creatively.

    c. Use facial expressions.

    d. Use gestures.

    e. End the story in an interesting way.

• Choosing Stories to Tell

First of all, you should choose a story from a book you have in your Story Center. It is important for oral stories in preschool programs to be connected to books. This helps young children as their literacy emerges to understand the concept that books are "written-down talk." It is also especially satisfying for children to discover the book from which the teacher told the oral story. The book thus serves as a followup for the storytelling activity.

Some books lend themselves to storytelling better than others. **Folk tales or formula tales are especially well suited to oral telling** because they are easy to remember. They are based originally on oral stories and frequently follow a formula that listeners recognize: easily identifiable characters who need to resolve a dilemma; tasks or trials that must be accomplished (often three); and a satisfying resolution in which the main character overcomes a difficult situation. Such stories are often easy to tell because 1) their formula structure lends itself to remembering the story easily, 2) the action is dramatic and to the point, and 3) the characters speak in dialog that the storyteller can remember and use impressively.

You may want to **choose a story with repetitive lines** that you say over and over, **with the children soon joining in**. In *Stone Soup*, the children can repeat the lines: "Soup from a stone, fancy that." In *The Three Billy Goats Gruff*, many lines in the story are repetitive. Audience participation is an important part of storytelling. Repeating lines in a story makes children a part of the storytelling itself.

In addition, you should **choose a story that you yourself like**. Not every book in your center may appeal to you personally, but if you intend to spend time learning the story and making it your own, you should choose a book you would enjoy sharing with the children because it has meaning for you. If you are lukewarm about the story, this attitude is likely to come across to the children, so choose with feeling and with care.

You may also want to choose a book for which you have a puppet. **Puppets are easier to handle in storytelling than in story reading, where you must also hold a book.** You can use a puppet: 1) as a character in the story +
to say its lines itself; 2) to make asides as you tell the story; or 3) **to become the actual storyteller and tell the whole tale itself**. The latter is especially +
effective if you are a bit shy about telling stories. Some teachers feel the same about telling stories as they do about singing: that they are not good at it, so they would rather not do it. If you let a puppet do the telling for you, then the children's eyes are on the puppet, not on you, and you may find it easier and even fun to tell a story. In order to be effective, storytelling should be a satisfying experience for both you and the children.

Try out a puppet ahead of time to see whether using it is comfortable for you. Not every storyteller likes to use puppets. Some tellers feel that the puppet distracts children's attention from the story. Not every story lends itself to telling with a puppet. Try out your story ahead of time both with a puppet and without one. Hand puppets can be purchased in children's book stores, toy stores, and museum gift shops. On the other hand, it is easy to make a hand puppet from a sock pulled over your hand, with eyes pasted on.

• Learning the Story

First of all, you need to **read the story through to yourself** noting the +
characters, dialog, and plot. Then, read the story orally to get the feel about how it sounds aloud. For young children, you will want to make the story simple; therefore, you will be including only the main characters and main elements, omitting everything else. You do not need to memorize anything other than perhaps the opening and closing sentences. Oral stories are more effective if you speak directly for the characters in dialog. Dialog does not need to be memorized. It is better spoken naturally by you. To convert any written story to an oral tale, you can:

1. Read the story through, noting characters, dialog, and plot.
2. Decide which characters to include and how to speak for them.
3. Decide how to begin the story to catch the children's attention.
4. Decide on three to five elements of the story to dramatize as you tell it.
5. Decide how to end the story with a twist, a joke, a surprise, a question, or a quotation.

For example, you could choose to convert the book *It Wasn't My Fault* by Helen Lester (1985) into an oral tale. Although it is not a folk tale, the story has the repetitive elements of a cumulative tale with one similar incident following another, making it easy to remember. As you read it through, you will note that there is one main character, Murdley Gurdson, who is always having unfortunate things happen to him that are always his fault. Finally, something happens that does not seem to be his fault, so he investigates it. There are four other characters representing the main incidents in the story: the bird that lays the egg on Murdley's head, the aardvark that screams and scares the bird, the pigmy hippo that steps on the aardvark's tail, and the rabbit in the hopping shoe that frightens the pygmy hippo.

+   Next, **read the story aloud, noting its rhythm, the dialog, and any repetitive lines** you would enjoy saying. As Murdley confronts several animals involved in the egg-laying incident, they all claim: "It wasn't my fault." This is a line you will want to repeat, having your listeners chime in as the story progresses.

+   Finally, you will be converting the written story to an oral tale by **focusing on the main characters and the main incidents**. You have read the story silently. You have read it aloud. Now close the book and tell the story privately. How did it go? Did you remember all the incidents? Were you able to speak for each of the characters? You must **decide whether to use a different voice quality** for each of the animals or to use your own voice. Whatever is comfortable for you will please your audience. Some tellers always use their own voice for every character, although they may slow down or speed up the dialog to differentiate their characters. Other tellers raise or lower their voices to distinguish specific characters.

+   What about **the beginning and ending of the story**? As a teller, you are free to begin and end the story as the book does or to make up your own beginning and ending. Try it out in different ways. This is called making the story your own. By the time you are ready to tell the story in front of your children, it will actually be your own—your story rather than the one in the book.

• Delivering the Story

+   Now you are ready to begin. To **get your audience's attention,** you may want to sit in a child's chair in the storyteller's circle rather than on floor level like the children. This can be your storytelling chair. Storytelling can be done successfully with a larger group of children than story reading because the children do not have to look at the pictures in a book. They will be making their own pictures in their mind's eye. And you will be making eye contact with all of them because you do not have to look at the book or show them the pictures. For a smaller group of children, you may want to sit on the floor at the children's level instead.

+   The best way to **begin a story is to start right in** as soon as the children have calmed down. You might consider whispering at first to help children focus their listening skills on your voice. Repeat the opening of the story if you think some of the children did not hear it. By now, everyone should be listening. Then, tell the story as you have practiced it. Use your voice creatively for the characters, just as you have practiced. In addition, use **facial expressions and gestures** where appropriate. Storytelling has been called   + "the theater of the face." (O'Callahan, 1983).

When you tell about Murdley Gurdson stepping out of one of his too-big shoes, for instance, you may want to turn your head as if looking around. When you tell about the egg landing on Murdley's head, you may want to squinch up your face or look up. You may want to shake your finger at each of the animals as Murdley confronts them one at time. Or you may want to hold out both hands with palms up while shaking your head every time you say, "It wasn't my fault." You may also want to perform hand motions for the animals as they eventually scramble the egg to eat. And finally, you need to think of a funny way to end the story as Murdley opens the closet door instead of the front door to let the animals out and everything in the closet falls on his head, but it truly was not his fault.

You may find yourself changing the story every time you tell it, depending on your audience. That is what makes storytelling so wonderful. It is a fluid art adaptable to any situation. At times, you may want to stretch out your story, at other times, to shorten it. Since it is your story because you have made it so, this is perfectly permissible. Finally, you will know that your children truly appreciate your efforts not only when they say, "Tell it again, teacher," but also when they ask to sit in the storyteller's chair to tell their own stories!

• Picture Books to Be Converted to Oral Stories

The Three Billy Goats Gruff by Paul Galdone (1973) is the classic story that lends itself to telling much better than reading. It is a story with a simple but dramatic plot: The three billy goats want to go up to the meadow to eat grass, but they have to pass over a bridge with a troll under it who threatens to eat them. The storyteller takes the parts of the three billy goats and the troll by changing voices, from a high, squeaky voice for the tiniest goat to a loud, gruff voice for the biggest goat and a roar for the troll. The sound of "trip, trap, trip trap" for the goats walking over the bridge can be done by voice, by clapping your hands, or by tapping on a table. This is an excellent first story with which to try out your skill as an oral storyteller. Your reward will be great when you realize how well your performance has captivated your audience.

Goldilocks and the Three Bears retold by Jan Brett (1987) is another fine story for telling aloud. Because this is such an old favorite, some teachers think that most of their children have probably heard it at home. In this day and age of television and with all the adult family members busy working, this may no longer be true. Your telling of the story will give a new dimension to children who have not heard it and an added dimension to anyone who has. Each teller puts something of him- or herself into the story, thus making it different. Read Jan Brett's version to yourself to give you insights into the bears' and Goldilocks's characters. Look for sound words you can dramatize in your story, such as "Plump!" when Goldilocks sits in the chair of "the little, small, wee bear" and it breaks (Brett, 1987). Your children will also enjoy looking at Brett's wonderfully medieval illustrations later, when you put the book on the shelf of your Story Center.

Another simple classic story for the teller to remember and retell easily is *Stone Soup* by Ann McGovern (1986). Children enjoy hearing how the hungry young man stops at the house of a little old lady who will not give him anything to eat, so he proceeds to make soup from a stone. This is a cumulative tale in which various vegetables and other ingredients are added to the bubbling soup pot, one by one. The storyteller repeats the whole list of ingredients each time a new one is added. Children love to hear this repetition and will soon be joining in if you encourage them. **A followup activity**

+ **is the actual making of stone soup in the classroom.** Tell the tale again as you make your own version of stone soup.

Another wonderful cumulative tale that is easy to relate is *Journey Cake, Ho!* by Ruth Sawyer (1953), an American Appalachian variant of the European story about the gingerbread man. The "journey cake" is a pancake that the old man and old woman give to Johnny, the bound-out boy, when they tell him he will have to leave because they no longer have enough food for him in their mountain cabin. The journey cake gets away from Johnny and rolls down the mountain, picking up a cumulative conglomeration of animals who chase it as it rolls. The storyteller repeats the rhyme of the journey cake, adding animals cumulatively as they join the parade. Your children will join in, too, before you finish telling the story. This is **an excellent story**

+ **to follow up by making pancakes with your children**.

A simple story that your children will readily respond to is Robert Kraus's *Whose Mouse Are You?* (1970). This story lends itself to telling aloud, especially if you have a mouse hand puppet. You can make your own puppet from a grey sock with big pink ears and white eyes added, or you can find a real mouse puppet in a children's bookstore. In this case, you will be the narrator asking the question, "Whose mouse are you?" In response, you then become the mouse puppet answering, "Nobody's mouse." The story continues with this sort of dialog between the narrator and the mouse. You do not have to memorize the dialog, only the order of the questions asked by the narrator. Your response can be your own and not necessarily the words in the book. If your children like the story, **one of them might want to par-**

+ **ticipate and be the mouse puppet** at another telling. Leave the puppet in the Story Center for the children to use in pretending.

Since alligator puppets are quite easy to come by, you might consider purchasing an alligator book such as *Keep Your Mouth Closed, Dear* by

Aliki Brandenberg (1966). This is the story of little alligator Charles, who swallows something every time he opens his mouth. As you tell the story with a puppet on your hand, you may want to use other props of the items that Charles swallows by accident: a wooden spoon, a sponge, Father's hat, a can of baby powder, an alarm clock, a zipper, and finally, the vacuum cleaner hose, which solves Charles's problem by sucking out all the things he has swallowed. Children respond well to the story, especially if they can participate with the items swallowed. The last item he almost swallows, but doesn't is a chocolate layer cake. You can use this book to lead into a food experience with a birthday cake—or perhaps something else equally as tempting that you have substituted for cake.

In this way, you can make your Story Center one of the most dynamic parts of the curriculum. If your children have truly made a real book/storytelling connection, you can consider their experience with your Appropriate Practices Curriculum successful.

IDEAS +
in CHAPTER 6

1. *Promoting reading in the home*
   a. Have a duplicate collection of lending books for children to borrow at the end of the day. (p. 125)
   b. Invite parents to the Story Center to listen and then take a turn at reading themselves. (p. 125)
   c. Send home a newsletter with names of books children are reading, and give directions for making book extension games. (p. 125)
   d. Have a book bee for parents to make book extension games. (p. 125)
   e. Have a "My Favorite Books" chart to keep track of books children have had read to them at home and in school. (p. 125)
   f. Take a field trip to the public library with parents to help. (p. 125)

2. *Setting up the Story Center*
   a. Use bright colors in the Story Center on rugs, pillows, furniture, posters, and so on. (p. 125)
   b. Have book extension puppets, puzzles, games, and posters displayed. (p. 125)
   c. Have a flannelboard on the wall at child's height or on a low easel. (p. 125)
   d. Have child-size bookshelves displaying fronts of books. (p. 125)
   e. Have inflated chairs, benches, sit-on foam animals, giant foam blocks, or junior couches to sit on. (p. 125)
   f. Have an old bathtub with pillows for a book-reading place. (p. 126)
   g. Have a core of favorite books always on shelves, but add new books from time to time. (p. 126)
   h. Hang books on colored ribbons from a horizontal rod or clothesline. (p. 126)

3. *Promoting language development*
   a. Have books that feature interesting words or funny sounds. (p. 128)

   b. Read *Goodnight Moon* in a whispery voice, and say goodnight to items in the classroom. (p. 128)

   c. Dramatize favorite books such as *Caps for Sale* by bringing in some caps. (p. 129)

   d. Bring in a tin pail when you read *Blueberries for Sal,* and drop items in it. (p. 129)

   e. Have books that feature repeated rhyming words or phrases. (p. 129)

   f. Follow-up *Jamberry* by going berry picking or by buying berries. (p. 129)

   g. Follow-up *The Lady with the Alligator Purse* by making pizza. (p. 130)

   h. Follow-up *Sheep in a Jeep* with a toy sheep and vehicle. (p. 130)

   i. Make flannelboard characters from paperback books. (p. 130)

   j. Tape record the reading of a book with a sound cue for turning pages. (p. 130)

   k. Use bathroom tissue tubes to whisper through after reading *The Surprise Party.* (p. 131)

   l. Make puzzles from paperback books. (p. 131)

4. *Promoting social development*

   a. Cut out flannelboard characters from *Best Friends.* (p. 132)

   b. Write a letter to a friend after reading *We Are Best Friends.* (p. 132)

   c. Divide up fruit after reading *Sharing.* (p. 133)

5. *Promoting emotional development*

   a. Make flannelboard figures from a spare copy of *The Temper Tantrum Book,* and use peel-off circle "smiley faces." (p. 133)

   b. Get hot pad holder animal hand puppets for use with animal books. (p. 133)

   c. Follow-up *It Wasn't My Fault* by making scrambled eggs. (p. 134)

   d. Read *Don't Worry, I'll Find You* before going on a field trip. (p. 134)

6. *Selecting books*

   a. Have hands-on experience first with books you plan to buy. (p. 134)

7. *Reading books*

   a. Do story reading with individuals and small groups only. (p. 135)

   b. Read to individuals and small groups at least once a day. (p. 135)

   c. Become acquainted with the book you are going to read. (p. 135)

   d. Decide how to introduce the book to get the children's attention. (p. 135)

   e. Read with expression. (p. 136)

   f. Read the same stories more than once. (p. 136)

8. *Doing followup book activities*

   a. Use paperback copies of books to cut up for puzzles, flannelboard characters, board games, paper dolls, stick puppets, and counting games. (p. 136)

   b. Make stone soup in the classroom. (p. 142)

   c. Make pancakes after telling *Journey Cake, Ho!* (p. 142)

   d. Have a child be the mouse puppet in *Whose Mouse Are You?* (p. 142)

9. *Telling stories*

   a. Adapt the story to the audience's responses by speeding up or slowing down. (p. 137)

   b. Become the various characters by changing your voice. (p. 137)

   c. Allow children to make pictures in their minds' eye. (p. 137)

10. *Choosing stories to tell*

   a. Choose folk tales for easy oral storytelling. (p. 138)

   b. Choose a story with repetitive lines. (p. 138)

   c. Choose a story you yourself really like. (p. 138)

   d. Use puppets for storytelling rather than story reading. (p. 138)

   e. Use a puppet to tell the story. (p. 138)

11. *Preparing for storytelling*

   a. Read the story silently noting the characters, dialog, and plot. (p. 139)

   b. Read the story aloud privately, noting rhythm, dialog, and repetitive lines. (p. 140)

   c. Focus on main characters and main incidents. (p. 140)

   d. Decide whether to use a different voice quality for each character. (p. 140)

   e. Decide on a beginning and ending. (p. 140)

12. *Delivering the story*

   a. Get your audience's attention. (p. 140)

   b. Start right in. (p. 140)

   c. Use facial expressions and gestures where appropriate. (p. 141)

REFERENCES CITED

Friedberg, B., & Strong, E. (1989). 'Please don't stop there!': The power of reading aloud. In J. Hickman & B. E. Cullinan, *Children's literature in the classroom: Weaving Charlotte's web* (pp. 39–48). Needham Heights, MA: Christopher-Gordon Publishers.

Janssen, D. H., & Beaty, J. J. (1988). *Storytelling Mark Twain style.* Columbia, MO: Janssen Education Enterprise.

Lester, H. (1985). *It wasn't my fault.* Boston, MA: Houghton Mifflin Company.

McKenzie, M., & Pinnell, G. S. (1989). Changing conceptions of early literacy learning. In J. Hickman & B. E. Cullinan, *Children's literature in the classroom: Weaving Charlotte's web* (pp. 25–38). Needham Heights, MA: Christopher-Gordon Publishers.

O'Callahan, J. (1983). Video: *Master class in storytelling.* Martha's Vineyard, MA: Vineyard Video Productions.

Salsbury, E. C. (1965). *Susy and Mark Twain: Family dialogues.* New York: Harper & Row.

Schwartz, J. (1981). Children's experiments with language. *Young Children 36* (5), 16–26.

OTHER SOURCES

Beaty J. J. (1990). *Observing development of the young child.* Columbus, OH: Merrill Publishing Company.

Cascardi, A. E. (1985). *Good books to grow on.* New York: Warner Books.

Hough, R. A., Nurss, J. R., & Wood, D. (1987). Tell me a story: Making opportunities for elaborated language in early childhood classrooms. *Young Children 43* (1), 6–12.

Howarth, M. (1989). Rediscovering the power of fairy tales: They help children understand their lives. *Young Children 45* (1), 58–65.

Klechner, K. A., & Engel, R. E. (1988). A child begins school: Relieving anxiety with books. *Young Children 43* (5), 14–18.

Kontos, S. (1986). What preschool children know about reading and how they learn it. *Young Children 42* (1), 58–66.

Oppenheim, J., Brenner, B., & Boegehold, B. D. (1986). *Choosing books for kids.* New York: Ballantine Books.

Smith, C. A. (1986). Nurturing kindness through storytelling. *Young Children 41* (6), 46–51.

CHILDREN'S BOOKS

Brandenberg, A. (1966) *Keep your mouth closed, dear.* New York: E. P. Dutton.

Brandenberg, A. (1982). *We are best friends.* New York: Greenwillow Books.

Brett, J. (1978). *Goldilocks and the three bears.* New York: Dodd, Meade & Company.

Brown, M. W. (1947). *Goodnight, Moon.* New York: Harper & Row.

Cohen, M. (1971) *Best friends.* New York: Macmillan.

Cohen, M. (1967). *Will I have a friend?* New York: Macmillan.

Degen, B. (1985). *Jamberry.* New York: Harper & Row.

Galdone, P. (1973). *The three billy goats gruff.* New York: Clarion Books.

Gomi, T. (1981). *Sharing.* San Francisco, CA: Heian International, Inc.

Gwynne, F. (1980). *The sixteen hand horse.* New York: Simon & Schuster.

Hines, A. G. (1986). *Don't worry, I'll find you.* New York: E. P. Dutton.

Hoban, T. (1985). *A children's zoo.* New York: Greenwillow Books.

Hutchins, P. (1969). *The surprise party.* New York: Macmillan.

Klasky, C. (1984). *Rugs have naps (but never take them).* Chicago: Children's Press.

Kraus, R. (1970). *Whose mouse are you?* New York: Macmillan.

Lester, H. (1985). *It wasn't my fault.* Boston, MA: Houghton Mifflin.

McCloskey, R. (1948). *Blueberries for Sal.* New York: The Viking Press.

Preston, E. M. (1969). *The temper tantrum book.* New York: The Viking Press.

Sawyer, R. (1953). *Journey cake, ho!* New York: The Viking Press.

Slobodkina, E. (1968). *Caps for sale.* New York: Scholastic Book Services.

Shaw, N. (1986). *Sheep in a jeep.* Boston, MA: Houghton Mifflin.

Westcott, N. B. (1988). *The lady with the alligator purse.* Boston, MA: Little, Brown.

TRY IT
YOURSELF

1. Set up your Story Center as described in this chapter with rugs, pillows, bright colors, posters, games, puppets, and a core of good early childhood picture books, displayed attractively.

2. Read to a small group in the center a book that will promote language development based on sound play. Have a followup activity that extends the learning based on the book.

3. Use a book with children to promote their social development. Follow up with an activity in another part of the classroom based on the book.

4. Tell a story based on one of the books in your center, speaking expressively for the characters in the book.

5. Tell a story using a puppet and doing a followup activity based on the book.

7

WRITING CENTER

LETTERS   I can say the alphabet
A–B–C–D–E,
I can print the alphabet
L–M–N–O–P,
I can write the alphabet,
Watch me make a loop;
I can eat the alphabet
When it's in my soup!

• • • • • • • • • • Writing as a Natural Development

Just as learning to read can develop naturally with young children in a print-rich environment, so can learning to write. The concept of emergent literacy discussed in Chapter 6 refers both to reading and to writing as emerging naturally within children when they are surrounded by reading and writing activities at home and in the preschool and encouraged to interact with those activities.

Why did we not know this about children before? If writing is truly a natural development, why did we fail to see it happening and encourage it to unfold naturally? And why do we still teach writing to children in the primary grades?

It is another case of seeing what we are looking for. In the past, adults generally assumed that children had to be taught to write. Therefore, we rarely paid attention to the pre-writing skills that young children have always displayed from infancy on. When children scribbled on paper, on frosted windows, or even in the mud, we dismissed it as nothing of real importance—merely something children did before they could draw, just as babbling was something children did before they could talk.

Now we know better. It soon became obvious that the more researchers looked for evidence of emergent literacy in young children, the more they found. First of all, they took a closer look at children's scribbling and discovered that it was not all the same. Infants scribbled differently from toddlers. Toddlers scribbled differently from preschoolers. In fact, there seemed to be a real progression from random scribbling, to controlled scribbling, to the writing of mock letters and words, and finally to real writing as children experimented and matured. Not only that, but the children themselves realized what they were doing. They could even tell the difference between scribbles that were drawings and scribbles that were writing! Many could even read their so-called "mock writing."

Now we understand that just as babbling is a foundation for speaking, so scribbling is a foundation for writing. And both speaking and writing are different forms of the same basic urge found in all human beings: the desire to communicate. We now realize that if we expect this progression from scribbling to writing to occur naturally, we must nurture it in the home and in the preschool classroom. **We must fill the children's environment with examples of writing and reading.** We must encourage and support any attempts at writing our children make, no matter how crude, no matter how primitive.

Just as we display attractively the children's art—even their scribbles and blobs—so we must also **display the children's writing—even their scribbles and lines**. In addition, we need to provide a Writing Center in our preschool classrooms so that children will understand these new expectations of ours: that we count on them to make natural and playful experiments with writing, as they do with art, blocks, and puzzles.

• • • • • • • • • • Writing in the Preschool Classroom

The print-rich environment discussed in Chapter 6 applies in equal measure to a classroom in which the natural development of writing is expected. Some examples of printed material that should be displayed in your classroom include:

Signs—
for Block Center buildings
for building safety
for playground safety
traffic signs

Children's names—
on cubbies
on children's art, writing
on children's placemats
on children's stories
on attendance chart
on helper's chart

Sign-up sheets—
computer turns
art projects
uses of equipment
activities
outdoor play equipment turns

Charts—
children's height, weight
growth of plants
weather
books read
recipes
menus
rules
experience charts
activity schedules

Bulletin board—
notices
letters, invitations, thank-you notes
cards
directions
messages

Labels—
on activity areas
on equipment shelves
on grocery items

Other—

picture books

children's stories

computer programs

self-regulating devices

maps

daily schedule

floor plan

first-aid kit

calendar

· · · · · · · · · · **Setting Up the Writing Center**

This activity area should be located as close as possible to the Story Center and/or the Computer Center. Writing activities can then be stimulated by or spill over into these two areas as children become excited about written communication.

The Writing Center should contain a table and chairs—or better still, a child-size desk. **A roll-top desk with pigeon-hole compartments is a natural stimulus for writing.** Children are excited to be sitting at such a grown-up desk. You may need to have a sign-up sheet for turns at the desk as you do for turns at the computer! The **compartments** of such a desk **should be filled with writing and printing tools and implements**:

Pencils: regular pencils, primary-size pencils, soft color pencils, and erasers that fit over their tops

Pens: ball-point pens of the "rolling writer" type

Markers: felt-tip markers of various sizes and colors (water-soluble ink types)

Pencil sharpeners: regular, fastened-down sharpener; small hand-held sharpeners of different types

Paper clips: container of large paper clips

Stapler: child-size stapler and staples

Rulers: several wooden and plastic rulers

Scissors: several pairs

Hole punch: several hole punchers and large brads for fastening

Rubber stamps: alphabet letters, rubber animal stamps, dinosaur stamps, flower stamps, and so on; address stamps, stamp pads with different colors of inks

The drawers of such a desk should be filled with:

Paper: blank typing paper, light-colored construction paper, carbon paper

Pads and tablets: small multicolor pads, writing tablets; pads with self-sticking pages

Notebooks: spiral notebooks, secretary's dictation notebooks, loose-leaf notebooks

Stationery: various kinds of note paper and matching envelopes; regular white envelopes

Cards: 3-by-5 cards of various colors

Paste: rubber cement, glue, cellophane tape

Peel-offs: blank peel-off labels; peel-off stickers with pictures and designs; large peel-off alphabet letters; address labels

Stamps: cancelled stamps of various kinds

A small school-type desk or a table with several chairs can also serve well in the Writing Center.

+ The area can be sectioned off with a shelf divider that can contain **sets of alphabet letters:** plastic, wooden, magnetic, sandpaper, and so on, and a sectioned box of movable alphabet letters. Other materials can include:
+ thick, soft, **colored chalk and several small chalkboards;** pencil box sets; alphabet books and other picture books to motivate writing.

+ One shelf might hold several **small cases for overnight lending** that contain a number of the writing tools and supplies mentioned above. These can be borrowed by children and returned the next day, as they do with duplicate picture books. Children need to be involved with pleasurable writing activities at home as well as in the preschool. Parents may not be aware of their children's desire and need to communicate in writing at this early age. Circulating such writing materials into the home not only supports their children's interests but also affords you an opportunity to involve the family in a developmentally appropriate activity they may not have been aware of (Rich, 1985).

Filling your center with writing implements like this is no different from stocking your Art Center with painting supplies. It delivers a powerful message to the children: that the teacher expects them to participate and experiment with pleasurable writing activities on their own, just as she does with painting activities in the Art Center.

+ Another table in the area can feature a typewriter. Either a **primary typewriter or regular adult typewriter** is preferred to children's toy typewriters, which are often difficult to use. Old, standard manual typewriters are often available very reasonably from used office equipment dealers—or perhaps from a parent. How will children use it? In the same way as they use the computer, the youngsters will experiment with the typewriter until they get it to work the way it is supposed to. Then they will type—with or without paper—often in play or pretending activities, but sometimes typing real words or their names.

+ Another piece of equipment in the Writing Center that can be used with surprising results is **a sand table**. Children like to smooth out the surface of sand and use it for scribbling, writing, and printing letters and their names. Or they may stamp letters into wet sand from the wooden or magnetic alphabet letters on the shelf. They also create scenes from the stories you have read or told them (Barbour, Webster, & Drosdeck, 1987). Sometimes, the signs they print on paper end up in the sand table to protect their structures or label their buildings. You may want to consider using a sand table for several months here in the Writing Center before shifting it to the Science Center for a completely different type of activity.

The walls of the Writing Center should feature **a variety of colorful posters or pictures with labels,** a bulletin board for mounting children's writing +
or your messages to them, magazine pictures of children writing, and the alphabet letters from A to Z in upper- and lowercase letters. Book posters are appropriate here as well. Obtain them from children's bookstores or order from:

Children's Book Council, Inc.
350 Scotland Road
Orange, New Jersey 07050

Their folder lists current posters and prices. Most are illustrations by outstanding children's book artists, either from their own books or in support of reading.

Depending on your wall space in the Writing Center, you may want **a hanging that contains letters.** Quilts or children's bedspreads featuring the +
alphabet can be hung on the wall. Colorful carpeting with squares of alphabet letters can be ordered through school-supply companies. Flannelboards to be used with alphabet letters can be purchased or homemade.

• • • • • • • • • • Scribbling and Mock Writing

All children everywhere scribble before they write, just as they babble before they talk, as previously indicated. The earliest marks they make usually occur before their first birthday and are often called random scribbling. If infants are given writing tools, they will grip them in a fist and make marks on surfaces in a random manner without even watching what they are doing (Lamme, 1984). If adults in the vicinity show excitement in the scribbles or praise the youngsters for their efforts, they will continue with great gusto. If, on the other hand, they are scolded or punished for marking up surfaces other than paper or chalkboards, they may discontinue their experiments with writing.

Mark Twain understood the importance of young children's scribbling and praised them for it. In a Christmas note to his daughter Susy, in which he pretends to be Santa Claus, he writes:

My dear Susy Clemens: I have received and read all the letters which you and your little sister have written me by the hand of your mother and your nurses; I have also read those which you little people have written me with your own hands—for although you did not use any characters that are in grown people's alphabet, you used the characters that all children in all lands on earth and in the twinkling stars use; and as all my subjects in the moon are children and use no characters but that, you will easily understand that I can read your and your baby sister's jagged and fantastic marks without any trouble at all. But I had trouble with those letters which you dictated through your mother and the nurses, for I am a foreigner and cannot read English writing well. You will find that I made no mistakes about the things which you and the baby ordered in your *own* letters—I went down your chimney at midnight when you were asleep and delivered them all myself. (Salsbury, 1965, 46)

With practice and maturity come control. By the time children have reached preschool age, they are usually able to do what is called controlled scribbling. Here, the child watches the marks he is making and places them where he wants them on the paper. The scribbles generally take the form of circles, lines, dots, and splotches, although some scribbles are emerging into the basic shapes of circles, squares, triangles, and crosses. At this point, scribbling often takes two different paths, one eventually becoming drawing, and the other, writing. Drawing scribbles are discussed in Chapter 8, "Art Center."

As young children gain more experience with print materials, they seem to recognize that writing occurs in horizontal lines, while art occupies whole spaces. Children in your class may thus begin making large, scribbled art products that they identify as particular objects, with small, linear scribbles underneath that they say tells the story. They have progressed to the named scribbling stage.

At this point, they will frequently ask an adult to write for them. They may want you to write down what their painting is about, to make a sign for their block building, or to write a note to Mom. Sometimes, they will scribble under or above your writing or ask you to write underneath their line of scribbles. Often, they will try to copy what you have written. Encourage them in this endeavor. *Copying* seems to speed up the writing process for young children, while *tracing* slows it down (Lamme, 1984). Nevertheless, since the development of writing is such a personal as well as spontaneous affair for the young child, encourage each one to proceed as he or she is doing. If tracing alphabet letters appeals to the child, let him continue doing it.

At the same time, children are becoming aware of what real words look like as well as the letters that make up words. At this point, letter awareness begins to follow a parallel development with scribbling in children's progression into conventional writing.

Children who take pleasure in the fun of writing will now often fill pages with lines of scribbling. You soon recognize this as their mastery level of in-

During the preschool years scribbling takes two different directions: one form becomes drawing, the other becomes writing. Most children can distinguish between the two.

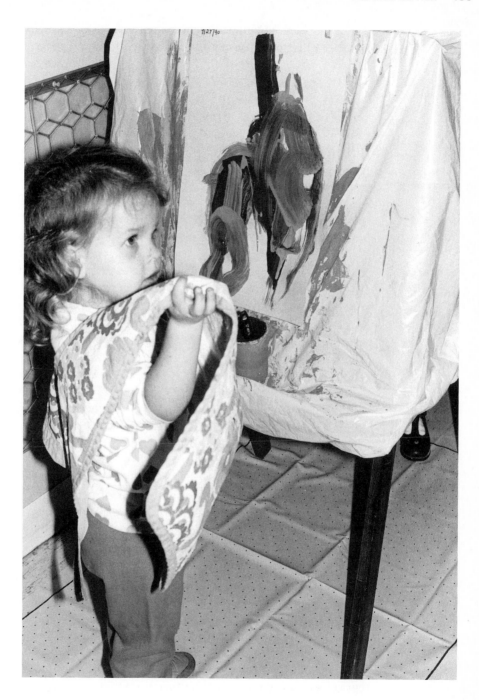

teraction, while their earlier scribbling was certainly manipulating the medium. Sometimes these children ask you to read their writing because they "can't read," and they believe that someone who can read should be able to decifer their writing! You might respond by asking them what they think it says. Your Writing Center should appeal to children at this mastery level because of the exciting array of writing implements and writing surfaces you have provided for their use.

If you are keeping an eye on your children's writing products, you will eventually note that some of their scribbles are beginning to resemble letters, and some may even resemble words. They also may notice what is happening and share their discovery with great excitement if they know it will please you. They have arrived at the so-called "mock letter and mock word" stage in their progression into writing. To form mock words, they often separate their scribbles with a line or a period after each one. Some children even draw a circle around each mock word. It is not up to you to correct these spontaneous efforts. They will eventually recognize how adults (you) divide lines of writing into words by leaving a space between each word.

Again, young children often fill pages with their mock writing. Now they are more likely to tell you rather than ask you what it says as they progress into the meaning level of writing development. They are still scribbling, although their scribbles resemble conventional writing more and more—just as the jargon stage of young children's language development resembles real speech. For preschoolers, this *process* of writing is much more important than any *product* they create. Nevertheless, they are usually pleased when you recognize their work and display it on a bulletin board. It is a motivation for them to continue writing. Think about it. Have you ever displayed a page of a child's writing scribbles on the wall in the same way as you do a child's art work? Children extract important messages from both the things we do and the things we do not do. They quickly understand what it is that the adults in their lives consider important as well as what they consider not important.

Letter Awareness

Letter awareness seems to follow a parallel development with print awareness in young children. In extracting this kind of meaning from their world, children first perceive print (writing) as lines (sentences). Later, their perception becomes more refined as they recognize the divisions in the lines that are words. Still later, they recognize that words are made up of letters.

The first letters they recognize are often those in their own names since adults sign children's names on their work and encourage children to print their own names. In the beginning, they often learn to make the first letter of their name and let that stand for their whole name. Soon, however, they are printing their entire name, although not always in proper order, in conventional forms of letters or in linear arrangement.

As with their early attempt at drawing, children's first printing of letters is a free-flowing sort of expression with letters of all sizes and shapes floating here and there on the page. A child named Kathy, for instance, may print a backward *K* somewhere on a sheet of paper. Then, she may print a larger *a* somewhere else, maybe nowhere near the *K*. She may not like the way that *a* turned out, so she makes another smaller one—or two. Then comes the *t*. For this, she turns her paper sideways, where there is more room, and makes a *t*. The *h* she makes is up in the corner, and the final *y*, which looks more like a *v*, is down near the bottom of the paper. She has written her name!

Because you know that the *process* of writing her name is more important than the final *product,* you accept her effort with pleasure just as it is. She will eventually refine her writing skills by combining what she has learned about mock writing with what she is learning about alphabet letters. Little by little, she will develop a sense of left-to-right progression, of linear writing, and of letter size, letter shape, and orientation.

If children are surrounded by letters, letter games, alphabet books, and letter activities, they will eventually learn to distinguish a number of alphabet letters. It is neither necessary nor appropriate to teach your children the letters of the alphabet in any formal sense. Let them **play around with letters, words, and writing** in your Writing Center and elsewhere in the classroom. If they ask you how to make a letter, show them. If they ask you the name of a certain letter, tell them. Thus, they will teach themselves to recognize the letters they need to know as they use them playfully and seriously in the activities they pursue.

• • • • • • • • • • Writing Activities to Promote Cognitive Development

• Alphabet Letters

For preschool children, the recognition and naming of letters is a cognitive concept that is related to their future reading achievement. Nevertheless, there is controversy regarding whether or not the teaching of the alphabet to preschoolers is appropriate. We realize that children can learn to read without knowing the alphabet. Why, then, should they have to learn it?

Preschool children want to and need to learn about letters. It is not necessary for them to memorize the names of the twenty-six alphabet letters in order, but it is important for them to develop the concept that speech can be written down; that such writing takes the form of words; and that words are made up of letters that have names. As literacy emerges naturally with children whose lives are surrounded by print, their recognition of single letters is a part of this spontaneous unfolding. Any formal teaching of the alphabet on the part of the teacher is as unnecessary as it is inappropriate. Children are going to learn about letters in spite of what adults do or do not do.

After all, your children want to recognize letters for all kinds of reasons. One reason is in order to use the computer's typewriter keyboard. They will be pressing one key at a time to make something happen on the monitor screen. They will need to know which key to press. The keys are identified by letters and numbers. They can **learn to find and identify letter keys if they begin with a simple alphabet computer program**. They will not only develop computer literacy on their own, but also letter knowledge.

Of the many ABC computer programs available, several seem attractive to children and teachers alike. Previously described on page 75 is *Stickybear ABC* (1982). Preschoolers have no trouble identifying not only letter keys but also new words such as *volcano* and *octopus*.

Another easy-to-use program is *Animal Alphabet and Other Things* (1986), in which a letter appears on the screen when the child presses the letter key (e.g., the letter *A*). Pressing the letter a second time causes the letter to turn into an appropriate animal (e.g., an alligator). Side 1 of the disk features all twenty-six uppercase letters, and side 2 shows the lowercase. When selecting alphabet computer programs, check to be sure that the entire alphabet is on one side of the disk. Young children have great difficulty otherwise.

A program with six activities and good graphics is *My ABC's* (1984), which includes letter and number recognition, letter matching, and dancing letters for any key pressed. Children like programs in which they have direct control over what happens. They also like programs in which something happens every time they press a key, as this one does.

Computer alphabet programs should be used in conjunction with hands-on alphabet activities in the Writing Center. Several sets of alphabet letters should be available (e.g., wood, plastic, magnetic, sandpaper, etc.) for matching and sorting games. You can make your own games by **tracing around a set of wooden or plastic letters onto a posterboard and letting children try to match the letters to their outlines**. Youngsters love to stretch out on the floor with the posterboard and the letters strewn about. This same activity can be created with **magnetic letters that you trace on a metal surface,** such as a refrigerator door or metal bulletin board. You can use a china marker or fingernail polish to do the tracing. Children enjoy pushing the magnetic letters into place on this vertical surface so that the letters fill up the entire outline.

Alphabet books are appropriate in your Writing Center, too, as long as you **check them out carefully**. This popular form of picture book comes out with new editions year after year. Some alphabet books feature glorious illustrations that turn out to be more of a showcase for an artist than a learning experience for young children. Others may be too difficult for preschoolers, or too simple. Borrow a few alphabet books from the library and try them out with your children before you purchase your own.

If you have guinea pigs in your Science Center, then your children may enjoy Kate Duke's *The Guinea Pig ABC* (1983). A large uppercase letter fills each page with one or two guinea pigs romping around it to illustrate the one descriptive word at the bottom of the page. Unlike most alphabet books that feature names of things, this book illustrates adjectives such as "G" for "Greedy" and "I" for "Itchy," for example.

Eating the Alphabet: Fruits & Vegetables from A to Z by Lois Ehlert (1989) is a wonderful, colorful, tasty expedition from "Apple" to "Zucchini." Each set of double-spread, horizontal pages contains an upper- and lower-case letter with several brightly colored fruits or vegetables to illustrate the letter. Using this book with small groups of children can lead into **a series of field trips to purchase one or two of the alphabet food items** each time + you go. Take the book along to identify the fruit or vegetable you want. For example, the "Aa" pages show apricots, artichokes, avocados, apples, and asparagus. Be sure to purchase enough of the food item for everyone. The Writing Center children can then divide up and serve the "letter food" to the rest of the children.

For example, **the children may want to create a "C" snack** for everyone + by cutting up carrots, celery, cucumbers, and cauliflower purchased at the store to be dipped into a dip that they have mixed. Thus, the abstract concept of letters becomes real to children when concrete, three-dimensional objects are involved. How else can you make letters come alive for children? What about **making alphabet soup**? +

Children also want to learn about letters so that they can print their own names. Some children already know how to print their names when they enter your program, but most three-year-olds are barely at the beginning of the writing process. They usually ask one of the classroom adults to sign their names to art products. As you sign a child's name, **ask him or her to sign his own name,** too. It may only be a scribble, but that is how writing + starts. You can tell the child that what he has written is his personal script and that what you have written is in conventional script.

Make letters personal, and you will quickly have your children's attention. **Use their printed names** in every way you can think of. The computer + program *Early Games* (1984) contains a game called "Names," in which a child types in his own name, presses the Return key, and then watches while his name flashes on the screen in exciting and colorful designs. Bring in a set of **alphabet blocks** and see whether the child can make his name from the blocks. Take an instant **photo of his block name,** and mount it on + the bulletin board in the Writing Center.

Read books that feature names, such as *Andy (That's My Name)* by +

Tomie de Paola (1973), in which little Andy comes along with a wagon containing the letters of his name. The big kids take the letters and make various words from them but will not let Andy play because he is too little. The book *A my name is ALICE* by Jane Bayer, with Steven Kellogg's hilarious illustrations (1984), contains names of critters from A to Z presented as pattern-play-type rhymes (e.g., "My name is Alice and my husband's name is Alex. We come from Alaska and we sell ants. Alice is an APE. Alex is an ANTEATER").

Have children **collect the alphabet letters they know**. Bring **in** (or have
+ the children bring in) **an empty tissue box** for their alphabet letters. The boxes can be painted by the children and labeled with their names. You can
+ **provide letter cards** for your children to use by taking an old set of playing cards, pressing them face down onto the sticky side of white contact paper, and cutting them out. Next, take a sheet of large press-on type letters and transfer one letter to the white face of each card. Keep these cards in a cigar box for the children to select when they want. Even if they do not really know the letters by name, they will soon learn them if you interact with individuals saying, "Oh, Daryl, look at all the alphabet letters you have collected! Do you know the names of any of them?" **Children can find their own let-**
+ **ters** for their box by cutting them out of old magazines that you provide for this purpose. Where else might they look for letters?

Some children may be interested in going farther with letters than merely collecting them. You may see them copying the letters they know on a sheet of paper—over and over until the page is filled. Then they take another sheet and fill that one, too. Do you understand what they are doing? Once again, they are interacting with materials at the *mastery* level. By now, you probably realize that whenever you see young children doing something over and over again, they have advanced to the mastery level. Remember to display their letter sheets on the Writing Center bulletin board.

Next comes the *meaning* level. How do children spontaneously transfer meaning to the letters they know? At first, they use one letter to stand for an entire word, such as their name. *K* means *Kathy*. Then they begin to use other letters to stand for words: *R* stands for *are*. *U* stands for *you*. At this point, they have cognitively begun to understand that letters stand for sounds as well as for words. Eventually, they realize that letters can be put together to make up words. They may print *KY* to stand for *key* or *HS* to mean *house*. Most children, however, reach this more advanced understanding at age five or six.

You can help your preschoolers extract meaning from the letters they
+ know by **reading appropriate story alphabet books** to them. Clyde Watson's *Applebet, An ABC* (1982) is a complete story about the *apple* that *Bet* picked, which went into the *cider* they drank on the way to the fair. In addition to single alphabet letters, this book also features combinations: *CH* for

cherry, *QU* for *quarrel*, and *SH* for *sh-h*. *The Bears' ABC Book* by Robin and Jocelyn Wild (1977) is the story of three little bears on a wild romp through a dump with an alphabet item that they discover and play with on each page, from A to Z.

Writing Activities to Promote Physical Development

Small Motor

Young children learn to hold and control a writing implement on their own. You do not need to teach them how. They start in infancy with a power-grip fist around the crayon or chalk and later switch naturally to a precision grip, using fingers and thumb. Your best help will come from the variety of writing activities and materials you provide in your Writing Center. Do not put out all your writing tools at once. **Add a new one to pique interest** once in a while, **with a new activity to introduce it**. For instance, add colored chalk and small individual chalkboards; or have a **wet chalk activity** with   + fingerpaint paper. The children can dip the chalk in a cup of water before writing on the paper, or you can wet the paper instead of the chalk.

Another time, have fingerpainting itself. To encourage children to do personal writing, let them **fingerpaint on small trays**. Their scribbled writing   + can be saved if they want by pressing a sheet of paper onto it and rubbing. Still another time, let them write in the fingerpaint with an implement such as a tongue depressor. Children can also **write with their fingers in trays of salt**. They especially enjoy erasing their marks by shaking the tray.   +

Writing Activities to Promote Social Development

The wonderful thing about writing is that it is a social activity for young children. They **all can write an invitation or a thank-you note on a large piece of newsprint,** dictating to you the words they want on their note or   + writing the words themselves in scribbled personal script with your translation underneath. Then, each child can sign his name and add a decoration if he wants. The note can be folded and mailed in a large envelope. Children enjoy writing together like this. They tell each other what they are doing, ask each other for help, and compare notes.

Communal notes such as this can be messages asking for permission to do something, thanking a parent or community helper for visiting, asking for information about a topic the children are pursuing, sending greetings to someone having a birthday, inviting people to come to a class picnic, thanking people for helping on a field trip, asking a high school student to come and play the guitar, thanking a librarian for the story hour she per-

formed, or sending a get-well message to someone in the hospital. **Bring
into the Writing Center all kinds of greeting cards** when this activity is in
progress.

+

Children may want to write notes or messages to one another as well.
They can help **make individual mailboxes from half-gallon milk cartons**
covered with colored paper, labeled with their names, and stacked on a
shelf. Children will be motivated to write if you give them reasons for practicing written communication. Write a note to each of them at least once a
week. Put it in their mailbox, and ask them to reply. This means you need
your own personal mailbox, as well, to receive their answers.

+

Another social skill that can be promoted through writing is turn taking.
Children can sign up to take a turn with the activities in the classroom,
with a special toy, with a piece of playground equipment, with a book, on
the computer, and so on. Put clipboards with pencils attached in the various areas of the classroom where turn taking is necessary. Have children
write their names under one another's and cross them off when their turn
is finished. Even if children are still scribbling in their own personal script,
they can sign their name this way. They will be able to identify their own sig-
nature whether or not you can.

+

• • • • • • • • • • • Writing Activities to Promote Language Development

Just as children acquire their language ability naturally by saying
sounds first and then single words, so they also acquire their writing ability
by making letters first and then words. They start with naming words in
writing, just as they do in language acquisition. They usually begin by
printing their own name, as previously mentioned. In a classroom that features a Writing Center, however, some children will eventually want to write
other naming words as well.

In order **to recognize naming words, young children need many experiences with them.** You will be reading books with them, of course, that are
full of words and illustrations of things that can be pointed to and named by
them. In addition, read from **books that feature naming words,** such as
The Strawberry Look Book by Richard Hefter (1980). In this book the Stickybears (Mama, Papa, and Little Bear) from the computer program series go
shopping at the supermarket, toy store, clothing store, furniture store, bak-
ery, and florist, as well as stopping at a restaurant and garage. Every item in
the full-page illustrations has its name printed directly on the object. Read
this book on a one-to-one basis with your children. Ask the child to point to
objects that you will name, and then invite the child to try his or her skill at
naming as you point to an object.

+

+

After reading this book, **make some simple name cards for objects in the classroom**. Print these name words on sheets of self-stick paper: words such as *chair, table, shelf, window, wall,* and so on. Do not expect the children to read these words. You do the reading, and ask children to stick the name word where it belongs. At the end of the day, you can reassemble these words for repeated use. Leave the words in a container in the Writing Center, and eventually the children will be able to play the game themselves.

Some children are sure to want name cards of their own. At this point, you can start a **personal name word can** for each child in the Writing Center. Cover an empty food can with colorful contact paper, and place it on the shelf as a container for each child's personal word collection. Start the collection by printing the child's name in large upper- and lowercase letters on a 3-by-5 card or self-stick sheet. Add other name words on cards when the child asks for them.

Make a set of name word cards that the children can borrow when they want them, showing popular commercial logo names from cans of food, cereal boxes, junk mail, supermarket ads, coupons, and so on. In addition to products, these word cards can also feature the names of fast-food restaurants, gas stations, cars, airlines, chain stores, and so on, if you feel this is appropriate. Interacting with commonly used name words like this is how children teach themselves to write and read, even though it may seem commercial.

Some children may want to **write name words on the computer**. The *Early Games* "Names" program described on page 159 can be used for words as well as children's names. In fact, children can type in more than one word and watch it being flashed on the screen.

As children reach the *meaning* level in their use of naming words, they respond well to games played with words. This is the time to **read rebus books to individuals and small groups** of children in the Writing Center. A rebus is a picture or symbol used in place of a word in a sentence. Children have to guess which word is being depicted by the rebus. A classic rebus story is Polly Cameron's *"I Can't," said the Ant* (1971), in which objects in the kitchen appear as rebus drawings in each of the rhyming sentences. *The Rebus Treasury* by Jean Marzollo (1986) contains familiar nursery rhymes and words to songs with a tiny rebus picture in each sentence. Mark Twain also wrote rebus letters to his young children when he was away from home. You can **write a rebus letter to your children and let them decipher the meaning**.

This also is the time to **use wordless picture books** with your children. We used to think that a wordless book would stimulate storytelling with young children, who would make up the words of the story to go along with the illustrations. Now we realize that most young children instead name or describe the objects they see in wordless book illustrations, rather than making up stories about them. It is word sense rather than story sense that children develop through wordless picture books (Hough, Nurss, & Wood, 1987).

Wordless story books that young children can enjoy include:

Rosie's Walk, by Pat Hutchins (1968)
A boy, a dog, and a frog, by Mercer Mayer (1967)
The Midnight Adventures of Kelly, Dot, and Esmeralda, by John S. Goodall (1972)
Do You Want to be My Friend? by Eric Carle (1971)

You can show your children that these books do not have words in them, that instead of words, the pictures tell the story. Ask them to look at the pictures as you turn the pages and to tell you what words they would like you to use when you tell them the story. **Write down the words they suggest on**
\+ **a note pad**. Then be sure to **use their words** as you tell the story from the pictures in the wordless book.

• • • • • • • • • • Writing Activities to Promote Emotional Development

To help your children control their negative feelings, you may be suggesting to them that they can express their feelings in words rather than by acting them out. Instead of striking out at another child in anger, for example, they can tell that child in words how they feel. Instead of becoming upset and crying when someone takes their toy, they can tell the someone how they feel.

Another way that strong negative feelings can be diffused is to **write**
\+ **down the words expressing the feeling**. You will be the one writing down the words. Ask the child how he feels when he is upset, and write down a word or two. Sometimes children will seem to project their feelings into the actual word you write. They may even want you to write their "feelings word" on a card for their personal word can. They can take out the word and look at it when they feel that way again.

If this is the case with your children, you may want to read to individuals or small groups another kind of alphabet book: *A is for ANGRY, an animal and adjective alphabet* by Sandra Boynton (1987). Each double-spread page shows a large, capital alphabet letter with an animal of the same letter clinging to it, with an adjective and a small animal underneath. For example, *B* is illustrated by a large bear, a small bunny, and the adjective *bashful*.

• • • • • • • • • • **Writing Activities to Promote Creative Development**

Children will be looking at stories in books, hearing stories told or read by you, making up their own stories, telling stories through a puppet, and tape recording their own stories. This creative outpouring on their part can also be written down. You will be the principal writer at first, although children can also be encouraged to write down their own stories in their personal script (scribbling and mock writing).

To encourage this kind of activity, you need to **write down** the **stories on an "experience chart"** that a small group of children may dictate to you. + Such a chart is a large piece of newsprint (sometimes lined) on an easel that teachers use for writing down dictated group stories. After a field trip is a good time to ask the children to tell the story of the trip while you write it down. After someone special has visited the classroom, you can ask the children to tell the story of the visit while you write it on newsprint. Later, you and the children can read back the story together. They may want the story in a class storybook that you can make, or they may want to **dictate a story for you to write in their own personal storybook**.   +

Make a blank book for each child with his name on front. In it the child can write his own personal script story or a story that he dictates to you. If you are taking instant photos every day of the interesting things that children are doing, mount a picture of a particular child on the front of his book and ask him to tell you the story about it. You can write as he dictates or let him write his own story.

• • • • • • • • • • **The Teacher's Role in the Writing Center**

• **Observing Developmental Levels**

Once the Writing Center is set up and equipped, the teacher needs to observe in an informal manner the children who are using the center, commenting on their involvement and encouraging them in their continuation of the activities. She can also determine whether particular children are interacting with writing materials at the manipulation, mastery, or meaning level in order to support them with activities that will extend their learning.

In order to record her observations on the Child Interaction Form, the teacher needs to be aware of the kinds of Writing Center activities that can occur at the manipulation level, the mastery level, and the meaning level. Table 7–1 lists a number of possibilities. Because children's pre-writing activities tend to be individual in nature, most interactions fall under the solitary play or parallel play categories. The gathering of data on the Child Interaction Form helps the classroom staff to plan for individuals as well as identify the kinds of new materials to be introduced in the Writing Center.

TABLE 7–1	Writing Center Activities: Levels of Interaction

Manipulation Level

Scribbling

Playing with alphabet letters or blocks without regard to their names

Playing with writing implements without writing

Playing with stamping, printing materials without regard to meaning

Playing with salt tray, sand table, or fingerpainting without writing

Making letters here and there on paper

Playing around with computer alphabet programs with no control

Playing with a typewriter without control

Mastery Level

Mock-writing the same words over and over, sometimes in a list

Filling a page with mock writing

Making a list of words

Writing/typing letter, name or word over and over

Tracing letters over and over

Playing with alphabet letters

Matching letters, categorizing letters

Stamping letters or pictures over and over

Making letters, names, words over and over on salt tray, sand table, fingerpainting

Playing with computer alphabet programs with control

Meaning Level

Writing name scribble on paper, salt tray, sand table, fingerpainting

Printing name or words with letters

Writing name or word on typewriter or computer

Arranging alphabet letters or blocks to make name, words

Stamping letters to make name, words

Making mock-writing sign, label

Making mock-writing message

Making mock-writing story and ''reading'' it back

Making up own games with computer alphabet programs

In addition to recording an individual child's interaction level, the teacher also needs to keep track of which children use the Writing Center regularly and which do not. Her own presence in the center may bring in children who have not yet experimented with writing. Her attention to individuals may encourage them to attempt this new skill. She may also offer a direct invitation to a child who has not become involved. Perhaps the child can write a note to his mother or father about the block building he has constructed. Children are more often motivated to attempt a new activity when it relates to them personally.

Finally, the sensitive teacher will keep her eyes and ears open to children's own ideas and suggestions so that she can structure the Writing Center to better serve the needs of individuals. She will make the center fun for preschoolers so that they will engage in writing activities with the same zest they bring to dramatic play or block building. She will understand that it is not her role to teach young children to write, but to set up a Writing Center to entice them to become deeply involved in pre-writing activities on their own.

IDEAS +
in CHAPTER 7

1. *Setting up the Writing Center*
   a. Fill the children's environment with examples of the children's writing and reading. (p. 150)
   b. Display the children's writing, even their scribbles and lines. (p. 150)
   c. Have a roll-top desk with pigeon-holes to stimulate writing. (p. 151)
   d. Provide sets of alphabet letters in wood, plastic, sandpaper, and magnetic materials. (p. 152)
   e. Provide colored chalk and individual chalkboards. (p. 152)
   f. Provide cases of writing materials for overnight lending. (p. 152)
   g. Provide a primary typewriter or a regular, standard typewriter. (p. 152)
   h. Have a sand table in the Writing Center. (p. 152)
   i. Feature book posters with labels in the Writing Center. (p. 153)
   j. Have an alphabet wall-hanging, quilt, or rug in the Writing Center. (p. 153)

2. *Promoting cognitive development*
   a. Let children play around with letters, words, and writing. (p. 157)
   b. Have simple alphabet computer programs. (p. 158)
   c. Trace around a set of alphabet letters and have children try to match the letters to their outlines. (p. 158)
   d. Have alphabet books, but check them carefully for their appropriateness for preschoolers. (p. 158)
   e. Take field trips to purchase alphabet food items. (p. 159)
   f. Create letter snacks for everyone. (p. 159)
   g. Make alphabet soup. (p. 159)
   h. Ask children to sign their own names, even if the name is a scribble. (p. 159)
   i. Make alphabet letters personal by using children's names in many ways. (p. 159)
   j. Take a photo of children's names made from alphabet blocks. (p. 159)
   k. Read books that feature names. (p. 159)
   l. Have children collect their own personal alphabet letters. (p. 160)
   m. Use playing cards, contact paper, and press-on type to make letter cards. (p. 160)
   n. Read appropriate alphabet story books. (p. 160)

3. *Promoting small motor development*

    a. Add a new writing tool and new activity to the Writing Center periodically. (p. 161)

    b. Have a wet chalk activity. (p. 161)

    c. Have children do fingerpainting writing on small trays. (p. 161)

    d. Have children write with their fingers on trays of salt. (p. 161)

4. *Promoting social development*

    a. Do a group thank-you note on newsprint. (p. 161)

    b. Bring in all kinds of greeting cards. (p. 162)

    c. Make individual mailboxes from half-gallon milk cartons. (p. 162)

    d. Have children sign up to take a turn. (p. 162)

5. *Promoting language development*

    a. Read books that feature naming words. (p. 162)

    b. Do a name card activity with objects in the classroom. (p. 163)

    c. Make a personal name card can for each child. (p. 163)

    d. Make name word cards from commercial logos. (p. 163)

    e. Have children use simple name games on the computer. (p. 163)

    f. Write a rebus letter to your children. (p. 163)

    g. Write down words children suggest for stories from wordless picture books. (p. 164)

6. *Promoting emotional development*

    a. Write down feeling words to help children diffuse strong negative feelings. (p. 164)

7. *Promoting creative development*

    a. Write children's dictated stories on an experience chart. (p. 165)

    b. Make blank books for children to use in dictating or writing their own stories. (p. 165)

REFERENCES CITED

Barbour, N., Webster, T. D., & Drosdeck, S. (1987). Sand: A resource for the language arts. *Young Children 42* (2), 20–25.

Hough, R. A., Nurss, J. R., & Wood, D. (1987). Tell me a story: Making opportunities for elaborated language in early childhood. *Young Children 43* (1), 6–12.

Lamme, L. L. (1984). *Growing up writing.* Washington, DC: Acropolis Books, Ltd.

Rich. S. J. (1985). The writing suitcase. *Young Children 40* (5), 42–44.

Salsbury, E. C. (Ed.). (1965). *Susy and Mark Twain, family dialogues.* New York: Harper and Row.

OTHER SOURCES

Beaty, J. J. (1990). *Observing development of the young child.* Columbus, OH: Merrill Publishing Company.

Morrow, L. M. (1989). *Literacy development in the early years.* Englewood Cliffs, NJ: Prentice-Hall.

Schickendanz, J. A. (1986). *More than the ABCs, the early stages of reading and writing.* Washington, DC: National Association for the Education of Young Children.

CHILDREN'S BOOKS

Bayer, J. (1984). *A my name is Alice.* New York: Dial Books.

Boynton, S. (1987). *A is for angry, an animal and adjective alphabet.* New York: Workman Publishing.

Cameron, P. (1971). *"I can't," said the ant.* New York: Scholastic Book Services.

Carle, E. (1971). *Do you want to be my friend?* New York: Thomas Y. Crowell.

Duke, K. (1983). *The guinea pig ABC,* New York: E. P. Dutton.

De Paolo, T. (1973). *Andy (that's my name).* Englewood Cliffs, NJ: Prentice-Hall.

Ehlert, L. (1989). *Eating the alphabet: Fruits & vegetables from A to Z.* San Diego, CA: Harcourt Brace Jovanovich.

Goodall, J. S. (1972).*The midnight adventures of Kelly, Dot, and Esmeralda.* New York: Atheneum.

Hefter, R. (1980). *The strawberry look book.* New York: Weekly Reader Books.

Hutchins, P. (1968). *Rosie's walk.* New York: Macmillan.

Marzollo, J. (1986). *The rebus treasury.* New York: Dial Books for Children.

Mayer, M. (1967). *A boy, a dog, and a frog.* New York: Dial Press.

Watson, C. (1982). *Applebet, an ABC,* New York: Farrar, Straus, and Giroux.

Wild, R., & Wild, J. (1977). *The bears' ABC book.* New York: Harper & Row.

CHILDREN'S COMPUTER PROGRAMS (by publisher)

Paperback Software
2612 Eighth Street
Berkeley, CA 94710
   My ABC's 1984 (IBM)

Random House Software
400 Hahn Road
Westminster, MD 21157
   Animal Alphabet and Other Things 1986 (Apple)

Springboard
7808 Creekridge Circle
Minneapolis, MN 55435
   Early Games 1984 (Apple, IBM, C64, Atari)

Weekly Reader Software
Middletown, CT 06457
   Stickybear ABC 1982 (Apple, Atari)

•••

TRY IT
YOURSELF

1. Set up a Writing Center in your classroom with shelves full of writing tools, equipment, activities, computer programs, books, posters, a typewriter, and a bulletin board as described in this chapter.

2. Set up a print-rich environment in other areas of your classroom with labels, signs, children's names, charts, sign-up sheets, bulletin boards, and other print materials.

3. Do an alphabet letter activity with a small group as described in the chapter with wooden, plastic, or metal letters, books, a computer program, cards, or a field trip.

4. Do a writing activity with a small group as described in the chapter, involving the children's actually writing a story, an experience, a letter, a note, or something else.

5. Make an assessment of five of your children as to the level of involvement they display in writing or printing letters (i.e., manipulation, mastery, or meaning) and describe how you determined their level.

ART CENTER

PAINTING AND TALKING

(Action chant)

I'm a dabbler.
  Dabble-dabble,
With a paintbrush,
  Dabble-dabble,
On an easel,
  Dabble-dabble,
Or the table,
  Dabble-dabble.

I'm a babbler,
  Babble-babble,
With a toy phone,
  Babble-babble,
On a doll bed,
  Babble-babble,
Or a table,
  Babble-babble.

See me painting,
  Dabble-dabble,
Hear me talking,
  Babble-babble,
With the children,
  Babble-babble,
As I'm walking,
  Dabble-dabble.

I can't stop now,
  Dabble-dabble,
With my painting,
  Dabble-dabble,
'Cause my talking's,
  Babble-babble,
Got me fainting,
  Babble-babble,
Plop! (fall down)

(dabble-dabble = wave right fist up and down as in painting)
(babble-babble = wave left fist up to mouth and away as in phoning)

• • • • • • • • • • Art in the Early Childhood Classroom

Young children seem to have a natural affinity for art, just as they do for speaking and writing, if their environment is full of interesting opportunities. Art, like language, is a means of communication and self-expression for children. It is visual, though, rather than verbal, and involves the elements of line, shape, color, and texture rather than words.

Because young children have an inborn drive to communicate, they continually work at the development of this ability in every possible aspect. They coo, cry, babble, and finally speak. They scribble horizontally, play with letters, and finally write. In art, they scribble, make shapes, combine shapes, and finally draw pictures. They experiment with colors and play around with textures. **If given a wide variety of materials as well as the freedom and time to discover how these work,** young children will teach themselves the art skills they need in order to communicate what they have to say.

Thus, art lends itself well to the activities of the self-directed learning environment, that is, as long as the adults in the classroom remember that the children are involved in a learning *process* rather than in creating an art *product*. Most three- and four-year-olds are not painting a picture as they

173

stand at the easel, wielding a paintbrush. They are instead manipulating the medium, as they did with blocks, computer programs, numbers, letters, and words.

They splash paint around on their paper, sometimes making a blob, other times painting lines or circles. Just as you are about to hang up their finished work to dry, they may cover over the whole painting with brown. "Why did they do that?" you may wonder. The colors were so pretty before they covered them over. You must remind yourself that most of the children are not creating paintings but are instead manipulating the medium of easel paint. They are trying out brushes, colors, lines, and strokes to see what happens when they use them. As they gain control, they will advance to the mastery level of involvement, doing the same kinds of shapes or designs over and over. Finally, some, but not necessarily all of the children, will evolve to the meaning level of art development and begin to paint identifiable objects and pictures.

• • • • • • • • • • The Development of Drawing Skills

All children around the world go through a similar sequence in the development of drawing skills. They begin with scribbles which they make on paper, tabletops, walls, steamy windows, or even in dirt with a stick. Their first scribbles are purely motor expressions: "endless lines done in a rhythmic, manipulative manner" (Beaty, 1990, 304), one on top of another, without even looking on. As the child gains arm and hand control, he or she will watch what he is doing and begin to control the placement of the scribbles on the paper.

Rhoda Kellogg, who collected thousands of children's drawings from around the world, was able to identify twenty basic scribbles and called them "the building blocks of art" (Kellogg, 1970, 15). From these scribbles, young children concentrate on a few favorite forms, repeating them over and over, often on top of one another as they master the use of brushes or crayons.

Shapes begin to emerge from the scribbles in the natural sequences of development. Kellogg identified six basic shapes in children's early art: the rectangle (or square), the oval (or circle), the triangle, the Greek cross (+), the diagonal cross (×), and an odd shape (Kellogg, 1970, 45).

By ages three to five, children are not only repeating these shapes but often combining them, one on top of another. It is intriguing to realize that these particular combinations are found not only in children's early art all over the world, but also in the rock drawings of early man throughout the world. One of the forms, the so-called "mandala," is a combination of a cross within a circle. Mandalas are commonly found on the walls of ancient caves, in early religious designs, and in the art of preschool children! What a universal human heritage our children are expressing in their natural development of drawing skills.

The sun is one of the next shapes to appear naturally in children's art, with the sun's rays evolving from the ends of a mandala cross, whose lines perhaps protruded outside the circle (although the cross itself no longer appears within the circle).

Next to evolve is the human, which is a sun with its rays becoming hair on top, an arm on either side, and two legs coming out the bottom of the circle. The human's eyes appear as little circles or dots within the sun. Some children draw a nose or mouth as well, but some do not. All children everywhere seem to make their first humans this way, with arms and legs attached to the head. Eventually, most children lengthen the two legs and place a horizontal line between them, making a more conventional body.

From ages four to six, other recognizable objects appear in children's art, drawn from their minds and not from what they see. Thus, young children's houses, dogs, cars, and trees are quite similar. As you might expect, children next fill art papers with their repertoire of objects over and over until they have mastered them. You will recognize that they have reached the meaning level of their drawings when they begin telling you spontaneously what their pictures are about.

• • • • • • • • • • Setting Up the Art Center

To help children advance through these levels of manipulation, mastery, and meaning on their own, you can set up the Art Center of the classroom so that children can choose and use it easily. **Have at least one, and preferably two, easels available at all times.** Easels are among the most inviting and usable devices for stimulating children's independent involvement with art. Paints and brushes can be ready and waiting for children whenever they choose to paint. **Children can learn to take their own easel paper** from a shelf or a pad and attach it to the easel with clips or clothespins. **When finished, they can hang their own papers to dry** over drying lines strung parallel on a homemade stand-up frame or from a commercial paint-drying rack.

Commercial easels come in various types and sizes: the traditional free-standing, two-sided easel, as well as wall easel, table easel, and adjustable easel. **Attach a clipboard with pad and pencil to the side of each easel so that children can sign up when the easel is in use.**

Paints available for child use will be on low shelves near the table(s) where they are to be used. They can include: mixed tempera paint of various colors in plastic jars or squeeze bottles, tempera markers with liquid paint and a flow-through brush on the top, watercolor sets in plastic boxes, and fingerpaints in plastic jars, along with brushes of various sizes, paint-mixing jars, and sponges. Trays of white painting paper, colored construction paper, and glazed fingerpaint paper can be located on the same shelves easily available to the children.

Keep materials in separate, color-coded containers with illustrated labels on the outside for easy selection and return by children. Some programs, because of space limitations, prefer to roll out **art carts with shelves containing necessary painting supplies**. Helper children can assist in loading the carts for the day's activities.

The materials in the Art Center should be those available for free use by the children. It is not necessary to put out at the same time all the art materials owned by the program. **Add new materials from time to time. Retire materials no longer used regularly.** Teacher's art materials such as powdered tempera paints or pottery clay should be stored elsewhere.

TABLE 8–1	Art Materials	
Tempera paints	Yarn	Scissor rack
Easels	Sequins	Masking tape
Fingerpaints	Glitter	Transparent tape
Fluorescent paints	Pom-poms	Sponges
Watercolor sets	Feathers	Stampers
Tempera markers	Felt shapes	Stamp pads
Pastel crayons	Styrofoam shapes	Pottery clay
Wax crayons	Craft buttons	Clay bucket
Felt-tip markers	School paste	Clay boards
Colored pencils	School glue	Clay hammer
Colored chalk	Glue sticks	Rolling pins
Chalkboards	Rubber cement	Plasticine
Easel brushes	White paper	Play dough
Hole punches	Kraft paper	Cookie cutters
Peel-off shapes	Construction paper	Painting aprons
Paper doilies	Manila paper	Painting trays
Weaving loops	Glazed paper	Mixing jars
Weaving frames	Tissue paper	Drying rack
Pipe cleaners	Crepe paper	Aluminum foil
Popsicle sticks	Newsprint	Cellophane paper
Corrugated paper	Food coloring	Wheat paste
Ribbon	Scissors	

Access to water is important for art activities. Locate the area near a   +
sink if possible, or arrange for buckets of clean water and rinse water to be
stored on a low stand for easy use by children.

Art activities can be integrated into the entire curriculum if materials   +
from your other learning centers are included in this area. Picture books
with colorful illustrations are especially attractive lead-ins to art activities
and should be available to children in both the Art Center and the Story
Center.

• • • • • • • • • • • Beauty and Aesthetics

The Art Center should also be the place where beauty and aesthetics begin. **An early childhood classroom should be both pleasing to look at and
beautiful to be in.** We know that children appreciate bright colors and airy   +
spaces. We realize that the adult staff also finds pleasure in beautiful surroundings. Let us, then, make our classroom a beautiful place to live and
work in, beginning with the Art Center and spreading into the entire environment.

A dull and gloomy environment puts a damper on happiness and joy. Although children themselves bring their own verve with them to the classroom, it is up to you to take advantage of their spontaneous delight by
arranging the environment with beauty in mind. It is not necessary to go
overboard with bright colors. Rather than **painting your walls** a bright yellow, for instance, you might consider **a lovely, light pastel color,** which is   +
more soothing yet able to accentuate the colorful activity areas you arrange.
Fresh wall paint may not be necessary (or possible if you are leasing your fa-
cility). Nevertheless, the walls can be cleaned and the activity areas made
colorful.

Rolls of corrugated cardboard in a variety of hues **can color code your
separate area walls or be used as a bright baseboard throughout the room**.   +
Self-adhesive vinyl paper comes in a variety of solid colors for covering
shelves, countertops, or tables. Matching curtains can be purchased or
made. **Homemade room dividers of folded packing-crate sections** can be
covered with colored burlap. Make your own bulletin boards the same way   +
out of cardboard and burlap with brown vinyl wood-print borders.

Do not overdo colors or clutter. Use your own sensibilities to decide how   +
much color to use and how many materials to have available at one time.
Sensory overload, that overwhelming feeling of too many clashing colors or
too much unnecessary material being displayed at one time, can affect both
children and adults. Keep your decorating scheme simple but beautiful.

One bulletin board in the Art Center can display a changing array of the
children's progress as they work through their artistic development from

scribbles to identifiable designs. If your bulletin board has a light blue backing, then you might consider mounting the children's art on yellow or even

+   pink backing paper. **Change the bulletin-board backing from time to time.** Change your color scheme perhaps once or twice during the year. If you are using corrugated cardboard or self-adhesive vinyl, this is not difficult to do. Children and adults alike respond to variety if it is not overdone.

+   **Picture-book posters can be mounted on cardboard backing and covered with clear food wrapping** for display in any of the activity areas. This art from modern children's books is as impressive and beautiful as any in an art gallery. Posters of animal photos, flowers, trees, and outdoor scenes are also appropriate.

+   **Talk to children about colors and natural beauty, starting with them personally.** Mention how you like the colors of the clothing they are wearing. Wear attractive clothing yourself. **Bring in flowers, seed pods, and**

+   **branches** for attractive arrangements that you can talk to the children about. Help them see the beauty around them, both within the classroom and outside. Did they notice the splash of red on the head of the house finch at the bird feeder? How many different shades of green can they see on the grass, trees, and bushes in the yard? Are there any colors like this in the classroom? Look out the window at the beautiful blue color of the sky. How can they bring this color into the classroom to make their indoor environment more beautiful?

• • • • • • • • • • Art Activities to Promote Physical Development

• Small Motor

The principal small motor development you will want to promote through art activities is the holding of a brush, crayon, or drawing tool and controlling the marks it makes. This involves the development of arm, hand, and finger muscles as well as the eye-hand coordination necessary to make the tool do what you want it to do. In addition to the easel materials and other art supplies available for children's independent use, you will want to provide special activities that focus on holding implements and using them for drawing purposes.

An interesting way to begin is to **introduce a small group of children** in

+   the Art Center **to the little picture-book boy Harold and his purple crayon,** created by Crockett Johnson. Make a stand-up cutout of Harold on a piece of cardboard by tracing a simple outline of Harold on it and painting it blue for his pajamas, flesh color for his head, and with a white wide-eyed look as shown in the books. Put a hole through his cardboard hand big enough to insert a purple crayon. Bring in several of the "Harold" books to read to the group while Harold watches. Those that are out of print can often be found in the public library.

Harold and the Purple Crayon by Crockett Johnson (1955) is the first of the stories, showing Harold starting out drawing scribbles with his purple crayon, but then continuing his purple line as he walks in the moonlight, drawing the objects he needs and the things he wants to see. Another day, read *A Picture for Harold's Room* by Crockett Johnson (1960) or one of the other "Harold" books.

At the same time, have one of your Art Center tables **covered with white paper for the children to scribble and draw on with purple crayons** after the story is finished. You may want to have available several shades of purple crayons, such as violet and magenta. Have everyone sign his name in purple before the next group comes into the area and you cover the table with clean paper. If they do not print letters, let them scribble their names in personal script. If children want to identify the objects they have created, just as Harold did, you can accept it, but this early drawing activity is not the time to ask children to tell about their art.

Another simple drawing activity with black paper and white chalk can be motivated by reading the stunningly illustrated white-on-black book *Song of the Horse* by Richard Kennedy (1981). A photocopy picture from the book can be mounted near the art table when you read the book to a small group. The story is a first-person narrative told by a girl about riding her wonderful horse, Spirit. The words may seem too advanced for your children on your initial reading to yourself, but try them out on your children anyway. They are poetry in prose: telling how "moles and mice rush from their holes to see what great event is happening, but we are gone. We are a phantom, a ghost."

Let children make white lines on their black paper to the thunder of horse's hooves, to the sound of the wind, to the shouting of the cheering world. Put on a record or tape with drumbeats if you want. You can also tape-record hoofbeats with a cassette recorder from a video Western movie. Classical music such as the *William Tell Overture* or the *Grand Canyon Suite* may also be appropriate, or you may want to make your own hoofbeats on a children's drum or tambourine. Because children's first drawings are physical rather than cognitive, let them make their lines to the rhythm without even looking on. Can black and white lines be beautiful? Ask your children.

Another simple drawing activity that children enjoy involves making the blue chalk or blue crayon background for the story *Where does the butterfly go when it rains* by May Garelick (1961). The poem is a story in rhyme asking where the various animals go when it rains. Its pages are white covered with blue from a crayon or piece of chalk rubbed sideways across them. The rain in the book is scratched across the blue background with a sharp instrument. Because the book does not tell where the butterfly goes, it also leaves the children with a challenge to find out.

Children enjoy **covering their white papers with blue from an**

+ **unwrapped crayon or piece of chalk rubbed sideways** back and forth
+ across the paper. Give them **a fingernail file to scratch** across their blue
crayoned paper to make the rain.

Other small motor art activities include tearing, folding, cutting, squeezing, spattering, pasting, and rolling out dough. Children enjoy **tearing up
+ sheets of colored construction paper into pieces to be used in collages**.
Let them help keep a collage basket full of torn colored paper. Torn tissue
paper, crepe paper, and colored aluminum foil can also be used. Have other
baskets full of collections of items for collages, such as styrofoam shapes,
colored pipe cleaners, feathers, seeds, pasta shapes, and pom-poms. These
can be pasted or glued to backing paper in free-form creations.

+ **Preschoolers like to fold paper,** too. Let them practice on small pads of
colored paper. These folded papers can then be torn or cut and pasted on
collages. Some children are skilled enough at cutting with scissors to cut off
the corners of the folded papers, which turn out to be holes in them when
opened up. If the papers are white, children may call them "snowflakes."

Let children learn to cut with scissors by having in your Art Center a basket or scissor rack containing forged steel school scissors rather than the
blunt preschool scissors so often seen. Forged steel scissors are not only
easier to cut with but also retain their sharpness. **For safe use, it is better
+ to have sharp scissors than dull or blunt ones.**

Beginning cutters have better luck at first if you hold the paper tightly between your two hands while they cut. Let them **practice cutting with wrap-
+ ping paper ribbon that you hold for them**. They can **cut it into confetti** for
later use on greeting cards or collages. After you get them started, let one
child be the ribbon holder and another be the cutter. They can take turns
cutting and holding. Once they are able to coordinate their cutting, let them
cut up the pages from pads of colored paper into collage pieces. Children
+ also like to **cut out pictures from old magazines**. Be sure to have a selection
of magazines next to the scissor rack.

Children can develop small muscle strength by **squeezing plastic bottles
+ of paint to make designs** on colored construction paper. Lines and squiggles of liquid color can cover the paper, or the paper can be folded and blotted together, making another kind of design altogether.

• Large Motor

The book *Color Dance* by Ann Jonas (1989) can be used in the Art Center
to motivate large motor activities with colors, or later, when the cognitive
concept of mixing colors is being explored. It is a gorgeous book of colors
showing three girls in red, in yellow, and in blue leotards dancing in pairs
and then together with filmy cloths of the same colors, demonstrating what
happens when you mix the colors. Finally, a boy in white and black joins

Children can develop small muscle strength through art activities, such as squeezing and stamping with sponges and fingerpaint.

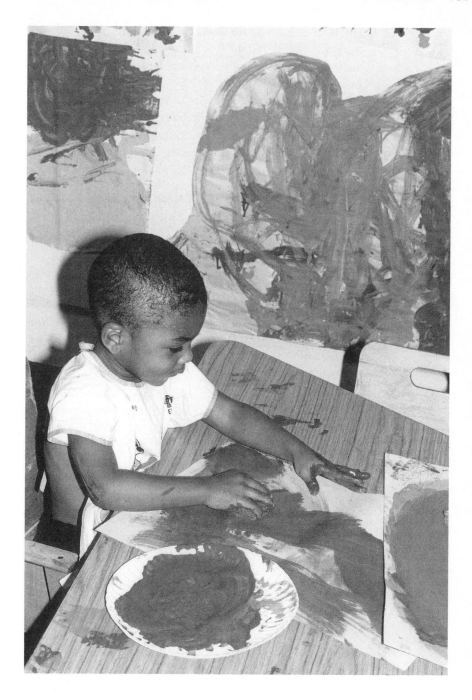

them to demonstrate what happens when white or gray or black colors are added.

Preschool children will eventually explore and experiment with what happens when paint colors are mixed together, but first, **let them twirl around physically with filmy cloths to music**. Then, let them return to the Art Center **and place one thin cloth over the other**. Can they see through them and discover a new color, as the children do in the book? Can they hold them up against the window and look through them.

If you don't want to use filmy cloths, what about umbrellas? The very simple book *Umbrella Parade* by Kathy Feczko (1985) has different animals walking out in the rain, each with a different color of umbrella. Bring in several umbrellas and let children have the physical experience of opening them. Then they can **parade around the classroom with umbrellas or paper parasols of different colors** after hearing this story. Afterwards, **cover one umbrella with another, and shine a light through from underneath**. Does this make a different color?

• • • • • • • • • • Art Activities to Promote Cognitive Development

The concept of color is a cognitive development that occurs in youngsters as early as four to six months of age (Richardson, Goodman, Hartman, & LePique, 1980, 123). Your concern in the preschool classroom is for children to learn to name and identify the various colors. This involves visual discrimination as well as knowing the names. Many preschoolers already recognize several colors. Others say the names of colors just as they say letter names of the alphabet, without really knowing what they mean.

In order for your children to put words and visual imagery together into a concept of color, **take one color at a time and let your children immerse themselves in it**. You might want to start with red because, as Kelly says, *Red Is Best* in the book by Kathy Stinson (1982). Read to your children why Kelly likes red stockings, red jacket, red boots, red mitts, red pajamas, red cup, red barrettes, and red paint the best, no matter what her mother thinks.

Ask the children to **bring something red to the class tomorrow**. Bring something red yourself, perhaps red flowers. Put red paint in the easel jars, and have red fingerpaint ready on one of the tables. Put out red interlocking bricks in the Manipulative/Math Center. Red toy fire engines can be parked in the Block Center for the children to use with their buildings. The program *Color Me* (1986) can be placed in the Computer Center for children to use with a joystick, mouse, or touch pad. In the Writing Center, red writing tools can be featured, such as felt-tip markers or colored pens and pencils. The children's scribbling can be mounted on red backing paper. Have red hats and shirts in the Dramatic Play Center. Color the water red in the water table. In the Story Center, put out the wordless book of Tana Hoban's striking color photos from city streets: *is it red? is it yellow? is it blue?* (1978). In the Music Center, teach a color song.

How long should you feature red? That will depend upon your children and your curriculum goals. After a week or so of red, you can continue with another color, perhaps green. You may decide to choose the particular color based on the season or a holiday.

When all of the colors have been introduced one by one, you will want your children to **experiment with mixing colors to make new colors**. Put   +
out two jars of different colors at the easel trough, perhaps yellow and blue, and let the children experiment to see what will happen. Daubs of yellow and blue fingerpaint can be placed on fingerpaint paper on one of the tables before the children arrive. You can read to the children in the Art Center the classic picture book *The Color Kittens* by Margaret Wise Brown (1977) about Brush and Hush, the kittens who mixed colors together to make all the colors in the world. But they could not find green until they accidentally poured a bucket of blue and a bucket of yellow together.

Mixing various paints together is a wonderful way for your children to experiment with colors. The idea is not for children this age to learn which colors make green and which make purple, but only to realize that new colors can be made by mixing other colors together. Children can also experiment with light or dark shades of a color by adding various amounts of white or black to the color.

Can your children make new colors with colored chalk? Let them try by   +
coloring with a piece of chalk on its side and then covering this with another color of chalk. **What about with crayons?** Unwrap a set of crayons to   +
use on their sides to see which new colors the children can create.

Bring in **food coloring for them to use in creating new liquid colors**. A   +
set of empty baby food jars in a tray can be half-filled with water by you and a drop or two of different food colors added to each. Have several empty jars, a cup of clear water, and a medicine dropper or two on the tray. One or two children can choose this color mixing experiment in the Art Center. Using muffin tins half-filled with different colored water is another variation.

This is the time for the children to **make various colors of play dough**.   +
Let them experiment every day with a different combination of colors by squeezing drops of food color directly into the play dough as they make it.

Can colored lights be blended to make different colors, too? Obtain   +
several colors of cellophane paper and bring in **a flashlight**. When the   +
room is darkened (as at nap time), shine the flashlight on the ceiling. Put blue cellophane over it, and then yellow cellophane. Children will be delighted to see that it really does turn green. You may want to read the book *Little Blue and Little Yellow* by Leo Lionni (1959), in which a blue cir-

cle and a yellow circle want to play together but are not allowed to by their different families. They sneak off together anyway, and of course, turn a new color: green. In this case, you will need two flashlights so that you can show each color separately as well as what happens when they come together.

Your Story Center should also feature Bill Martin, Jr. and illustrator Eric Carle's classic picture book *Brown Bear, Brown Bear, What Do You See?* (1983). Each of the animals sees another animal of a different color on the next page. A brown bear, redbird, yellow duck, blue horse, green frog, purple cat, white dog, black sheep, goldfish, mother, and beautiful children are the objects to be seen. Once the children have heard the story and seen the pictures, they will be answering the "What do you see?" question themselves, even before you turn the page.

• • • • • • • • • • Art Activities to Promote Language Development

Children can listen to and use the color words they are learning about. Read them stories and poems about color. **Let them make up color stories of their own.** Be prepared to tape-record or transcribe on paper the stories they tell you. Read from the wonderful book of color poems called *Hailstones and halibut bones* by Mary O'Neill (1961) whenever you are featuring a particular color in the classroom. The poems include "What Is Purple?"; "What Is Gold?"; "What Is Black?"; "What Is Brown?"; "What Is Blue?"; "What Is Gray?"; "What Is White?"; "What Is Orange?"; "What Is Red?"; "What Is Pink?"; "What Is Green?"; and "What Is Yellow?". The children may want to make up their own poems about the colors they know.

Talk to the children about the designs they are making in their art experiments, and listen to what they say about them. Tease their imaginations into projecting **what they think their designs look like**. Read the book *It Looked Like Spilt Milk* by Charles G. Shaw (1947) to motivate their ideas. Each blue page of the book shows a white form that looks like an object but is not the object. Children may want to make their own *It Looked Like Spilt Milk* book by **squeezing a bit of white paint onto a blue paper and then folding the paper and pressing it together**. What do they say that their white blobs look like?

As the children look at the illustrations in the color stories you are reading to them, they may become interested in **illustrating their own books about colors**. In the story *Swimmy* by Leo Lionni (1963), the artist does stampings of paper doilies to illustrate his "forest of seaweeds" that the little fish swims through. Your children may want to **put paint of various colors on paper doilies and then turn them over onto a white paper and stamp or rub them** so that the imprint of the doily remains. They can also roll over them with the rolling pins they use for play dough.

It is not necessary for children to tell you a story about their art products. Once you realize that most children's paintings are the result of a *process* rather than a *picture* that the child painted, your own comments about their art should be appropriate. Instead of saying, "Rachel, what a lovely picture of four suns! Do you want to tell me about it?" the teacher might rather **make comments about the child's efforts,** such as, "Rachel, you really worked hard with colors this morning!" Or she might comment **in terms of the art vocabulary** she would like the children to understand, "Rachel, those yellow shapes you have painted are really bright! Did you notice the interesting pattern of circles and lines you drew?"

If the children want to talk about their art products, do not discourage them. However, the art can speak for itself. It is not necessary for the child to describe it. Your comments using art vocabulary words such as lines, shapes, colors, patterns, and textures, as noted above, may eventually become part of their own vocabulary. Once children understand that such things are more important to teachers than their telling a story about their work, they will begin to talk about their paintings in similar terms.

If children want to write stories about their drawings or have you write their dictated stories, do not discourage this. Some children may really have a story they want to tell. However, this is not the purpose of most of their art efforts. Their finished product may have no value for them at all since it was the art process itself that was most meaningful.

· · · · · · · · · · Art Activities to Promote Emotional Development

· Water Play

Art can be used to promote emotional development in young children in both direct and indirect ways. The direct, hands-on experiences involve using art as a therapeutic means for releasing negative feelings. When children are feeling out of sorts, **water play can be a very soothing art activity**. Put a pan of water on one of the art tables with a variety of small, thin, colored sponges nearby. Let them soak the sponges and squeeze them out as much as they want. Then show them how the **sponges can be cut up** into little pieces with scissors **and used in collages** when they dry out or be glued into **sculptures** or a Christmas tree. They may want to cut up a bucket full of sponges to play with in the water and later dry out for use in art projects such as these.

Put several small pans of water on an art table with a set of food-coloring containers, several empty pouring bottles, a small pitcher, several funnels, and egg beaters. Have the same number of children as you do pans of water so that each can play with his own water, **experimenting with mixing colors, beating them up with an egg beater,** and **filling and pouring colored water into bottles**. Since this is not a permanent activity that can be saved

and displayed on a bulletinboard *per se,* you may want to **take photos of the**
+ **children's colored water for bulletin-board display or for a personal book**
they may be making.

• Dough

+ **Dough, Plasticine, and clay are also excellent therapeutic materials**
for releasing negative emotions. They can be squeezed, pounded, rolled,
punched, kneaded, pulled, and pressed into various shapes. Each has a different tactile sensation, a different resistance, and a different degree of ease
or difficulty in manipulating it. Thus, each of these materials will give children a different experience. In addition, each is still another therapeutic
material that can allow children to release tensions and work out emotions.

Use them one at a time at different times during the year, but be sure to
try each one with your children. Since dough is easiest to make and use,
many teachers limit art modeling material to dough. Dough is not the same
as clay, however, and should not be substituted for clay. It is worth any time
and effort you might expend to provide a real clay experience for your
children.

Modeling dough ("play dough") can be made according to various recipes.
A favorite one is:

2½ cups flour	2 teaspoons alum
½ cup salt	2 tablespoons cooking oil
2 cups water	

Pour two cups of boiling water over the dry ingredients. Stir together and
add cooking oil. When cool to the touch, turn the dough onto a lightly
floured surface, and knead with your hands until smooth. Store in an airtight container. Do not refrigerate. For a larger group of children, double
the recipe.

+ **In the beginning, make the dough before the children arrive.** Give each
child at the art table a chunk or ball of dough to experiment with. **Let them**
+ **manipulate the dough with their hands at first.** At another time, you can
add other implements such as rolling pins and cookie cutters, but the initial experience is the time for them to have the opportunity of manipulating
the medium without other concerns interfering. Let them see what it feels
like to squish it between their fingers, to roll it into a ball, to flatten it into a
pancake, to pull it to pieces, or to knead it into different shapes. Remember,
using modeling dough (like using paint) is a *process* for young children.
Don't expect them to make something. Some may want to tell you what their
dough shapes look like, which is fine but not necessary.

The next time you make a new batch of dough, you might consider doing
it at the art table with a small group of children on hand to help measure,

stir, and divide up the prepared dough for the number of children who will use it. **Have a recipe chart** that you have made posted near the table for your helpers to see, with the ingredients illustrated with simple drawings of cups, flour bag, salt box, water, and oil container. Do not use food colors yet. This is more effective later on, when the children can make their own dough and experiment with colors.

+

• Clay

Young children love to have their hands on natural clay (pottery clay) as well. It is an entirely different medium from dough. Buy it ready mixed, and keep it in an airtight container or plastic bag. Being water based, it dries out when exposed to air. Keep it moist with a damp sponge, but if it gets too moist, expose it to air again. A child-size piece of clay can be cut off the large lump with a wire or stout twine held in either hand and pulled through it. **Encourage children to work clay with their hands in any way they want.** At first it is dense and may be difficult to work, but soon, the children will be punching and poking it, twisting and rolling it into satisfying shapes. Their shapes can be set out to dry and then painted if they want. It may take a week or two for them to dry. Use very thin tempera paint because the clay absorbs it.

+

Working with pottery clay is more messy than dough, and some children are uncomfortable with this. Show them how easily it can be brushed off like dust when it dries. Again, children will be manipulating the medium in their early efforts with clay rather than modeling something. After they are used to working it with their hands, you can **add other implements, such as tongue depressors, nails, and forks**.

+

• Plasticine

This material is sometimes called oil clay because of its oil base. It is denser than natural clay and does not dry out, although it can become hard. It has an entirely different feel from clay or dough. **Children can punch, poke, knead, roll, and model this clay as they do to the other forms.**

+

• Fingerpainting

Another excellent **medium for releasing pent-up emotions in a nondestructive manner is fingerpainting**. Children can stand over a table with their sleeves rolled up and get their whole bodies involved with the sweeping arm motions that may cover the entire table with paint. Or they can sit quietly, spreading the paint around and around on a paper or tray in front of them.

+

They can use both hands at once, fingers only, fists, palms, or sides of hands to make lines, swirls, circles, zig-zags, handprints, and fingerprints. They can wipe out the lines they have made, mix two colors of paint together to make new colors, or draw a picture. If children want to save their finger-paint creations, they can do them on glazed art paper and hang them up to dry, or they can press a sheet of paper onto their designs on the tabletop and make a rubbing of their art.

Fingerpaints can be purchased commercially or **made** by teachers and children together **from soap powder** mixed to the proper consistency with water and then sprinkled with tempera paint powder or mixed with food col-

+ oring; made from **liquid starch** with color added; or made from **wheat paste** (wallpaper paste) mixed with water and poster paint.

• Artists

Children need to gain another kind of appreciation for the emotional side

+ of art: that **art is** also **done by** people called **artists;** that artists have feelings about things; and that they express those feelings in their art.

A wonderful introduction to the artist is the simple, touching story of *Emma* by Wendy Kesselman, illustrated by Barbara Cooney (1980). Emma is a grandmother with four children, seven grandchildren, fourteen great-grandchildren, and a lot of time on her hands in between their visits. She secretly takes up painting pictures of the things she remembers from where she grew up and the things she liked from where she lives now. What a surprise for her relatives when they find out, and what a surprise for Emma at their reactions.

A different kind of story is told by children's book illustrator Tomie dePaola in his book *The Art Lesson* (1989). It is dePaola's own story of his yearning to become an artist from his earliest years: of how his family bought him crayons, but his teachers had other ideas, until at last the art teacher came to school for his first real art lesson. After this, your children may want to search the library for other dePaola books.

• • • • • • • • • • • Art Activities to Promote Social Development

As they do in other activity areas, the children can learn to share and to

+ take turns with art materials. **Activities in sharing can be planned** when the teacher puts out four art papers on the table but only one box of crayons or one jar of paste that needs to be used by all. Children can also learn to sign up for turns at the easel or at the water table, as previously noted.

Art lends itself especially well to children's social development through group activities. Small **groups of children can do group fingerpainting** to-gether on one large sheet of paper. A **group collage** can be made together, or

+ a **group mural**. Several children can do a painting project together, such as painting a large cardboard carton to be a playhouse. Others can cut out pictures from magazines and paste them in a **class scrapbook**. Children working together like this learn to plan, to explain their ideas, to solve problems, to cooperate.

• • • • • • • • • • Art Activities to Promote Creative Development

All the art activities mentioned in this chapter are designed to promote creativity in young children. Creativity is enhanced when children can accomplish things on their own, through their own choices and their own efforts. Teachers can provide the materials and occasionally some of the ideas, but it is then up to the children themselves to explore, experiment, and follow their own artistic notions. To assist children's development of creativity, teachers' best method of support is encouragement rather than direction.

Teacher-directed art may have a place from time to time when the object is to help children learn to follow directions or to enhance their small motor skills. Yet even then, free-choice art materials should always be available for those who want to pursue their own artistic impulses. Creativity connotes freedom—for both children and teachers. It is the underlying element of the Appropriate Practices Curriculum in a self-directed environment.

• • • • • • • • • • The Teacher's Role in the Art Center

Although the preschool teacher's primary role in the Appropriate Practices Curriculum may not be the traditional one of sitting at an art table with the children, directing them on how to cut out orange pumpkins or red hearts, she is nevertheless responsible for what goes on in the Art Center. She needs to set it up in the first place with appropriate materials for the children's easy selection and return. She then needs to observe individual children to determine the level at which they are interacting with materials in order to support their further development. As with Writing Center activities, children may pursue different types of activities in the Art Center at different levels of interaction. In order to record these levels on the Child Interaction Form, the teacher needs to be aware of the kinds of activities that can occur in art at the manipulation, mastery, and meaning levels.

Once the teacher has identified the level of interaction for the different children in the Art Center and recorded it on the Child Interaction Form, she can use the information to promote the continued progress of the children. For Barbie, who is beginning to draw circles, lines, and crosses on the easel instead of her usual scribbles, the teacher might decide to offer encouragement in Barbie's mastery phase by providing colored chalk and a

TABLE 8–2	Art Center Activities: Levels of Interaction

Manipulation Level

Making random marks on paper

Covering paper with color

Making scribbles

Swishing hands and fingers around in fingerpaints

Playing with paste, glue

Playing with play dough, clay

Playing with computer drawing program without control

Scribbling on chalkboard

Tearing, cutting paper randomly

Playing with stamp pads and stamps

Mastery Level

Making shapes, lines, marks over and over with paint, crayons, markers, chalk

Making shapes and designs in fingerpaints

Putting paste/glue on paper (sometimes picture side)

Making definite shapes with play dough over and over

Cutting out play-dough cookies

Making lines, shapes on computer drawing program; changing colors

Tearing, cutting paper into many pieces

Stamping pictures, designs on paper over and over

Meaning Level

Making sun with rays

Making sun people with rays as arms, legs, hair

Making animals, trees, flowers

Making houses, rainbows, vehicles

Pasting pictures

Creating a named object with play dough, clay

Making named lines, shapes on computer drawing program, or telling story about drawing

Tearing, cutting paper and making a collage or named form

Naming stamped pictures or telling story

chalkboard as well. For Tom, who spends most of his time making cars from play dough, the teacher might decide to bring in another modeling medium, such as clay or Plasticine.

The teacher's records will show not only the level of the children's interaction with materials but also their favorite kinds of materials. Those who prefer to draw can continue drawing with crayons, markers, pencils, chalk, and paintbrushes as such materials are added to the center. Modelers can be encouraged to transfer their skills from play dough to clay to Plasticine as the year progresses.

Art in the early childhood classroom can thus be an activity of great satisfaction for both children and teachers. If you are successful in your center setup, then children can become deeply involved in activities that are highly meaningful to them personally. Art can become a wonderful means of communication and self-expression for them. For you, your observation of children at work in the process of art exploration and discovery can be equally as meaningful. Young children have much to teach us if we are open enough to learn from them. Their fresh, new ideas, their inquisitiveness and experimentation, and their original uses of materials can give us new insights into the creative process and our role in supporting it.

IDEAS +
in CHAPTER 8

1. *Setting up the Art Center*
  a. Give children a wide variety of materials, the freedom, and the time to discover how these work on their own. (p. 173)
  b. Have at least one, and preferably two, easels available at all times. (p. 175)
  c. Make it possible for children to get their own easel paper and hang finished papers to dry. (p. 175)
  d. Attach a clipboard with pencil to the side of each easel for children to sign up for turns. (p. 175)
  e. Have paints available on low shelves near tables where they will be used. (p. 175)
  f. Have art carts which children help load with painting materials. (p. 176)
  g. Add new materials from time to time and retire old materials. (p. 176)
  h. Have access to water. (p. 177)
  i. Integrate art activities into the entire curriculum. (p. 177)

2. *Beautifying the classroom*
  a. Make the classroom pleasing to look at and beautiful to be in. (p. 177)
  b. Color-code learning centers with corrugated cardboard. (p. 177)
  c. Do not overdo colors or clutter. (p. 177)
  d. Change the bulletin board backing from time to time. (p. 178)
  e. Picture-book posters can be mounted on cardboard and covered with clear food wrapping. (p. 178)
  f. Talk to children about colors and natural beauty, starting with them personally. (p. 178)
  g. Bring in flowers, seed pods, and branches for attractive arrangements, and talk about them. (p. 178)

3. *Promoting small motor development*
  a. Introduce a small group of children to Harold and his purple crayon. (p. 178)
  b. Cover the art table with white paper and put out various purple crayons for children to use in scribbling. (p. 179)

    c. Let children make white lines on black paper to the thunder of horse's hooves. (p. 179)

    d. Have children cover white paper with blue chalk or crayon rubbed on its side and scratch it through with a fingernail file. (p. 179)

    e. Have children tear up sheets of colored construction paper for collage material. (p. 180)

    f. Have children fold and cut paper. (p. 180)

    g. Use sharp scissors rather than dull or blunt ones. (p. 180)

    h. Practice using scissors by cutting ribbon into confetti. (p. 180)

    i. Have children cut out pictures from old magazines. (p. 180)

    j. Have children squeeze paint out of plastic bottles to make designs. (p. 180)

4. *Promoting large motor development*

    a. Let children twirl around with filmy colored cloths to music. (p. 182)

    b. Bring in colored umbrellas or paper parasols and shine a flashlight through one over another of them. (p. 182)

5. *Promoting cognitive development*

    a. Introduce one color at a time and let children immerse themselves in it throughout the classroom. (p. 182)

    b. Have children bring something of the same color to class. (p. 182)

    c. Let children experiment with mixing paint colors to make new colors. (p. 183)

    d. Let children try to create new colors with chalk, crayons, and food coloring. (p. 183)

    e. Have children make different colors of play dough. (p. 183)

    f. Bring in colored cellophane and flashlights to make different colors. (p. 183)

6. *Promoting language development*

    a. Let children make up color stories. (p. 184)

    b. Have children tell what designs look like to them. Let them squeeze paint onto a paper, fold, and press it. (p. 184)

    c. Have children illustrate their own book of colors. (p. 184)

    d. Have children stamp with paint-covered paper doilies. (p. 184)

    e. Comment on children's art in terms of art vocabulary (lines, shapes, colors, patterns, textures). (p. 185)

7. *Promoting emotional development*

    a. Use water play as a soothing art activity. (p. 185)

    b. Have children cut up colored sponges for a collage, sculpture, or Christmas tree. (p. 185)

    c. Have children experiment with mixing and pouring liquid colors using egg beaters and bottles. (p. 185)

    d. Take photos of children's colored water play for the bulletin board or personal books. (p. 186)

    e. Use dough, Plasticine, and clay as therapeutic materials to help children release negative emotions. (p. 186)

   f. Make play dough before the children arrive. (p. 186)

   g. Let children manipulate dough with their hands at first. (p. 186)

   h. Use a simple, illustrated recipe chart when children make dough. (p. 187)

   i. Encourage children to manipulate clay with their hands at first; later, add other implements. (p. 187)

   j. Have children punch, poke, knead, roll, and model Plasticine clay. (p. 187)

   k. Use fingerpainting as another medium for releasing pent-up emotions in a nondestructive manner. (p. 187)

   l. Make your own fingerpaints from soap powder, liquid starch, or wheat paste. (p. 188)

   m. Have children learn that art is done by artists who express their emotions through their art. (p. 188)

8. *Promoting social development*

   a. Plan activities for sharing art materials. (p. 188)

   b. Have children learn social skills through group fingerpainting, group collages, group murals, and group scrapbooks. (p. 188)

REFERENCES CITED

Beaty, J. J. (1990). *Observing development of the young child.* Columbus, OH: Merrill Publishing Company.

Kellogg, R. (1970). *Analyzing children's art.* Palo Alto, CA: National Press Books.

Richardson, L. I., Goodman, K. L., Hartman, N. N., & LePique, H. C. (1980). *A mathematics activity curriculum for early childhood and special education.* New York: Macmillan.

OTHER SOURCES

Bos, B. (1978). *Don't move the muffin tins: A hands-off guide to art for the young child.* Roseville, CA: Turn the Page Press.

Brashears, D. (1985). *Dribble drabble: Art experiences for young children.* Fort Collins, CO: DMC Publications.

Feeney, S., & Moravcik, E. (1987). A thing of beauty: Aesthetic development in young children. *Young Children 42* (6), 7–17.

Haskell, L. L. (1979). *Art in the early childhood years.* Columbus, OH: Merrill Publishing Company.

Jenkins, P. (1980). *Art for the fun of it.* Englewood Cliffs, NJ: Prentice-Hall.

Schirrmacher, R. (1986). Talking with young children about their art. *Young Children 41* (5), 3–7.

CHILDREN'S BOOKS

Brown, M. W. (1977). *The color kittens.* New York: Golden Press.

Carle, E. (1983). *Brown bear, brown bear, what do you see?* New York: Holt, Rinehart and Winston.

dePaola, T. (1989). *The art lesson.* New York: G. P. Putnam's Sons.

Feczko, K. (1985). *Umbrella parade.* Mahwah, NJ: Troll Associates.

Garelick, M. (1971). *Where does the butterfly go when it rains?* New York: Scholastic Book Services.

Hoban, T. (1978). *is it red? is it yellow? is it blue?* New York: Greenwillow Books.

Johnson, C. (1955). *Harold and the purple crayon.* New York: Harper & Row.

Johnson, C. (1960). *A picture for Harold's room.* New York: Harper & Row.

Jonas, A. (1989). *Color dance.* New York: Greenwillow Books.

Kennedy, R. (1981). *Song of the horse.* New York: E. P. Dutton.

Kesselman, W. (1980). *Emma.* New York: Harper & Row.

Lionni, L. (1959). *Little blue and little yellow.* New York: Astor-Honor.

Lionni, L. (1963). *Swimmy.* New York: Pantheon Books.

O'Neill, M. (1961). *Hailstones and halibut bones.* Garden City, NY: Doubleday.

Shaw, C. G. (1957). *It looked like spilt milk.* New York: Harper & Row.

Stinson, K. (1982). *Red is best.* Toronto, Canada: Annick Press Ltd.

CHILDREN'S COMPUTER PROGRAMS

Mindscape, Inc.
3444 Dundee Road
Northbrook, IL 60062
    Color Me 1986 (Apple, IBM, C64)

TRY IT
YOURSELF

1. Set up the Art Center of your classroom as described in this chapter with easels, shelves full of materials children can choose and use, and at least one kind of material new to the classroom.

2. Make your classroom beautiful to look at by following some of the suggestions in this chapter about colors, posters, and so on.

3. Do an art activity with a small group of children that begins with your reading to them one of the children's books suggested in this chapter.

4. Set up a color-mixing activity for your children to discover on their own how colors can combine to make a new color.

5. Set up a clay activity for your children, and observe what they do with it.

MUSIC CENTER

MAKING
MUSIC

(Action chant)

Can you whistle, whistle, whistle?	(Nod head)
Can you hum, hum, hum?	(Rock side to side)
Can you shake it like a thistle?	(Shake body)
Can you strum, strum, strum?	(Strum imaginary guitar)
Can you tap your fingers lightly?	(Tap fingers)
Can you drum, drum, drum?	(Slap hands on knees)
Can you move around politely?	(Tiptoe in place)
Can you run, run, run!	(Run hard in place)

• • • • • • • • • • Music in the Early Childhood Classroom

Children are as atuned to music as they are to art. Music, too, is a medium for their communication and self-expression. Children enjoy moving to a beat and playing rhythm instruments. They take pleasure in using their voices as instruments as well as making sounds with other parts of their bodies.

Too often, though, music in the early childhood classroom is a passive or controlled experience for children. It is a record or tape they hear being played. It is a piano the teacher plays. Sometimes they learn to sing along to the music or move to the directions of the singer. But seldom do they have the chance to make their own music on their own terms in order to play around with tones and tunes and beats—in order to express themselves and their feelings in rhythm and melody.

The self-directed learning environment offers them this opportunity. The Music Center is set up for children's exploration. Materials are provided to give them experience in manipulating, mastering, and making their own meaningful music. The Appropriate Practices Curriculum gives them the freedom to explore on their own and the time to become as deeply involved with music as they do with blocks and books and paints.

• • • • • • • • • Natural Musical Development in Young Children

The elements of music that young children are involved with include *tone*, *rhythm*, and *melody*. The *tone* of a song has to do with its loudness or softness (dynamics), its shortness or length (duration), its highness or lowness (pitch), and its quality (timbre). Through maturity, exposure to sounds, and practice, children develop the ability to recognize and discriminate among tones and to imitate them as well as to produce their own original tones in their singing and music making.

The *rhythm* of music has to do with its fastness or slowness (tempo), its pulse (beat), and its long and short or light and heavy accents (pattern). *Melody* has to do with a particular flow of tones in a certain rhythm. Children develop their ability to recognize and to reproduce rhythm and melody in the same way as they develop tone: through maturity of physical, cognitive, and language abilities, as well as through being exposed to these elements of music and having a chance to try them out. This natural development follows a sequence somewhat similar to that of a child's acquisition of language skills. After all, speaking and singing seem to have a common origin, much like drawing and writing.

• Birth to Six Months

Infants are aware of music from the beginning, as shown by their different responses to different kinds of music. Lullabies tend to calm them down, whereas lively music makes them more active. Infants themselves vocalize by crying that varies in pitch, loudness, and rhythmic patterns. They experiment with other sounds such as coos, gurgles, and squeals, and finally begin to babble by repeating long strings of sounds: "ba-ba-ba-ba" (Bayless & Ramsey, 1987). If someone is singing to them regularly, infants' vocalizing often sounds a bit like crooning, especially at nap or bedtime. They are attracted to rhythmic sounds such as the ticking of a clock and to melodious sounds such as musical toys. Tones of voice attract them, too, especially the voice of their primary caregiver (Jalongo & Collins, 1985).

• Six Months to Two Years

Infants and toddlers show more awareness of musical sounds and will turn toward them and listen intently. Some may indicate the music they like best as well as what they do not like. They may move their bodies in response to music, rocking or swaying and even clapping their hands, but not necessarily in time with the music. Some may attempt to imitate sounds, and as their babbling becomes a favorite activity, it may resemble a song. Many infants prefer vocal to instrumental music at this age. Toddlers often seek out the sounds that please them most, including music on television programs. In addition, they will try to locate particular objects such as pots and pans or cups and bowls for sound making activities (Bayless & Ramsey, 1987).

• Two to Three Years

Toddlers may attempt to dance to music by bending knees, swaying, and swinging arms. They respond well to pattern repetition and can learn simple fingerplays. Two-year-olds may experiment with their voices and often sing or hum at play. They may join in a favorite nursery rhyme or song and

TABLE 9–1	Natural Musical Development in Young Children

Birth to Six Months

Calm down to lullabies
Become more active to lively music
Vocalize with crying that varies in pitch, loudness, and rhythmic patterns
Experiment with sounds: coos, gurgles, squeals
Begin to babble: repeat a string of sounds
May imitate crooning at bedtime
Attracted to rhythmic sounds: ticking of clock, musical toys
Attracted to tones of voice, especially caregiver's

Six Months to Two Years

More aware of musical sounds: turn toward them; listen intently
Move bodies in response to music: rock, sway, clap
Babbling becomes favorite activity
May imitate sounds
May prefer vocal music
May seek out sounds that please them
Look for and use sound-making objects (e.g., pots and pans)

Two to Three Years

Dance to music by bending knees, swaying, and swinging arms
Respond to pattern repetition
Can learn simple fingerplays
Sing or hum at play
Know words to nursery rhymes
Play toy xylophones, drums, and so on

Three to Four Years

Have better voice control
Know song lyrics
Can follow rhythm
Understand loud–soft, fast–slow
Can dramatize songs
May sing own words to familiar tunes

Four to Five Years

Listen actively to music
Sing complete songs from memory
Have better rhythm and pitch accuracy
Respond to group singing
May sing alone for group
Play rhythm instruments to accompany singing
May create own tunes

get many of the words right. They are showing increasing interest in listening to musical instruments and the phonograph and often enjoy making musical sounds on toy xylophones, drums, and tambourines (Bayless & Ramsey, 1987).

• Three to Four Years

Their increased cognitive and language development gives three-year-olds better voice control, rhythmic responses, and mastery of song lyrics. They are beginning to understand the basic musical concepts of loud–soft, fast–slow. They may also love to dramatize songs or try out different ways to interpret songs rhythmically. Music has, in fact, become an important means to express and communicate ideas that are beyond their language abilities. They may spontaneously make up their own songs with repetitive words and a tune resembling ones they know (Jalongo & Collins, 1985; Bayless & Ramsey, 1987).

• Four to Five Years

Children at this age are active listeners of music. Their attention span is longer, and with encouragement, their desire to become involved in musical activities increases. They can sing complete songs from memory with greater pitch control and rhythmic accuracy because of their development of the concepts of high–low pitch and long–short tones. They are more responsive to group singing and may even enjoy taking a turn to sing alone. They can play many kinds of rhythm instruments, often to accompany songs, and they may even create tunes of their own (Jalongo & Collins, 1985; Bayless & Ramsey, 1987).

This is how children develop musical abilities naturally. All children everywhere progress through the same sequence of development, although their individual rates of progress may differ. Some children progress rapidly and may be singing whole songs at two-and-a-half years. Others take their time and may not have developed much rhythmic or pitch accuracy, even at age five. It is not up to you to teach them how. Instead, children will continue their natural development if their preschool classroom is filled with music and happy sounds and if the Music Center itself encourages them to participate in exciting musical activities.

• • • • • • • • • • • Setting Up the Music Center

Music in the self-directed learning environment takes place not only in a designated activity center but also in the entire classroom. The Music Center contains materials and activities for individuals and small groups to investigate sound, rhythm, and melody on their own. A large space in the classroom is also used for group singing games and creative movement. The other activity centers are eventually infiltrated with music and sound as the children bring new songs and rhythms with them into the Block, Dramatic Play, Art, and Story Centers, and the teachers who visit these centers respond with their own personal music.

"Make music personal" should be the theme of your music activities. First of all, it needs to be personal in your own life. Do you enjoy music? Then **bring in records or tapes of the music you enjoy to share with the children** at appropriate times. Soft music is appropriate at nap time. Rock music is appropriate at times when the children are actively engaged in the learning centers. Certain classical music may be appropriate at times when others moods are desired. The teacher may want to use her own personal cassette recorder to share this music.

The Music Center itself should contain a **cassette recorder** for the children's use. **Children can learn to use it and not abuse it,** as they learn with the computer. A simple, illustrated rules chart on the shelf near the recorder can tell them how. Both the Music Center and the Story Center should have their own recorders not only for prerecorded tapes, but also for recording the children's own productions. You may want **a clipboard nearby** for children to sign up for use of the recorder. Have **earphones** available if the tapes are for personal rather than group use.

Your music center should be set up to **promote** the following activities: **listening, sound exploration, rhythm, and music making**. Its contents will change as the children explore different elements of music. In addition to the cassette recorder or record player, the prerecorded tapes, and blank tapes on a low countertop, the shelves in the center may contain sound-making materials, musical instruments, rhythm instruments, materials for children to use in making their own instruments, picture books with a musical theme, and hooks holding costumes, scarves, and other materials for creative movement. Illustrated labels will help children to choose and return particular materials to their shelves or hook spaces, just as they do in the other activity centers.

You may choose **not to display all your rhythm instruments at one time**. If the children are investigating drumming sounds, then drums and similar instruments may be the only ones out. On the other hand, you may be displaying materials on the shelves of your Music Center that have never even been associated with music. In addition to using the shelves in your Music Center, you may choose to **display instruments on a pegboard with hooks and an outline of the instruments drawn on the board** so that children can match instruments to their outlines and return them to their places when finished. Some programs with limited space prefer to use a music cart (like the art cart) that can be rolled out and later put away.

• • • • • • • • • • **Musical Activities to Promote Emotional Development**

• A New Approach to Music with Young Children

To make music meaningful for children, you should **make it personal**
+ **for them** as well. Your musical activities can be centered around the things
that your children respond to personally. This will not only attract their attention but also help to promote their positive self-image. Thus, you might
focus classroom music on:

Themselves, their feelings, their toys, their clothing, their food
Their families
Their friends
Their pets, other animals
Their homes, their rooms
Their school
Their car, the school bus
Objects in their environment: trees, flowers, wind, rain

For example, we know that young children are fascinated by *shoes:* their
own and everyone else's. A child will often tell you he is wearing a new pair
of shoes, whether or not he really is. This may happen because little children are so close to the ground that shoes are the first thing they notice
about a person. With this in mind, you might **consider featuring shoes and**
+ **"shoe music" in your music center.** Not your everyday sort of musical activity, you may protest, but that is exactly the point: To make music meaningful for young children, you need to make it personal—and pleasurable.
Why should you do the same ordinary "rhythm band" kinds of music activities when you have a world of intriguing things to choose from—when you
have your own wonderful, creative young children and their fascinating interests to tap into?

How, then, can you use shoes for music making? First of all, consider the
elements of music you will be featuring in the Music Center and the classroom: listening, sound exploration, rhythm, and music making. What can
you do with a shoe? Well, you can:

Try it, buy it, tie it, buckle it, Velcro it, walk in it, run in it, hop in it, jump
in it, skate in it, dance in it, slide in it, slop in it, stomp in it, tiptoe in it,
tromp in it, work in it, play ball in it, flip-flop in it, climb tall in it, swim deep
in it, run long in it, fall down in it.

Remember, no matter what you do with a shoe, make "shoe music" fun
for yourself as well as for the children.

• Listening

Acquire a collection of shoes of all kinds and make a tape of shoe sounds for children in the Music Center to listen to. Here are some of the shoes you might collect:

Regular leather tie shoes	Bowling shoes
Patent leather buckle shoes	Roller skates
Ballet slippers	Ice skates
Tap-dancing shoes	Snowshoes
Sneakers	Swim fins
Rain boots	Cowboy boots
Snow boots	Motorcycle boots
Work boots	High-heel shoes
Jogging shoes	Slippers
Baseball or football shoes	Flip-flops
Stilts	Crutches
Golf shoes	

Take a blank tape, sit down at a table when the children are not around, and record some of these shoes walking, clumping, tapping, rolling, or whatever on your table. You can hold the shoes with your hands and clump them around. Have the same shoe make its same sound many, many times on your tape before you switch to the next shoe. Remember, it may take your children longer than you think to match the sound with the shoe. It is not necessary to tape the sound of every shoe you have collected, only a representative few. When you have finished your tape, wait awhile, and then try it out on yourself to see whether you can match the sound with the shoe. Make the tape over again if necessary, eliminating shoes that cannot be identified easily.

Put the same shoes on your Music Center shelves, along with the "shoe music" tape, and **ask your children to guess which shoe made the sound**. This should be a fun activity, not a chore. Talk with children who are enjoying this activity on their own and tell them when they have guessed one. This is not a "right-or-wrong" activity—no activities should be "win-or-lose" in your classroom. Rather than tell a child that she has not identified any of the sounds correctly except the roller skate, you can congratulate her for guessing the roller skate and encourage her to try again and see which other shoes she can identify. Let her try each shoe itself with her hands and the table of the Music Center, and have a partner play the tape while both listen to the sounds.

At the same time, you can bring the book *Shoes* by Elizabeth Winthrop (1986) into the Music Center and read it to the children who are listening and trying to identify shoe sounds. It is a simple and wonderful rhyming story about a variety of shoes from high to low, illustrated with pictures of children using all kinds of shoes in all kinds of ways.

Leave the book on the Music Center shelf for children to enjoy on their own. In the meantime, make a second tape or even a third one with other sets of shoes for chidren to match. Put these shoes in the Music Center in a separate container from the first ones.

• Sound Exploration

+   Would children like to **make their own shoe music**? They can tape record their own sounds of the shoes from the shelf of the Music Center, or they can take the tape recorder to the Dramatic Play Center and record children walking in the various kinds of shoes displayed there. (Be sure you have a wide variety of men's and women's shoes in stock.) Or they can record the sounds made by the dolls walking in the Dramatic Play Center. Would they also like to record the sound of their own shoes walking? They could say into the tape recorder: "This is what Jonathan's blue sneakers sound like," and then make the recording. Afterward, you might listen to the tape with them, talking about *loud* and *soft* sounds made by particular shoes.

A picture book that might stimulate making shoe sounds is *The Grow-ing-up Feet* by Beverly Cleary (1987), about Jimmy and Janet, who go to the shoe store to buy new shoes but find that their feet are not ready yet. They end up with a pair of red rain boots instead, but they cannot wear them because it does not rain. Their father solves the problem by squirting puddles with his hose. The children may want to start a pretend **shoe store in the Dramatic Play Center,** or they may want to **record the way shoes and boots sound in the water of the water table or a shallow pan of water in the Mu-**
+   **sic Center**. If the Art Center wants to get into the shoe act, it can sponsor a footprint session with children **making paint footprints on a large sheet of butcher paper** by having the youngsters step barefoot into a pan of paint and walk on the paper. Or they may want to make shoe and boot prints **in wet sand in the sandbox**. In this case, let children take off a shoe or boot to make the prints.

• Rhythm

Because each of the classroom activities needs to be integrated into all of the activity centers, you might start your rhythm activities in the Story Center by reading the 1989 Caldecott Medal winner, *Song and Dance Man* by Karen Ackerman (1988). It is the wonderfully touching story of Grandpa, who gets out his trunk and puts on a "song and dance show" in his attic for his visiting grandchildren. Be sure to have a pair of tap shoes for your chil-

dren to experiment with after you read this book. You might **invite an instructor from a local dance studio** to visit the class and demonstrate a tap dance. Or better still, **a student taking tap-dance lessons** could come to the   +
class and do a dance for the children.

• Music Making

Music making with shoes involves dance and music. This time, the teacher can **tape record children wearing different kinds of shoes dancing or moving to music**. Use a second tape recorder, a record player, or a radio   +
for the music. What different ways can the children move? Can they slide, clump, tiptoe, stomp, hop, raise themselves up and down on their toes? Special-needs children using a wheelchair, braces, or crutches can participate with their special shoe sounds being recorded, too. **Bring in a pair of children's crutches and let the youngsters try them out,** making shoe   +
music.

Another **music-making activity is a group game called "Pass the Shoe."**   +
Children sit on the floor in a circle and sing or chant the song:

PASS THE SHOE

Arranged by
Diana Black

Pass the shoe from me to you, to you.

Pass the shoe and do just as I do.

As they sing, they pass a shoe from child to child around the circle. When the song stops, the child with the shoe must do something, such as making a motion of some kind (e.g., patting the head or some other part of body, rubbing tummy, clapping hands, nodding head, waving hand, raising arms up and down). Everyone in the circle then copies this motion. The shoe is then passed around again to the singing of the song, and the game continues in the same way.

Musical Activities to Promote Physical Development

Other dance and whole-body-movement activities are discussed in Chapter 12, "Large Motor Center." Here, we consider small motor coordination activities involved in playing instruments. Most children love to make music. Whether they are blowing on toy horns or beating toy drums, young children tend to expend great energy in their production of sound. This is not surprising when we realize that those who love music most are generally the music makers themselves. With youngsters at the preschool age, it is even more important that they have the opportunity to make their own music rather than merely listen to the music someone else has made. Music for them is a means of expression that even their language cannot yet afford them.

Give them the opportunity to become physically involved in your Music Center activities first by making music with their hands and then by extending these hand skills to music making with instruments. Start with clapping. **Can children clap to the rhythm of their names?** You be the leader of a small group of youngsters, and let them all join in clapping to every syllable as each one in the group says his own name rhythmically: "My-name-is-Bar-bar-a-what-is-your-name?" Another time have them clap to two different rhythms: "I-see-you-Bob-by. (speed up) How-are-you-to-day?" Besides clapping hands, children can also sit in a circle and **clap their hands against their legs to a chant**. Use the chants at the beginning of each chapter to do leg clapping. The chant "Blocks" (Chapter 3) asks the children to clap on the fourth line of every verse.

What other kinds of sounds can they make with their hands? They might **ball their hands into a fist and make "pounding music"** on the table or the floor to the beat of a song on the record player or to the chants they know. For the "Painting and Talking" chant (Chapter 8), they could say the words on every other line and pound out the rhythm for "dabble-dabble" and "babble-babble." Can they make "knuckle music" as well?

• Instruments

Rhythm instruments that can be played with hand beats include drums (bongos, tom-toms) and tambourines. There are many kinds, both commer-

cial and homemade. Since your children may be too young to make complete drums with paper or skin heads, you can **collect empty coffee cans, salt boxes, and oatmeal boxes that they can paint and use as tom-toms**. +
The simplest **homemade drum** is **a coffee can covered tightly with a double layer of wrapping paper,** secured around the can with twine or a heavy +
rubber band. **Tambourines can be made from pie tins** with holes punched +
in the sides and bottle tops dangling from the holes on strings.

Tom-toms can be beaten to music with two hands, while tambourines are usually held with one hand and beaten with the other. Talk to the children about loud and soft sounds as well as light and heavy beats. It is **important for young children to explore a single instrument at a time**. When children +
play all the instruments in a rhythm band at the same time, all they hear is noise. Children can learn more about sound making and rhythm when they all use the same kind of instrument. Let them beat their hand drums to a variety of music: marches, waltzes, rock, country, and folk music.

Other instruments played by hand shaking include: maracas, hand bells, and jingle bells. Children can also **make musical shakers from margarine containers** filled with different ingredients (nails, seeds, paper clips, jingle +
bells). Put the various kinds of ingredients on the Music Center table in separate containers, and let children try them out before making a final choice for their own shaker. Tape on the tops securely, and let the children paint their musical shakers. Again, let children shake them to the beat of a variety of musical tunes.

Some instruments are played with sticks, including drums, xylophones, and rhythm sticks themselves. Commercial drumsticks come with purchased instruments. Otherwise, children can use pencils, toy sticks, or wooden dowels.

Other hand instruments include string instruments that you strum. Commercial guitars, ukeleles, and autoharps are usually played by the teacher as accompaniment to singing. But **autoharps can be strummed by a child sitting next to the teacher** while the teacher presses the chords. +
Have them try strumming with a felt pick, a plastic pick, or their thumb. How does each pick sound?

Homemade strumming instruments are more interesting to preschoolers. Make a collection of shoe boxes. Remove the tops. Cut four small slots equidistant in the top at either end. String four rubber bands around the box so that they are held in place by the slots. The **children will enjoy playing in a strumming band if everyone has a shoe-box strummer**. They can +
be strummed with a thumb or the stem of a wooden match.

If children are interested in the strummer, they will want to hear you read *Max, the Music-Maker* by Miriam B. Stecher and Alice S. Kanell (1980), about Max, who finds musical sounds everywhere: clicking a stick against a fence, tapping empty glasses, drumming on pans with a ladle, and finally, making a "rubberbandjo." Children may also want to hear you read and sing *The Banza: a Haitian Story* by Diane Wolkstein (1981), a folk tale about a little goat who must confront ten hungry tigers with nothing but a banza (banjo). The banjo is magic, and the little goat Cabree sings a song that terrifies the tigers until they all flee.

From all these experiences come children's heightened interest in rhythm and music as well as a strengthening and coordination of the small muscles.

• • • • • • • • • • Musical Activities to Promote Social Development

One of the reasons music may be so enjoyable to young children is that it is so often a social experience. Everyone sings the same song together. Everyone plays the musical game in a group. That kind of togetherness makes music something special for people. To create such a feeling of togetherness in your classroom, it is not necessary to begin with a music period in which everyone leaves the activity centers and comes to the circle space to learn a new song. Instead, you can infiltrate music into the entire classroom during the free-choice period by **starting a song yourself that everyone can sing**
+   **while continuing to engage in his own activity**.

Choose a song you have sung together before so that most of the children know the words, such as "The Alphabet Song." Children will join in as they hear others from other parts of the room singing. You and your co-workers can walk around singing to encourage everyone to participate. Do this spontaneous kind of singing whenever the mood strikes you, and you will soon have children also starting their favorite songs. In other words, it is not necessary to *wait* for a music period in order to enjoy singing. When people are happy, they can express it anytime in a song: "If You're Happy and You Know it, Clap Your Hands."

Neither is it necessary for you to be a performer in order to sing with the children. You remember that they are in the process period of their musical development. They are manipulating the medium of musical tones, pitch, rhythm, and melody. Some of them are mastering these musical elements by repeating them over and over. Only a few children will be at the meaning stage of music, where they create a product: for example, a song of their own. **If you find that you are uncomfortable singing, ask a co-worker to**
+   **sing with you**. The two of you can then blend in with the children when they join in. If you make a mistake—laugh! Really, there is no such thing as a mistake in music for you or your preschool children. Make music fun for yourself and the children.

+   One of the most delightful kinds of group music is **musical fingerplays**. Some are nursery rhymes put to music and finger movements. Others are old favorites. You should **have a repertoire of these songs to sing during**

transition times when children are waiting for something new to happen. +
One of the nicest collections of favorite fingerplays is *Eye Winker, Tom
Tinker, Chin Chopper: Fifty Musical Fingerplays* by Tom Glazer (1973). It
contains the words, piano arrangements, guitar chords, and fingerplay directions for such familiar songs as:

Down by the Station
Eensy Weensy Spider
Go in and out the Windows
Here We Go Round the Mulberry Bush
Hickory, Dickory, Dock
I Had a Bird and He Pleased Me
I Know an Old Lady Who Swallowed a Fly
I'm a Little Tea Pot
Jack and Jill Went Up the Hill
The More We Get Together
Old MacDonald Had a Farm
On Top of Spaghetti
Pop Goes the Weasel
Ten Little Indians
There's a Little White Duck Sitting in the Water
This Old Man
This Train is Bound for Glory
The Wheels on the Bus
Where Is Thumbkin?

**Copy down the words of each on a 3-by-5 card, and keep them in a file
box on top of a room-divider shelf** for use when children are restless or +
when you want to make a transition from one activity to another. Children
learn such fingerplay songs by singing them over and over with you as the
leader. It is not necessary to use a piano or, in fact, any instrument. Musical
fingerplays are more pleasurable when done informally with everyone singing together and enjoying themselves. The children will let you know which
ones are their favorites by asking for them again and again. In this case, **it
is easier for children to learn the words and actions when they are together in a group**. This could be at circle time or when they are waiting to +
go somewhere. Give children many experiences with musical fingerplays before you start musical games. Musical action chants are similar to musical
fingerplays, except that children move their whole bodies. The appendix includes simple original tunes for the chants found at the beginning of each
chapter.

Most classrooms use records or tapes for children's musical games. +
Children listen for the directions on the record and then follow them, with

the teacher leading. Some are concept games involving colors, body parts, or numbers. Others are traditional circle games, such as "The Farmer in the Dell" or "Skip to My Lou." Such games give children experience in listening and following directions. This is one kind of musical activity many young children enjoy, but it should not be the only one. In this case, the children are not the music makers but only the followers. Music is more meaningful and more pleasurable when children make it themselves or when it has something to do with them personally.

+   Other musical games **involve children more directly when they make the music themselves by singing** rather than using a record. This means they must sing and perform the actions at the same time, a task more difficult for preschoolers than for older children. These are usually circle games in which the children walk around the circle (e.g., "Ring Around the Rosey"), move their bodies while standing in a circle (e.g., "Do the Hokey Pokey"), or sometimes sit in a circle (e.g., "Pass the Shoe").

+   Some children may be uncomfortable with any kind of music or group activities. **They should not be forced to join in.** Music is a wonderful socializer that may eventually entice the shy child to join the group if he or she realizes he is not being forced or singled out. You realize that your children are only at the beginning of their development of the social skills necessary for playing in a group, getting along with other children, sharing toys, and waiting for turns.

• Puppets

+   Such **shy children may be more comfortable in group singing or musical games if they can hide behind something**. Have them or any child that wants bring a hand puppet to the group, and let the puppet sing for them.

+   In fact, one of the fun musical activities can be **a weekly "puppet sing"** at

+   which all the children **make a simple sock puppet or paper-bag puppet** that they bring to music circle time for singing. Have a basket full of socks that each child can select from. Let them stick eyes and noses on their socks from sheets of peel-off colored stickers of different kinds (e.g., circles, stars, triangles, smiley faces). They can name their puppets if they want. Another week, have them make paper-bag hand puppets in the same way.

• Pictures

Another method for including uncomfortable children in group singing activities is to **have each child choose a picture of an animal, hold it up,**

+   **and sing for his or her animal** at music circle time. Again, they can name their animal and even sing in the tone of voice they think their animal would use. Those who want can hold their animal pictures in front of their own faces when they sing. Another week, let them select from pictures of people. Children enjoy singing for "grandpa" or the "police officer"!

• Blowing Instruments

Hiding behind an instrument is still another way to help children feel more comfortable when making music. Few children, even the shy ones,   +
can resist blowing on a musical instrument. Purchase a set of **kazoos, whistles, or harmonicas,** enough for everyone in your class, and let them blow   +
on their instruments to tunes you play on the record player or tape recorder. They may want to march around playing their instrument. You may want to record their songs on a second tape recorder. When they are finished, collect all the instruments and sanitize them by cleaning with alcohol-treated wipes.

Homemade blowing instruments are enjoyable to use. Buy a set of combs and a roll of wax paper. A square of **wax paper can be folded over a comb for children to hum tunes on**. It may take some time for your youngsters to   +
learn the trick of humming on a comb. They laugh at the tickly feeling the sound vibrations make through the wax paper. Talk about this with the children. **Have them feel the vibrations that humming makes on their throats** by putting their hands on their throats. Can they tell the difference   +
in vibrations between high humming and low humming? A hearing-impaired child will be able to feel the sounds he may not be able to hear. Children can throw the wax paper away when they are finished playing on their combs and use new paper another time. Leave paper and combs on the Music Center shelf for children to experiment with on their own.

Children also enjoy blowing through "tooters" made from cardboard paper-towel or tissue tubes. They can make "toot-toot" sounds or try to fol-   +
low a real song with their horns. Use the tubes as they are, or punch holes in them as in a flute, or fasten a square of wax paper over the end with a rubber band. You can put cellophane tape around the blowing end to prevent it from getting wet and soggy. Have children's names on the tooters, and ask them to use only their own to prevent the spread of germs. Have a "tooter band" with all the children joining in. Even shy children will often participate because of the instrument. Again, such music can be taped and played back for the children to listen to. Do they hear the difference between comb music and tooter music?

What songs can they toot? Let them try some old favorites with you leading the way on your own tooter:

Row, Row, Row Your Boat   *This Old Man, He Plays One*
Three Blind Mice   *Twinkle, Twinkle Little Star*
My Bonny Lies Over the Ocean   *Yankee Doodle*
London Bridge Is Falling Down

· · · · · · · · · · **Musical Activities to Promote Language Development**

Musical activities to promote language development are involved chiefly with remembering and singing the words of the songs, making up new words to songs, and reading stories about music. Realizing that music in the preschool classroom needs to be *personal* in order to be meaningful to young children, you can focus your singing activities on people, places, and pets that have personal meaning to your children. Start with the children themselves.

· Songs

Songs can be sung about children's names, features, clothing, pets, fa-
+ vorite **activities,** and favorite **foods.** Where can you find such songs? You and the children can make them up. Yes, **make up words to familiar tunes**
+ **about things of interest to the children.** Both you and they will use and appreciate such songs as much as you do your homemade musical instruments. Such instruments are often appreciated and used more than purchased instruments because they are so much more personal.

Some examples of songs made up about children's names and sung to familiar tunes include:

(To the tune of Twinkle, Twinkle Little Star*)*
Cindy, Cindy, there you are,
How I wonder where you are;
Show us now how you can run,
Then come in and have some fun;
Cindy, Cindy, there you are,
How I wonder where you are.

(To the tune of Where Is Thumbkin?*)*
Where is Randy, where is Randy?
Here he is, here he is;
How are you this morning?
How are you this morning?
Come right in!
Come right in!

(To the tune of Lazy Mary, Will You Get Up?*)*
Brian Ridley, will you stand up?
Will you stand up, will you stand up?
Brian Ridley, will you stand up,
So early in the morning?

(To the tune of Here We Are Together*)*
    Here we have Samantha, Samantha, Samantha,
    Here we have Samantha with a smile on her face;
    Look this way and that way,
    Look that way and this way,
    Here we have Samantha with a smile on her face!

Use one song at a time, singing it over and over and inserting the different children's names. Soon they will be familiar with the tune. You can sing directions or welcome or some other message to the children in this way. Be sure to write down the basic words you use to a particular tune so that you remember them next time. Any of the songs named in this chapter can be used in a similar way. Children are delighted to hear their names used in a song. They will help you compose the words to a new tune if you ask them.

You can also **make up games using familiar songs and making up your own words**. Find out something about the children's pets, and then make up guessing-game songs:

(To the tune of London Bridge Is Falling Down*)*
    Someone I know has a dog, has a dog, has a dog,
    Someone I know has a dog, and his name is Spot.
    Who do you think has a dog, has a dog, has a dog?
    Who do you think has a dog with the name of Spot?

(To the tune of Mary Had a Little Lamb*)*
    Someone has a pretty cat, pretty cat, pretty cat,
    Someone has a pretty cat by the name of Tiger.
    Who do you think has a cat, has a cat, has a cat?
    Who do you think has a cat, by the name of Tiger?

Make up words to familiar tunes about holidays, seasons, exercises, or anything of interest to your children.

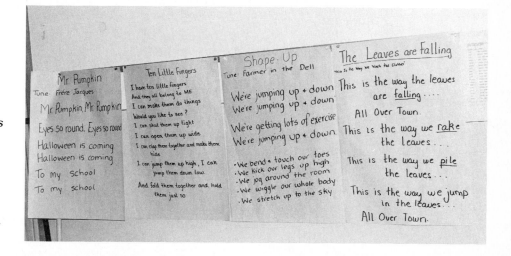

Be sure to make up a guessing-game song for every child in the class so that no one feels left out. Use the same tune for everyone. If they all do not have pets, then choose something else of interest to a particular child. (e.g., sneakers, a special toy, hairstyle, a favorite food). If the singing game catches on, play it over and over until the children remember and can sing the words on their own.

+ **Print the words of the songs you and the children are singing in the newsletters you are sending home** to the children's families. If you do not have a newsletter, send home the words on a separate paper so that families will know what their children are learning in school. Perhaps the children will want to sing the same songs with their families.

• Books

A very simple but wonderful book of snow sound words is *Ben's Snow Song: A Winter Picnic* by Hazel Hutchins (1987). Little Ben goes with his brother, sister, mother, and father on a skiing expedition. Ben in a sled, the others on skis, "shhsskree" down the slopes. The text presents words and phrases like a prose poem down the sides of striking illustrations. Read *Ben's Snow Song* in winter and ask your children to contribute their own winter songs. **They can also make a list of sounds or smells or feelings**
+ **about the season or the weather they are experiencing.** "Do all songs need to be sung to music?" you can ask your children.

Lizard's Song by George Shannon (1981) is a song that needs to be sung. Lizard sits every day on his rock and sings a song about his home. Bear tries to learn lizard's song but cannot remember it. When he captures Lizard and takes him to his den, he realizes that one must really sing his own song about his own place. This is the time to **help your children create their own**
+ **songs about their homes**. Once again, they can make up words to familiar tunes with your help:

> *(To the tune of* The Farmer in the Dell*)*
> *The Babcocks live on Fifth Street,*
> *The Babcocks live on Fifth Street,*
> *Hi, ho, the derry-o,*
> *The Babcocks live on Fifth Street.*

> *(To the tune of* Oh, Do You Know the Muffin Man?*)*
> *Oh, do you know where Lisa lives?*
> *Where Lisa lives, where Lisa lives?*
> *Oh, do you know where Lisa lives?*
> *She lives at 543 Elm Street.*

(To the tune of There's a Little White Duck Sitting in the Water*)*
> *There's a great apartment house,*
> *Over there on Eighth Street,*
> *There's a great apartment house,*
> *Over there on Eighth Street,*
> *There's a great apartment house,*
> *Over there on Eighth Street,*
> *And that's where Jeremy lives!*

• • • • • • • • • • **Musical Activities to Promote Cognitive Development**

Your children have been involved with cognitive activities in every aspect of music described thus far. The concepts of high and low, of loud and soft, of fast and slow are ideas they have touched on with rhythm, sound exploration, instruments, and singing. In addition, they can explore these concepts by trying out various objects in their environment for sound. Have children **explore by tapping with the objects in the Music Center**. What   + kinds of sounds do they make? Are they loud or soft? High or low? The results of their tapping explorations can be tape recorded and listened to.

If such exploration has captured the attention of your children, bring in a variety of **empty glass containers, and let children tap on them**. Is there   + a difference in sound? What is it? Why is it different? What will happen if you fill each of the containers with the same amount of water and then tap? Can the children predict the outcome? What will happen if you take a number of the same containers (e.g., glasses), fill them with different amounts of water, and then tap? Can the children help make a series of glasses with sounds from high to low by changing the amount of water in each? **Try the same kind of exploration with sand in the glasses instead of water.** Can   + the children predict what will happen this time? This kind of experimentation is the same kind as scientists do when they want to find out about the properties of objects.

• • • • • • • • • • **Musical Activities to Promote Creative Development**

Creative development through music is promoted whenever the children are free to do their own musical activities, whether through making up words to songs, making shoe music, singing and playing songs on their own, exploring sounds, experimenting with pitch, or making instruments. Another way you can promote creativity is to **combine music with other areas of your classroom** such as the Story Center or the Art Center. A num-   + ber of professional artists actually **paint to music**. Your children can do the   + same.

Maurice Sendak is a well-known children's book artist who paints his illustrations to classical music. Since some of his books take place at night, it can be a magical experience for your children to **listen to the stories being read while "night music" is played,** and later for them to **manipulate "night" kinds of art materials** while the same "night music" is played. *Where the Wild Things Are* by Sendak (1963), in which Max makes mischief, is sent to bed, and escapes into a world of fantasy where he becomes king of all the wild things, can be read to the background music of Moussorgsky's *Night on Bald Mountain.*

+

Put out some dark materials in the Art Center at the same time, for example, sheets of black and white construction paper, white chalk, charcoal sticks, black colored pencils and felt-tip markers, black and white easel paint, or anything else the children suggest. Play the same music as they experiment with the art materials. Again, we realize, most children will not be painting a picture but manipulating the medium of art materials that represent night.

Sendak's book *In the Night Kitchen* (1970) is another wonderful night story, this time about Mickey, who falls out of his bed and into a fantastic kitchen where he gets covered with dough. **You could play Tchaikovsky's *Nutcracker Suite* as you read the story** and later in the Art Center **as children make their own play dough**.

+

The 1988 Caldecott Medal winner, *Own Moon* by Jane Yolen, illustrated by John Schoenherr (1987), is a touching story of a father who takes his young child out into the snowy woods one moonlit winter night to look for a great horned owl. You could play Mozart's *Eine Kleine Nachtmusik* ("A Little Night Music") as you read and when children experiment with "night" art materials. Perhaps they would like to try cutting paper to be moons and snowflakes or fenceposts and shadows and pasting them into a collage. Be sure to accept whatever the children are able to cut since most preschool children are not skilled at making real objects.

· · · · · · · · · · **The Teacher's Role in the Music Center**

Once again, the role of the teacher in the Music Center may not be the traditional one of conducting a music period for the entire group. Instead, she will set up the center as described in this chapter so that children can become involved in music on their own as much as possible. She will also interact with individuals and small groups in the center in order to stimulate their involvement in personal music listening experiences, sound exploration, rhythm experiments, and music making in general. She will help them learn to record and play back their sounds, rhythm, and songs.

When classroom plans call for it, the teacher will bring in materials for making and using rhythm instruments. She will work both with individuals and small groups in the Music Center as well as the total group at circle time, promoting social musical experiences such as musical games, singing with puppets, and playing instruments.

• Observing Developmental Levels

Observing children's interactions with music to determine whether they are at the manipulation, mastery, or meaning level is not as obvious with music as it is with blocks, for instance. Yet the sensitive observer is often able to record children's interactions when the youngsters are involved with materials such as rhythm instruments. Typical interactions might include some of the following:

TABLE 9–2	Music Center Activities: Levels of Interaction

Manipulation Level

Playing around with drums, rhythm sticks, shakers, tone blocks, triangles, clackers in inappropriate ways
Using homemade tooters to blow air through, not making musical sounds
Snapping rubber-band strummers to experiment with sound or touch
Running mallets up and down xylophones, not striking separate notes
Banging on drums, tom-toms, bongos

Mastery Level

Using drums, bells, triangles, tone blocks in appropriate ways
Playing instruments over and over, almost as if practicing
Playing notes separately over and over on xylophone, rubber-band strummer
Using mallets to strike bells, cymbals, drums, tone blocks, triangles over and over
Swishing sand blocks together
Holding tambourine and tapping or shaking it
Rubbing rhythm sticks back and forth

Meaning Level

Playing single instrument appropriately to accompany own song
Beating drum in rhythm to music
Choosing and using particular instrument to make own music
Marching and playing instrument on own
Playing a melody on the xylophone
Playing tape or record and accompany music with instrument
Making up original ways to use bells, castenets, maracas, tambourines
Humming real song through kazoo, cardboard tooter, comb harmonica

As the teacher records her observations on the Child Interaction Form, he or she can begin to make plans for individual children. For children at the manipulation level, she may want to leave certain instruments in the center for an extra amount of time until the children learn how to use them. Those at the mastery level can be encouraged to try their hand at mastering several different kinds of instruments. Children at the meaning level who are making music on their own might be motivated to tape record their productions. Several children may, in fact, want to join forces to **record their**
+ **own rhythm-band music**. While music will remain a process for most of the children, some of those at the meaning level will want to preserve their accomplishments like this in the form of a tape recording.

• Modeling a Love for Music

Music will fill the classroom at appropriate times if the teacher encourages children to sing while they work by taking the lead herself. Hum your favorite tunes. Whistle if you know how. Can the children also whistle while they work, as the dwarfs did in *Snow White and the Seven Dwarfs*? **Play**
+ **this music and see how many of the children can make whistling sounds.** In addition, the teacher will use her repertoire of transition songs throughout the day. Finally, the teacher will be playing records and tapes as background music to set the mood for reading certain books or working on special projects. It will be a happy mood, indeed, in classrooms where teachers model their own love of music.

IDEAS+
in CHAPTER 9

1. *Setting up the Music Center*
    a. Bring in records or tapes you enjoy to share with children at appropriate times. (p. 201)
    b. Show children how to use and not abuse a cassette recorder. (p. 201)
    c. Have earphones available and also a clipboard for children to sign up for recorder use. (p. 201)
    d. Promote listening, sound exploration, rhythm, and music making. (p. 201)
    e. Display only a few of the rhythm instruments at one time. (p. 201)

2. *Promoting emotional development*
    a. Make music personal for the children. (p. 202)
    b. Consider featuring shoes and shoe music in your Music Center. (p. 202)
    c. Acquire a collection of shoes, and tape record what they sound like being walked in. (p. 203)
    d. Ask children to guess which shoe made the sound. (p. 203)
    e. Have children make their own shoe music and tape it. (p. 204)
    f. Have a pretend shoe store in the Dramatic Play Center. (p. 204)

g. Record the way boots sound in the water table. (p. 204)

h. Have children make paint footprints on paper and in sand. (p. 204)

i. Invite a guest to demonstrate tap dancing. (p. 205)

j. Tape record children moving to music wearing different kinds of shoes. (p. 205)

k. Bring in a pair of crutches and tape the sound they make being used. (p. 205)

l. Play the circle game "Pass the Shoe." (p. 205)

3. *Promoting small motor development*

a. Lead the children in clapping out the syllables of their names. (p. 206)

b. Have a leg-clapping circle activity to a chant. (p. 206)

c. Have children perform and then record their "pounding music." (p. 206)

d. Collect boxes and cans for tom-toms. (p. 207)

e. Make drums from coffee cans and wrapping paper. (p. 207)

f. Make tambourines from pie tins. (p. 207)

g. Explore a single rhythm instrument at a time. (p. 207)

h. Make musical shakers from margarine containers. (p. 207)

i. Have children strum an autoharp while the teacher plays. (p. 207)

j. Make shoe-box strummers and have a band. (p. 207)

4. *Promoting social development*

a. Sing a familiar song encouraging everyone to join in while they work in the various activity centers. (p. 208)

b. Ask a co-worker to sing along with you. (p. 208)

c. Make a collection of musical fingerplay songs to use during transition times. (p. 208)

d. Write fingerplays on 3-by-5 cards and keep them in a file box on top of the room divider for easy use. (p. 209)

e. Bring children together in a group to learn new songs and fingerplays. (p. 209)

f. Use records or tapes for some musical games. (p. 209)

g. Involve children directly in making music. (p. 210)

h. Do not force children who are uncomfortable to join in. (p. 210)

i. Shy children can hide behind some interesting object when singing. (p. 210)

j. Have a weekly "puppet sing." (p. 210)

k. Sing for animals in pictures. (p. 210)

l. Bring in kazoos, whistles, and harmonicas to help children make music. (p. 211)

m. Make comb harmonicas for playing. (p. 211)

n. Feel the vibrations that musical sounds make. (p. 211)

o. Make "tooters" from paper-towel tubes. (p. 211)

5. *Promoting language development*

a. Make up words to familiar tunes about children's names, families, clothing, pets, and so on. (p. 212)

b. Use one song at a time, singing it over and over and inserting different children's names. (p. 213)

c. Make up guessing-game songs about the children's pets. (p. 213)

     d. Print the words of the songs you are singing in the parents' newsletters. (p. 214)

     e. Have children make a list of sounds, smells, or feeling words about a season. (p. 214)

     f. Help children create songs about their homes. (p. 214)

6. *Promoting cognitive development*

     a. Children can learn the concepts of loud/soft, high/low, fast/slow by tapping with objects. (p. 215)

     b. Bring in glass containers, fill with water and later sand for tapping sounds. (p. 215)

7. *Promoting creative development*

     a. Have children listen to stories and paint to music. (p. 215)

     b. Play "night music" while children manipulate "night" art activities. (p. 216)

     c. Have children listen to the *Nutcracker Suite* when Sendak's *In the Night Kitchen* is read and play dough is made. (p. 216)

     d. Make a "night collage" after hearing the story *Owl Moon*. (p. 216)

     e. Have children record their own rhythm band music. (p. 218)

     f. Try whistling after hearing the song *Whistle While You Work*. (p. 218)

REFERENCES CITED

Bayless, K. M., & Ramsey, M. E. (1987). *Music: A way of life for the young child.* Columbus, OH: Merrill Publishing Company.

Glazer, T. (1973). *Eye winker, tom tinker, chin chopper: Fifty musical fingerplays.* Garden City, NY: Doubleday.

Jalongo, M. R., & Collins, M. (1985). Singing with young children! Folk singing for nonmusicians. *Young Children 40* (2), 17–22.

OTHER SOURCES

Haines, B. J. E., & Gerber, L. L. (1988). *Leading young children to music.* Columbus, OH: Merrill Publishing Company.

Hitz, R. (1987). Creative problem solving through music activities. *Young Children 42* (2), 12–17.

Moomaw, S. (1984). *Discovering music in early childhood.* Boston, MA: Allyn & Bacon.

CHILDREN'S BOOKS

Ackerman, K. (1988). *Song and dance man.* New York: Alfred A. Knopf.

Cleary, B. (1987). *Growing-up feet.* New York: William Morrow and Company.

Hutchins, H. (1987). *Ben's snow song: A winter picnic.* Toronto, Canada: Annick Press.

Sendak, M. (1963). *Where the wild things are.* New York: Harper & Row.

Sendak, M. (1970). *In the night kitchen.* New York: Harper & Row.

Shannon, G. (1981). *Lizard's song.* New York: Greenwillow Books.

Stecher, M. B., & Kanell, A. S. (1980). *Max, the music-maker.* New York: Lothrop, Lee & Shepard Books.

Winthrop, E. (1986). *Shoes.* New York: Harper & Row.

Wolkstein, D. (1981). *The banza.* New York: The Dial Press.

Yolen, J. (1987). *Owl moon.* New York: Philomel Books.

TRY IT
YOURSELF

1. Set up the Music Center in your classroom as described in this chapter with sound-making, rhythm, and music-making materials that children can choose and use and at least one activity or material new to the classroom.

2. Do a new musical fingerplay with the children during a transition time.

3. Do a new "name song" with the children using every child's name. Tape record it and play it back.

4. Set up a sound exploration activity that involves making a rhythm instrument. Tape record the children playing it.

5. Play a record or tape of classical music that sets the mood for reading a particular book or doing a particular project, and then do it.

10

SCIENCE CENTER

P E T S   *(Action chant)*

Minnie's got a guinea pig,   (March in place throughout)
Tony's got a turtle,
Holly has a hermit crab,
Jackie's got a gerbil,
Aaron has an ant farm,
Baron's got some guppies,
Karen's got a kitten,
Now she wants some puppies;
Pets, pets everywhere: (March and clap)
What am I to do?
I don't need another pet,
I've got you!   (Stop suddenly and point to someone)

Science in the Early Childhood Classroom

Few other activities in the early childhood classroom illustrate quite so vividly as does science the idea that young children acquire knowledge through self-discovery. Science, in fact, means investigation as far as young children are concerned. It is less about plants and animals or weather and water than it is about "finding out." How do preschool children find out about the world around them? Not through reading. Not through viewing a video. Not through hearing the teacher tell them. Those are methods that somewhat older children may find helpful. But youngsters younger than seven learn most appropriately about their environment by interacting physically with the objects within it. It is a hands-on approach that involves investigation with their five senses. In other words, for young children, science is a process of finding out.

Sensory Exploration

All children everywhere are well equipped for the task of investigating their environment. They bring with them into the world five wonderfully acute senses with which to explore: sight, sound, smell, taste, and touch. Infants put their senses to work almost immediately as they investigate every object with their mouths to see whether it will supply them with food. Preschoolers often focus on the sense of touch: twisting things with their hands and trying to take apart every new object they encounter. Even children with sensory handicaps such as impaired vision compensate for that lack by developing extra-acute hearing or touch.

The Appropriate Practices Curriculum can lead your youngsters to suc-

223

cessful scientific investigation of their environment if it taps into their natural mode of sensory exploration and if it provides them with the opportunities and the tools to explore fascinating objects with each of their senses.

• Sight

The sense of sight can be applied in several ways to your children's scientific investigations. First of all, they need to observe and notice things in their environment. If they are investigating water, for instance, they need to take a sweeping look to see any water in evidence in their classroom environment.

+ As you sit with a small group of children in the Science Center, **ask them what water they can see in the room**. The children may name the water dripping from a faucet in the sink, the water in the aquarium, the water in the water table, the water in the guinea pig's dish, or the water in the toilet (although the child who notes this may be challenged by another child who is quick to say, "You can't see it from here!") Others may see the bucket of water in the Art Center for rinsing paintbrushes or the pitcher of water being used to make play dough. You will want to record this water list so that children can carry their water explorations even further.

+ As they investigate the sight qualities of water, children may want **to view it through a magnifying glass**. What other vision tools can they use to help them see water better? "Would a pair of binoculars be good for viewing water?" you can ask the children. Listen to their answers. Many of the children may not know what binoculars are. But someone may reply, "Binoculars are good to see water if it's far away." That person may have used **binoculars** with his or her family. Perhaps a family member could be invited
+ to **go on a "water-viewing" field trip** with the group.

• Sound

Sound may be the next sense children will use, although this depends upon the object being investigated. "What sound does water make?" is a question you can pose to your group. Someone will be quick to tell you that it "splashes." "What does a splash sound like?" you may wonder aloud. "There are different kinds of splashes," someone else may say, so you will
+ need to investigate and **listen to water sounds up close**. One of the children can turn on a faucet—first slowly, and then fully. Have the children close their eyes so that they cannot see, only hear. Can the youngsters hear the difference? Can anyone turn on the faucet so lightly that the water drips? You can **tape record all these different sounds for later listening and**
+ **sound-identification fun**.

Once children are caught up in the fascination of sensory investigation, there is no end to it. Someone will want to pour out the paintbrush rinse water to hear the kind of sound it makes. Put that on the tape, too. Record the bubbling of the water in the aquarium and the water sounds children are making at the water table. Can they **blow bubbles through straws in the water table**? Does the guinea pig's water make a sound when he drinks it? Someone is also sure to want to record the flushing of the toilet.

• Smell

Children use smell all the time to help them identify and discriminate among the things in their world. All of us do. We often do not acknowledge our use of smell, and we often downplay its role because it is the polite thing to do. Research has shown us, however, that mothers can identify by smell alone which shirt out of several belongs to their particular baby. Babies also have this ability regarding their mothers.

Your preschoolers will enjoy **sniffing at different kinds of water to see whether there is a difference**. They may not find much of a difference with water in your classroom, although the aquarium water may smell of algae. Take them on **a water-collecting field trip,** and let them smell pond water and river water.

• Taste

If something is edible, young children will want to try it. By ages three, four, and five, they are not so likely to put everything new into their mouths as babies do. Still, they will be interested in **trying out the various samples of water that you provide to see whether there is a difference in taste**. Obviously, you will be providing samples that are pure and not harmful. Does bottled water from the supermarket taste different from tap water? This may be the time to experiment with taste changes in water by dissolving various-flavored drink powders in it. The color changes, too, the children may note. What happens when food coloring is dissolved in water? Does this change the taste as well as the color? Try different colors.

• Touch

Exploring a substance through touch can also be a stimulating experience for preschool children. **Pour a pitcher of very warm water into one place in the water table when the chidren are not looking, and ask them to find it.** Attach a **variable spray to your water faucet, and let children feel it at different settings**. Can they use words that describe the different feelings of sprayed water (from a fine mist to a steady stream)? You may need to help out. Let them **use egg beaters in the water table without soap bubbles**. Does the water feel any different before and after it has been beaten?

• • • • • • • • • • Curiosity

In addition to the sensory apparatus that is their natural inheritance, young children also are equipped with a strong drive to find out everything they can about their world. We call this drive curiosity. Every child is born with it. Some children, however, seem to have a greater degree of curiosity than others. This drive to find out is equivalent in many respects to young children's other inborn drive: to communicate. Youngsters acquire language naturally because of their drive to communicate, but they must hear language spoken around them in order to acquire their native tongue. They must be encouraged to speak, to imitate sounds, to take part in conversations if they are to become successful speakers.

In like manner, young children must be encouraged to explore their environment in order to acquire knowledge about it. Furthermore they must not be continually discouraged from exploring if they are to preserve this precious sense of curiosity and wonder. At home, it is possible that some children are scolded if they touch things. In the classroom, when such children act in an out-of-bounds manner, it could be because they are too severely restricted at home.

Other children who show no curiosity at all about the new things around them in the classroom may also have learned this behavior from being too restricted at home. If this is the case, then you should consider **talking with**
+   **parents about how children learn through exploration** and how they might explore at home. You should also think of ways to reawaken children's natural curiosity in the classroom. This drive in young children to find out needs to be nurtured and encouraged.

+   You can start by **being an "exploring" behavior model for the children** yourself. Pretend you know little or nothing about the objects in the classroom. How would you go about using your senses to explore things? Join in with the children in the great adventure of discovering the life around them. You, too, can be a scientific investigator.

• • • • • • • • • • Setting Up the Science Center

To be successful in enticing all the children into the Science Center, you should set it up based on topics of real interest to them. As you did with mu-
+   sic, you should **make science personal**. Focus the children's scientific explorations on themselves and their nearby world, and you will gain their attention and interest. That means you will be investigating such topics as:

The children themselves
  Their bodies
  Their clothing

Their food, drink
Their shadows

The children's pets
Dogs, cats, fish, birds, rabbits
Insects, snakes, gerbils, guinea pigs
Hermit crabs, frogs

The schoolyard
Trees, grass, flowers, dirt, stones
Birds, insects

The weather
Wind, rain, clouds, sun, snow

You will be **stocking your Science Center with** all kinds of **tools for investigating, measuring, containing, collecting, and recording things**. +
Some of the items may include:

TABLE 10–1	Science Materials

For investigating:

Goose-neck lamp	Plastic tubing
Stool magnifying glass	Straws
Hand magnifying glass	Sponges
Binoculars	Filter paper
Incubator	Screen
Mirrors	Sieves
Prism	Funnels
Hammer	Sponges
Tweezers	Scissors
Flashlights	Magnets

For measuring:

Balance	Stopwatch
Postage meter	Spring scale
Folding ruler	Twine
Tape measure	Yardstick
Wind-up ruler	Hourglass

For containing:

Margarine cups	Cigar boxes
Plastic trays	Shoe boxes
Plastic jars	Adhesive tape boxes
Plastic bottles	Egg cartons

TABLE 10–1	Science Materials (Continued)

For collecting:

Paper bags	Pouches
Plastic bags	String bags
Jars, boxes	Knapsacks
Collecting nets	Dippers

For recording:

Cassette recorder and blank tapes
Instant print camera
Notebooks, pads, writing tools
Chart paper
Twine, string
Cellophane tape
Scissors

+ One of the shelves in your Science Center will contain **a collection of books on** some of the **topics you might want to investigate**. As new topics emerge during the year, additional books will be added. You can start with books about:

Trees	Amphibians	Sun
Flowers	Snakes	Stars
Animals	Shells	Rocks
Birds	Insects	Water
Butterflies	Clouds	Air

The books can be story books you will be reading to the children as well as information books for yourself and the children with illustrations the children will enjoy looking at.

The center itself will need shelves for containing the tools you will be using, a bookcase or shelves for the books, display space on shelves or countertops for collections, work space on a table. **space for an aquarium, a**
+ **terrarium, and animal homes** for gerbils, a guinea pig, rabbits, or an ant farm. All the items in the Science Center will be marked with illustrated labels for easy identification by the children.

• • • • • • • • • • • The Scientific Method

Because young children come prepared to explore and investigate things with all their senses, it is easy to channel their energy along the lines real scientists use in their research:

1. Pose a problem or a question about something.
2. Guess or predict what will happen if . . .
3. Conduct the investigation.
4. Observe.
5. Draw conclusions.
6. Record the results.

For example, suppose Mary Jo comes in one snowy winter morning with something exciting that her father has told her on the way to school: that every snowflake is different—there are no two snowflakes alike. Can that be true? Mary Jo and a few other children want to **investigate that idea scientifically**. Sit down with them in the Science Center and **talk about how they can try to find out. Listen** to what the children have to say. **Jot down their ideas.**

Doug thinks that it cannot be true because nobody in the world could look at every snowflake. Mary Jo thinks her dad is right because he is always right. Andrea does not know. Jonathan wants to go outside, get a bucket of snow, and bring it in and look. The teacher poses the question: What will happen if we bring a bucket of snow inside? Will we be able to see the snowflakes? Will we be able to tell whether they are different? The children think that we will, so they bundle up, go outside, and get a bucket of snow.

Back in the classroom, it is soon obvious that they have a mass of snow, but no snowflakes. Where are they? What do they look like? Before the children can take off their winter wraps, Jonathan exclaims: "I see a snowflake! It's on Mary Jo's scarf! And there's another one!" Before the other children get a chance to look closely, though, the snowflakes have melted into the scarf. Now what to do?

After talking it over with the teacher, the children come to a new conclusion: that you cannot see snowflakes by bringing snow inside because they are so small they melt right away. So they decide to look at them outside. "You have to catch snowflakes when they are falling," announces Jonathan, "because on the ground they are all mashed together."

"You can catch them on my scarf," suggests Mary Jo. But what about the other children who have no scarves? How can they catch any snowflakes? "Is there **some kind of dark cloth in the room that we can take outside to catch snowflakes?**" wonders the teacher? The children scurry around to look. Doug comes back to the Science Center with three personal-size flannelboards from the Story Center.

"Will we be able to see the snowflakes we catch when they are so small?" wonders the teacher. The children say that they will be able to see them but that they will not be able to tell whether the snowflakes are different because they are so small. They decide that each child should also **take a magnifying glass outside to look at snowflakes**. Out they go again, armed with their scientific investigating apparatus. This time, each child catches snowflakes and looks at them through a magnifying glass. The children have to come under the shelter of the eaves so that the snow does not cover their boards or their glasses. They exclaim over the beautiful shapes of the snowflakes. They really are different!

+   Back in the classroom, the four children discuss their investigation with the teacher. **When they have made their conclusions** about whether it is true that each snowflake is different, the teacher **gets out the tape re-**
+   **corder,** and **each child reports his or her findings**:

> **Mary Jo** says: "The snowflakes I saw were all different."
> **Andrea** says: "I saw a lot of pretty snowflakes."
> **Jonathan** says: "My snowflakes were in clumps so I couldn't tell."
> **Doug** says: "My snowflakes were different, but nobody can see all the snowflakes in the world."

The teacher marks on the outside of the tape "Snowflake Research: 12/13." Perhaps some of the other children will want to continue this investigation.

The teacher then gets out the book about Robert Frost's poem *Stopping By Woods on a Snowy Evening* (1978) and reads it to the children. They love Susan Jeffers's snowy illustrations, especially the jewel-like snowflakes on the page that says: "and downy flake." Jonathan likes it that the old man makes angel's wings in the snow, just like the wings on the birds in the picture. Mary Jo likes it that the "grandpa" takes seeds to the birds in the woods because there are no seeds on the trees in the winter. Doug wishes he was there to feed the man's horse, like the children in the picture. Andrea says she didn't know horses had blankets like the one that the man put on his horse. (The teacher hadn't noticed this!) All the children wished they could have a ride in a horse sleigh like the one in the book. The teacher decides privately to look into such a possibility for a field trip.

They all want to cut out snowflakes in the Art Center, so the teacher goes over with them to show them how to fold and cut the paper.

· · · · · · · · · · · **Science Activities to Promote Cognitive Development**

The cognitive concepts most appropriate for preschool children to **inves-**
+   **tigate** involve **the properties of objects** (their shape, size, color, texture, sound, and odor); the actions of objects (how they move, react, balance, stand up, grow, eat); and the likenesses and differences among objects. Preschool children **need not be so concerned about "why" things are the way**
+   **they are, but rather "how" they look, act, and interact**.

When Jeffrey hears Ezra Jack Keats's story *Whistle for Willie* (1964), he wants to know about jumping off your shadow like Peter does in the story. The children talk with the teacher about shadows. Does everyone have a shadow? Can you run away from your shadow? The teacher invites the group over to the Science Center, where she pulls down the blinds and turns on the filmstrip projector. She shines the light from the projector on the children so that they can each see their shadows. Then, she shines the light so that each child **makes a shadow of his or her hand on a piece of white paper taped against the wall**. Can they make it bigger than their real hand? Smaller? The children are fascinated. Then, the teacher puts the projector on a higher shelf and shines it so that a child's shadow shows on the floor. **Can you jump away from your shadow?** Everyone wants to try it.

The children are most interested in the fact that shadows can be bigger than they themselves are. They all want to draw pictures of their hands, showing them bigger than they are. One of the classroom assistants volunteers to trace around a big shadow of each child's hand. The children have trouble holding their hands still enough, but finally the tracings are drawn. Jonathan holds his hand like a monster's! Some of the children decide to color their hand drawings, so they take them over to the Art Center.

The teacher realizes that she has struck a common chord of great interest with the children and decides to extend the experience. The next day, she brings in another Ezra Jack Keats book, *Dreams* (1974), and reads it to the same group of children who made their hand shadows. It is the story of an inner-city boy, Roberto, who brings home a paper mouse he has made in school and places it in an upstairs window of his apartment at night. When he is awakened in the middle of the night by a dog chasing Archie's cat into a box in the street below, Roberto accidentally knocks the paper mouse off the windowsill, and it tumbles down the side of the building, making weird and gigantic shadows from the streetlight as it falls, scaring the dog away.

Again, the children are delighted. This time they want to make Archie's mouse. The teacher is prepared and has brought in sheets of gray construction paper that she helps them twist into a cone fastened by cellophane tape. They look at the picture of the paper mouse in the book and decide to make the head and nose by bending down and taping the pointed top. Then they want pink ears taped onto their cones, which the teacher helps them make. Now, black dots for eyes and black lines for whiskers complete their mice. The teacher closes the blinds and hangs a sheet at the end of the Science Center. One child operates the projector while another child stands on a chair between the projector and the sheet, holds up her mouse as high as she can, and lets it go. Yes, the **mouse really does make tumbling shadows**. They try getting closer to the light and then closer to the screen to make the shadows bigger and smaller.

What can the children conclude from all this? That light shining on things makes shadows. That you can make big shadows and small shadows, depending on how close you stand to the light or to the surface where the shadow is.

All the children in the class eventually have a chance to make their own shadows with the lamp and then their own paper mouse, just like Roberto. The teacher later adds a simple but effective new book to the Science Center: *Shadows* by Tao Gomi (1981). One of the assistants brings in an appropriate poem to read: "My Shadow" from Robert Louis Stevenson's *A Child's Garden of Verses* (1957). Finally, the teacher brings in Marcia Brown's strikingly illustrated African story of *Shadow* (1983) and reads this prose poem of African beliefs about "shadow," who is sometimes white!

The children's study of shadows does not end there. One of the parents **reads about the children's experiments with shadows in the parents' newsletter** and volunteers to come in and show the children **how to make**

+   **shadows of animals with their hands**. The children continue to look for and find shadows of all kinds of things, inside and out. "One thing leads to another" in science, as pointed out by Maryann Ziemer (1987, 44), so of course, these curious children become excited about outside shadows of themselves, the trees, and the playground equipment made by the sun. The teacher is delighted, for she realizes that their curiosity has indeed been piqued by their investigation of shadows and that this can then lead them in other directions.

The teacher also understands that her role as facilitator in preschool science activities is to listen to the children's comments and questions and to set up the Science Center for them to explore things of great interest to them or to help them find the answers to their questions. One thing really does lead to another in preschool science, she realizes, and it is often her job

+   to **listen and then follow the children's lead**—especially when their interests take them in a direction that seems an appropriate area for study.

The **children's sudden discovery of shadows made by the sun** seems **an**

+   **ideal lead-in to the study of weather**. Keeping in mind that science is a process of finding out rather than a study of a subject, this teacher realizes that she herself knows little scientific information about the sun. That makes her somewhat uncomfortable. What can she tell her children about the sun? Then she stops for a moment and realizes that her lack of knowledge on a certain subject makes no difference at all. In fact, it is all to the good. What she really knows about is how young children learn by exploring on their own. She feels that she can **tap into their drive to find out**—their cu-

+   riosity—**and explore with them whatever it is they need to know**.

+   **From the library she finds exactly the right book** to answer some of their questions as well as whet their appetites still further: *Sun up, Sun down* by Gail Gibbons (1983), about a day in the life of a little girl from sunrise, with the sun making a long shadow of the girl, through midday, with no shadow at all, until evening, with a long, thin shadow from the opposite direction. A late afternoon rainstorm brings clouds that cover the sun and then a rainbow.

One of the questions to arise from this book is: Can a person's shadow

move if the person does not move? **The teacher does not answer this question but asks the children what they think.** Some say yes, and some say no. +
The teacher asks her habitual question: **"How can we find out?"** They decide to make shadows again in the classroom with the projector light. They find out that they can make a person's shadow move by moving the light. +

But what about sun shadows? Will they move too, if the person stands still? This time, the teacher suggests that a child **sit on a chair in the sun with her shadow on the sidewalk**. How can they tell whether the shadow +
moves? "It's going to take too long to find out," one child comments. "Let's **draw around** Barbie's **shadow with a piece of chalk,**" suggests the teacher, +
"and then wait and see whether the shadow moves out of its outline. Barbie will have to hold very still." This experiment is not only successful for Barbie, but everyone wants his shadow drawn on the sidewalk!

From shadows, to clouds, to weather, to rainbows, these children continue following their interests. The teacher often brings in a story book to set the stage, but sometimes, when interest is already high, she brings in an object or a tool to investigate the topic. **For rainbows, she brought in a prism to break up sunlight into rainbow colors,** and later, a crystal to hang +
in the window for the sun to shine through. Some children knew how to **paint rainbows** in the Art Center. Others listened to the story *Arrow to the Sun* by Gerald McDermott (1974) and **made up their own Indian rainbow dance**. +

This teacher continues to listen to the children's questions and comments to help her lead her class in an appropriate direction in science. She finds that one topic usually leads to another topic over the course of the year. Some of the cognitive concepts the class has explored include:

How much rain falls when it rains? (They made a rain gauge.)
Why do earthworms come out of the ground when it rains? (They
   started a terrarium with earthworms in it.)
What other things live under the ground? (They went on a field trip and
   started an ant farm.)
How can we get seeds to grow? (They made germinating dishes and grew
   bean seeds.)
What happens when you cook beans? (They made tacos from a recipe
   chart.)

· · · · · · · · · ·**Science Activities to Promote Emotional Development**

Whenever classroom activities are **focused on a child personally, they help promote his positive self-concept,** thus making him feel good about +
himself as a person. A favorite personal science activity that one classroom often conducts as a year-long project is an **"adopt-a-tree"** experience. The +

schoolyard is a large one with many maples and oaks and several pines. The teacher has each one of the trees located and labeled with a color-coded circle on a large newsprint chart she has made. Early in September, the children choose a tree to be their adopted tree for the year. The teacher takes a picture of each adopted tree with its child standing next to it. The chart is then mounted on the wall, along with the tree/child photos next to the proper tree-circle.

The children make a special visit to their trees once a week, after which different things happen, depending upon the children, their questions, and the direction that their interests take them. Some of the tree activities include:

Choosing tree, introducing self, hugging tree
Talk about taking care of tree, how trees help us
Naming of each tree by its child
Doing a sensory study of the tree: (close eyes)
    What can your nose tell you about your tree?
    What can your fingers tell you about your tree?
Looking at tree closely (with magnifying glass, with cardboard tube
  "viewer")
Looking at tree from a distance with binoculars
Making adopted-tree scrapbook
Making bark rubbings
Collecting leaves, needles, twigs, fallen branches
Making leaf rubbings
Pressing leaves and displaying in clear food wrapping
Comparing leaves from different trees; from same tree in different
  seasons
Identifying tree in tree book
Collecting nuts, seeds, pine cones
Counting, sorting, weighing seeds and cones
Making seed collage
Taking photos of trees in different seasons
Looking for living things in the tree
    Squirrels/nests
    Birds/nests/holes/eggs
    Insects/spiders/webs/wasps/nests
    Caterpillars/cocoons
    Fungus/moss/lichens
Activities about squirrels, birds, insects, caterpillars
Hatching butterfly from cocoon or chrysalis
Hatching eggs in incubator
Making bird feeders

Putting out seeds, suet, peanut butter for birds in winter
Putting out string, yarn, strips of cloth for nests in spring
Tape recording sound of wind in tree, birds' songs
Creative movement to tapes of wind in trees
Making popcorn strings to decorate trees at Christmas
Reading stories about trees
Making up stories about personal trees
Planting seeds from tree
Collecting things around tree in different seasons
Thanking tree for giving shade, seeds, homes for animals and birds, air
   to breathe, beauty

• • • • • • • • • • Science Activities to Promote Social Development

One teacher noted that many of the science activities pursued by her children were individual projects, such as the "adopt-a-tree" experience. She felt that science could be socially oriented as well, so she watched for an opportunity to **involve small groups of children in a learning experience that would call on their social skills**. She wanted individual children to be involved with other children so that they would have to take turns, wait for turns, and help one another. Care for the environment and for one another had been a theme in the classroom throughout the year. But sometimes young children forget about others when they want something for themselves. The **teacher decided to start with teams of two children each**.

Because the children showed a great deal of interest in looking for insects around their trees, she felt that **a "pets-in-a-jar" project** might be a good one **to help children learn to work together**. The teacher brought in enough jars for **every two children to have one**. She also provided **one collecting net** (an aquarium fish net) **for every team** of two children. She and her assistants each took with them **one trowel** or small digging tool and **a magnifying glass** that the children could **borrow and return**.

Before they went outside on an insect-collecting field trip, the teacher read to the total group a book that had become a favorite of individuals in the Science Center since their interest in insects had begun: *The Icky Bug Alphabet Book* by Jerry Pallotta (1986). The large, realistic, whole-page illustrations by Neil Pallotta gave the children a good idea of what certain insects looked like. The teacher **talked about the fact that these pictures were larger than life** and that the insects the children might find would be much smaller. The youngsters had already seen ants around their trees and now knew exactly where to look for them. The teacher knew that ants in this region were not a stinging variety; otherwise, she would not have promoted this project.

+ In addition, the teacher **talked to the children about teams and team-work**. A team of two children would be working together to collect insects. Each team would have one collecting jar and one collecting net. They would need to take turns. What would they put in their jars besides insects? The children came up with some ideas: grass, sticks, leaves, bark, dirt. One child said, "Whatever the bug is on." "Don't forget to put the cover on the jar so your bug doesn't get out," another child reminded the others.

+ The children decided ahead of time that **they would keep the insects they collected for only a few days** to look at them inside, but that then, **they would let them go so the insects wouldn't die**. Again the teacher and children talked together about care for our environment and care for one another.

The collecting expedition was a great success. Children are closer to the ground than adults and seem to have an eye for tiny things that adults sometimes overlook. They found a number of large black carpenter ants, small brown ants, a spider, a cricket, several caterpillars, a ladybug, a cocoon under a piece of bark, a small, dark beetle, and a little toad.

Back in the classroom, they talked about where each team had found its insect (or amphibian) and how the team collected it. Only one team had trouble sharing during the collecting. Brad said that Allen had grabbed the net out of his hand. Allen replied that the toad would have gotten away if he had not acted so quickly. Now he said, "Sorry," to Brad. The teacher fastened netting over the jars so that the "bugs" would have air but could not escape. The children wanted to keep their collection until the end of the week, so they talked about putting in appropriate food (leaves, crumbs) and water (a damp piece of sponge). They learned that their toad would eventually have to have insects to eat. They decided to keep the caterpillars and the cocoon to see whether the caterpillars would make cocoons and whether the cocoon would hatch into a butterfly or moth. They also decided that those particular jars that they kept would belong to the class and not only to the team that had collected them.

+ After the children had let their other collections go free, they wished they had something in the jars to look at again. The teacher suggested collecting more ants, this time to make an ant farm. They had been talking about ants, how they lived in a colony underground, and how each ant had a certain task to perform to help the colony. Instead of having teams of children this time, each with one jar of ants, she told the children she would bring in two large, gallon jars and that they could **sign up to work with other children** on one of the two ant farms.

+ One of the adult staff members worked with each group of children to make their ant farms. Before they went outside, they **discussed** what **the tasks would be to make an ant farm**:

1. Put a block in the middle of the jar to force the ants to tunnel against the glass so that their tunnels can be seen.

2. Fill the jar about half full of dirt.

3. Find an anthill or opening in the ground and dig up the ants. Be sure to get white ant eggs, ant cocoons, and wriggling larvae in addition to the ants. Look for an ant larger than the rest, who is the queen. Put all of these in the jar. (If the queen is not in the jar, the ants will tunnel awhile, but the colony will eventually die.)

4. Put a piece of wet cotton on top for moisture.

5. Cover the top of the jar with fine netting, and tie it tight.

6. Bring the jar inside, and tape a piece of black construction paper around the outside of the jar for a few days to encourage the ants to build their tunnels against the outside of the glass, where it is darkest, but where you will be able to see them best when the paper is removed.

7. Add drops of water when the cotton dries out, but not too much; otherwise, it will become moldy.

8. Keep the jar away from direct sunlight or the radiator.

9. Feed the ants every other day by putting bits of food on a piece of cardboard and removing old food. Try different things like bread crumbs, cereal, pieces of vegetable or fruit, or a spoon of honey. Do not overfeed.

Before they went outside, the children **decided which child would perform which task**. "Just like the ants!" said one girl. After the ant farms became active, the children **took turns feeding the ants and reporting on what was happening**. They named the colonies "Underground City" and "Tunnel City."

· · · · · · · · · · **Science Activities to Promote Language Development**

Talking about science projects, learning new names of things and new words to describe things, listening to stories read about science topics, making up stories about plants, animals, birds, and insects, talking about who will do a certain task: All of these are science activities that promote language development in young children. Perhaps the scientific activity most directly related to language, however, is recording the results of the children's explorations.

+   The **results can be recorded in several ways**. Children can discuss which conclusions they can make about their project, and then each one can **tape**
+   **record** what he or she learned. For growing things that they want to keep
+   track of (including themselves), children can **make a simple chart** on which heights are measured and shown with lines and labels. Another satisfying activity may be the **keeping of a journal** about their study, like scientists do.

+   For instance, **each of the children kept a "tree diary."** The teacher would write down the date, and then the child would scribble in his notebook or dictate to the teacher after he had made his weekly visit to his tree. When children did not know what to say, the teacher prompted them with open-ended questions, such as,"What did your tree look like today?" Most entries were quite simple: "My tree looked cold," or "Wet." But one said: "The leaves are starting to come out. They are all curled up."

The children also wanted to keep **two group journals for the two ant**
+   **farms**. They **took turns making entries**. Some children had things to say every day. Later, children often looked back over these notebooks and made comments about them to other children, teachers, and their parents. Photos, drawings, and cutouts from magazines also found their way into these journals. One child exclaimed: "We made a real book!"

· · · · · · · · · · · **The Teacher's Role in the Science Center**

Although it seems obvious that young children learn science concepts through self-discovery, the teacher's role is nevertheless a crucial one. Self-discovery could hardly take place if the teacher was not deeply involved in:

1. Setting up the Science Center so that children can use it easily in their investigations.

2. Listening carefully to children's comments and questions to help decide which direction the children's explorations might take.

3. Trying to arouse children's curiosity in the world around them by bringing into the Science Center intriguing objects; displays of natural beauty; appropriate books; guessing games about science objects; animals, insects, and fish.

4. Assisting children in exploring with all five senses.

5. Helping children use the scientific method.

6. Helping children record their results.

7. Extending science opportunities in new directions where appropriate.

8. Making science interesting to young children by making it personal.

The teacher's role in the Science Center is to encourage children to explore with all five senses, and to talk about what they find.

Because the teacher understands that science is a process for finding out, she will be involving the children in trying to find out all they can about themselves and the things in their environment. Yet when children bring in outside interests they have heard about, she also takes note of these and tries to integrate them into the Science Center or other activity centers. Children who are excited about the space shuttle may want to hear stories about it in the Story Center or to make a clay space shuttle in the Art Center. Or they may want to pretend to be space explorers in the Dramatic Play Center.

Not all the children are ready to glean meaning from science projects like this. They may be at the manipulation or mastery levels of learning rather than at the meaning level. It is important for teachers to observe children in the Science Center working with materials and to record their actions on the Child Interaction Form. Teachers can then interpret this data by indicating "Accomplishments," "Needs," and "Plans" for individuals and groups. Such interactions in the Science Center might include:

TABLE 10–2	Science Center Activities: Levels of Interaction

Manipulation Level

Playing around with magnifying glasses, magnets, prisms, rulers, balances in inappropriate ways
Using a magnifying glass for an eyepiece
Using a magnet for a toy gun
Looking through wrong end of binoculars
Pulling out wind-up ruler and snapping it back
Filling up collecting bottles, boxes, bags with items and dumping them out
Knocking on the side of an aquarium or terrarium to see what will happen
Collecting piles of leaves or seeds and throwing them
Shining flashlight in other people's faces

Mastery Level

Using magnifying glasses, magnets, prisms, rulers, balances appropriately
Lining up stones, shells, and so on and observing one at a time through magnifying glass
Pulling out wind-up ruler, measuring something, and rewinding it, over and over
Piling up items on balance till they balance, dumping them off, and repeating action
Picking up nails with magnet, taking them off, and repeating action

Meaning Level

Looking at insect through magnifying glass and telling what it looks like or what kind it is
Displaying shells, stones, seeds in a collection and telling something about them
Looking through binoculars, focusing on something, and describing what is seen
Measuring something and describing results
Making up story or book about adopted tree
Identifying bird, fish, insect, butterfly, and finding its picture in book

From this data, teachers can make plans for activities in the Science Center. If most of the children are playing around with the measuring implements, the teacher may want to postpone the measuring of the room until the children have taught themselves to use the implements. If children are just beginning to master their use of the balance, the teacher may want to provide them with other collections of items to balance, for instance, nails, buttons, counters, doll-house furniture.

When children begin to take the lead in science exploration by bringing in interesting items or suggesting places to go and things to see, the teacher will realize that her science curriculum has really caught on. She or he then needs to take the role of follower, listening carefully to the comments and questions of these energetic explorers and supporting their boundless curiosity with new paths of wonder they all can follow.

IDEAS +
in CHAPTER 10

1. *Using the sense of sight*
   a. Ask children what water they see in the room. (p. 224)
   b. Have children view water through a magnifying glass. (p. 224)
   c. Go on a water-viewing field trip. (p. 224)

2. *Using the sense of sound*
   a. Have children listen to classroom water sounds. (p. 224)
   b. Tape record all the different water sounds for later listening and sound-identification fun. (p. 224)
   c. Blow bubbles through straws in the water table. (p. 225)

3. *Using the sense of smell*
   a. Have children smell different kinds of water to see whether there is a difference. (p. 225)
   b. Go on a water-collecting field trip. (p. 225)

4. *Using the sense of taste*
   a. Have a water-tasting session with bottled water and tap water. (p. 225)

5. *Using the sense of touch*
   a. Pour very warm water into the water table and have children find it through touch. (p. 225)
   b. Put a variable spray on your faucet and have children feel it. (p. 225)
   c. Have children use egg beaters in the water table without soap. (p. 225)

6. *Reawakening curiosity*
   a. Talk to parents about how young children learn by exploring their environment. (p. 226)
   b. Be an exploring behavior model yourself for the children to see. (p. 226)
   c. Make science personal for the children. (p. 226)

7. *Setting up the Science Center*
   a. Stock the Science Center with tools for investigating things, measuring things, collecting things, and recording things. (p. 227)
   b. Supply a collection of books on topics to be investigated. (p. 228)
   c. Have space for an aquarium, terrarium, and animal homes. (p. 228)

8. *Promoting the scientific method of investigation*
   a. Listen to what children have to say about snowflakes and jot down their ideas. (p. 229)
   b. Catch snowflakes outside on a dark cloth and view them with magnifying glasses. (p. 229)
   c. Talk about children's findings and conclusions, and then tape record them. (p. 230)

9. *Promoting cognitive development*
   a. Concentrate with children on *how* things look and act rather than *why* they do for children this age. (p. 230)
   b. Make a shadow of a child's hand on a white paper on the wall. (p. 231)
   c. Have children try to jump away from their shadows. (p. 231)
   d. Write about children's science investigations in the parents' newsletter. (p. 232)
   e. Invite a parent to demonstrate how to make animal shadow pictures with hands. (p. 232)
   f. Listen to children's comments and questions about things, and then follow their lead in setting up science activities. (p. 232)
   g. Use the children's present interests as a lead-in to another topic that has some connection to the first. (p. 232)
   h. Tap into children's drive to find out. (p. 232)
   i. Find story books in the library for every topic you are exploring. (p. 232)
   j. Do not answer every question from the children, but ask them, "How can we find out?" (p. 233)
   k. Have a child sit on the sidewalk in the sun while you trace around her shadow to see whether it moves. (p. 233)
   l. Bring in a prism and let light shine through it. (p. 233)
   m. Have children who know how, paint rainbows. (p. 233)
   n. Read *Arrow to the Sun* and make up a rainbow dance. (p. 233)

10. *Promoting emotional development*
   a. Focus science activities on a child personally to help improve his or her self-image. (p. 233)
   b. Have each child adopt his own tree for the year. (p. 233)

11. *Promoting social development*
   a. Involve small groups of children in a science activity that calls on their social skills. (p. 235)
   b. Have a team of two children do a "pet-in-a-jar" project, each team with one jar and one net. (p. 235)
   c. Lend a trowel and magnifying glass to different children. (p. 235)
   d. Talk about the size of insect pictures in books in case the pictures are larger than life. (p. 235)
   e. Talk to children about teams, teamwork, and their tasks during the collecting field trip. (p. 236)

  f. Talk to children ahead of time about letting their insects go after a few days. (p. 236)

  g. Two groups sign up to make an ant farm. (p. 236)

  h. Discuss the tasks that are necessary to make the ant farm. (p. 236)

  i. Take turns feeding ants and reporting on what is happening. (p. 237)

12. *Promoting language development*

  a. Record the results of a scientific exploration by tape recording, charts, and journals. (p. 238)

  b. Keep a "tree dairy." (p. 238)

  c. Keep a group journal for the ant farms, taking turns making entries. (p. 238)

REFERENCES CITED

Ziemer, M. (1987). Science and the early childhood curriculum: One thing leads to another, *Young Children 42* (6) 44–51.

OTHER SOURCES

Arnold, L. B. (1980). *Preparing young children for science: A book of activities.* New York: Schocken Books.

Brown, S. E. (1981). *Bubbles rainbows & worms, science experiments for preschool children.* Mt. Rainier, MD: Gryphon House.

Rockwell, R. E., Sherwood, E. A., & Williams, R. A. (1983). *Hug a tree, and other things to do outdoors with young children.* Mt. Rainier, MD: Gryphon House.

Simon, S. (1975). *Pets in a jar, collecting and caring for small wild animals.* New York: The Viking Press.

Smith, R. F. (1987). Theoretical framework for preschool science experiences. *Young Children 42* (2) 34–40.

Sprung, B., Froschl, M., & Campbell, P. B. (1985). *What will happen if . . .* New York: Educational Equity Concepts.

CHILDREN'S BOOKS

Brown, M. (1983). *Shadow.* New York: Charles Scribner's Sons.

Frost, R. (1978). *Stopping by woods on a snowy evening.* New York: E. P. Dutton.

Gibbons, G. (1983). *Sun up, sun down.* San Diego, CA: Harcourt Brace Jovanovich.

Gomi, T. (1981). *Shadows.* San Francisco, CA: Heian International.

Keats, E. J. (1974). *Dreams.* New York: Collier Books.

Keats, E. J. (1964). *Whistle for Willie.* New York: The Viking Press.

McDermott, G. (1974). *Arrow to the sun.* New York: The Viking Press.

Pallotta, J. (1986). *The icky bug alphabet book.* Watertown, MA: Charlesbridge Publishing.

Stevenson, R. L. (1957). *A child's garden of verses.* New York: Grosset & Dunlap.

TRY IT
YOURSELF

1. Set up the Science Center in your classroom with tools for investigating things, for measuring things, for containing things, for collecting things, and for recording things, as discussed in this chapter.

2. Do an activity with a small group of children that encourages them to explore with one or more of the five senses.

3. Read a story book to a small group of children to stimulate their interest in a personal science topic, and come prepared to follow up on this interest with materials or a project they can do.

4. Write down the questions and comments you hear children making about the scientific investigating they are doing, and make plans to extend this activity based on these comments.

5. Take children on a collecting trip, and record the results in one of the ways mentioned in this chapter.

DRAMATIC PLAY CENTER

Who am I?
Let me see—
I am Wonder Woman on TV;
I am a dancer on the stage,
I am a rock star—all the rage;
Today I'm the mother who pours the milk,
Yesterday, a princess dressed in silk;
Tomorrow I don't know what I'll do—
Do you?

• • • • • • • • • • Dramatic Play in the Early Childhood Classroom

Dramatic play is one of the most complex kinds of play that young children engage in—and perhaps the most important. In dramatic play or imaginative play, as it is sometimes called, young children use *pretending* to investigate their world. They engage in "make-believe," creating pretend roles for themselves, pretend places for their roles to be enacted, and pretend situations to respond to.

It is difficult for many adults to understand the why's and wherefore's of dramatic play among young children because it is such a brief phenomenon—coming to a peak around ages four, five, and six, and fading away by age seven. Most adults have long forgotten their own foray into the world of make-believe and are a bit suspect of anyone—even young children—who engage in fantasizing. Isn't that some kind of escape from reality? Is it really healthy for young chidren to pretend to be someone other than themselves?

It is not an escape from reality for young children, and it is healthy for young children to pretend to be someone else. Pretending for young children before the age of seven is a necessary prelude to the life of reality that they will be leading. Imagining and pretending are creative tools all children are endowed with in order to investigate the world around them. Through pretending to be someone else, they find out what it is like to be themselves. Through pretending to be somewhere else, they find out what it is like to be where they are. A real paradox, but true.

If they are girls, they often try on the roles of mother, baby, sister, aunt, grandma, nurse, doctor (sometimes), teacher, or female superhero such as Wonder Woman. If they are boys, they often try on the roles of father, brother, uncle, doctor, police officer, repairperson, race car driver, or male superhero such as Superman or Batman.

"Wait a minute," says the adult mind, "Aren't those roles rather sexist?" They may indeed be sexist according to an adult frame of reference, but you must remember that young children are not operating in an adult frame of reference. These are the spontaneous roles young children may choose for themselves in order to investigate their world. Yes, some girls do try out the roles of race car driver or Batman, just as some boys try out female roles. Teachers of young children accept any role that young children want to try as long as it is not one of violence or harm to anyone.

"What can young children possibly learn by pretending?" you still may wonder. The answer is that so much is gained through dramatic play in every aspect of child development that a listing of possibilities seems the only way to approach the question:

In social development:
Cooperation
Social roles
Prosocial values such as honesty, service, loyalty, truthfulness
How to gain entrance to a group
How to be a leader
How to deal with a strong leader
How to negotiate
How to deal with people you disagree with

In cognitive development:
Concepts such as work, play, order, time
Concepts of travel, transportation
Concepts of illness, doctors, emergencies
Roles of family members, workers
Problem solving
Planning

In language development:
How to carry on a conversation
How to speak as a different character
Meanings for and uses of many new words
How to express feelings in words
Use of words as a substitute for actions

In emotional development:
Positive self-concept
How to express strong feelings in acceptable ways
How to control negative tendencies
How to deal with conflict

In physical development:
Mastering of certain motor skills (running, jumping, climbing, tricycle
    riding)

In creative development:
Divergent thinking
Novel solutions to problems
New ideas, plots, characters

Children who are able to engage in dramatic play with others learn to be cooperative and flexible. They soon realize that in order to keep the play flowing smoothly, they may need to compromise, to take an alternate approach, to accept someone else's ideas, or to accede to another child's wishes. For the egocentric young child who is often used to having his own way, the joy of the play itself seems to make most sacrifices worthwhile.

Dramatic play allows a child to be whomever he or she chooses. He can be boss, drive a car, soar through the air, come in late, eat what he wants, and command other people—as long as he can negotiate these roles with the other players. She can be boss, too, do what she wants, go where she wants, and command other people—as long as she can negotiate these roles. Thus, for young children who are, of course, controlled by adults in their real lives, dramatic play offers a powerful outlet for their feelings of helplessness in the world around them.

Because they play around with new ideas and novel solutions to problems, children who engage in such pretending are able to develop abstract thinking, creativity, flexibility, the ability to communicate, and the ability to get along better with their peers. Not every child takes to dramatic play easily, but children who engage in highly elaborate kinds of imaginative play seem to reflect higher levels of development themselves, and there is evidence that a high fantasy predisposition in children is linked to creativity (Garvey, 1977, 97).

• • • • • • • • • • Setting Up the Dramatic Play Center

This area of the classroom is somewhat different from the other activity areas. Rather than being an area of shelves full of materials and tables for use in investigating the materials, the Dramatic Play Center is more like a stage setting for children's spontaneous pretending. Because many of their roles center around home and family, **there should be a family area** available to stimulate such role playing.   +

The traditional kitchen area with child-size stove, refrigerator, sink, table, and chairs is still considered one of the most appropriate settings for dramatic play. Other props in this area can include a full-length mirror, a cradle or baby's bed, a telephone, an ironing board, a high chair, and a doll buggy. A corner storage area for child-size broom, mop, dustpan, bucket, and sweeper add other possibilities to the roles. **Cups, pots and pans, and cooking utensils can be hung on a pegboard with an outline or cutout of the item** for matching and classifying by the children. Cutlery can be stored   + in a plastic container or drawer with dividers to give children an additional opportunity for sorting and classifying. Plastic food, fruit, vegetables, and even pizza are available if you choose to use commercial props.

Dress-up clothes can hang separately on hooks; hats may hang on peg-   +

boards or a hat tree; purses, belts, wallets, shoes, jewelry, and other dress-up items have shelf space with illustrated labels so that children can see what is available and return items easily when they are finished. The dress-up clothes themselves should include both men's and women's clothing: dresses, skirts, tops, slacks, shirts, jackets, vests. Teen-age sizes are easier for young children to manage.

    A second "room" in the Dramatic Play Center **can be a sort of generic sitting room** with chairs and perhaps a child-size couch or bench around the outside. A table with a lamp (no cord) and a telephone is useful. Some low shelves with various props may help to divide this area from the kitchen. A pull-out counter or a folding play screen with a counter is another valuable addition. This area can serve as the setting for an infinite number of play situations if it is flexible. For example, it can become a:

Doctor's office	Bank
Shoe store	Gas station
Bus or train (or terminal)	Restaurant
Supermarket	Theater
Repair shop	Laundromat
Science museum	Hospital
Barber/beauty shop	Fire station
Post office	Airport
Business office	Zoo or pet store
Ticket office	Check-out counter

    Additional props in the area will vary with the kinds of pretending the children and you wish to promote. Bring in (or **have parents contribute**) a number of **empty shoe boxes, bags, and old shoes when you set up as a shoe store**. Be sure to have **a toy cash register for any store setup**. Children can help collect empty food boxes, cans, and jars for a supermarket. The typewriter from the Writing Center can be used for an office setup.

    If the size of the classroom does not allow for this second dramatic play space, then **consider a combination space shared with the Large Motor Center**. A commercial **junior gym,** sometimes called house gym, makes an excellent pretending area. The square wooden climbing device with a loft on top, a ladder up, and a slide down allows for a variety of imaginative play situations as well as large motor skill practice. Children use both the loft and the area under the loft for pretending. Some classrooms build their own lofts with ladders, steps, or climbers for getting up and down. Other classrooms have a **wooden or cardboard playhouse** tucked away in a vacant corner **or a tent** erected for varied use in dramatic play.

    Although pretending with miniature objects such as figures of people and animals, Barbie dolls, doll house equipment, and cars, trucks, and trains may take place in other areas of the classroom, the Dramatic Play Center focuses on roles and plots the children choose to investigate spontaneously using full-scale materials.

• • • • • • • • • • Dramatic Play Activities to Promote Social Development

Before young children can participate in spontaneous dramatic play, they need to have reached a certain level of social development that will allow them to become involved in this cooperative play. Child development specialists have long noted that young children seem to go through a sequence of social behavior categories based on their maturity and experience with other children, which begins with unoccupied or onlooker behavior and progresses through solitary play, parallel play, and finally, cooperative play (see pp. 29–30).

These social behaviors are observed when children engage in dramatic play as well as the other activities of the classroom. Sometimes children are onlookers or solitary players because they are ill at ease in the classroom setting. This is often the case of beginning three-year-olds, who are more used to a home setting and adult association than they are to a classroom with a lively group of peers. Sometimes children are onlookers or solitary players because they are immature and have not yet developed the cognitive and language skills that allow them to pretend with a group. Other times children resist joining group dramatic play because they simply do not know how. They have not had the experience of taking on a role and pretending with other children, or they do not seem to know how to gain access to a group of experienced players.

The activities you provide in your Dramatic Play Center can help such children to become involved socially in pretending with others. Although this will be spontaneous dramatic play on the part of the children, you can help set up the play through the props you supply and the initiating activities you provide.

Dramatic play based on a travel theme is something that appeals to most of the children because they themselves have traveled in a car, bus, or train (or subway). It is also an especially attractive activity for **newcomers to dramatic play** because they **can participate easily as passengers,** an undemanding role for beginners.

To initiate such an activity, you can invite a group into the Dramatic Play Center and **read them a book on travel in a vehicle,** such as *The Train* by David McPhail (1977). Little Matthew spends his days playing with his own model train and his nights dreaming about working on a real train. Ask your children whether they would like to **have their own train** and how they would set it up. A driving bench (stationary bench with a steering wheel mounted at one end) makes a fine engine for the engineer. Seats for the passengers can be lined up two by two behind the engine. An engineer's cap, a conductor's cap (police cap), a paper punch, and paper tickets are other props the children can use.

+   As the children take roles and set up the train activity, you can **invite one or two onlookers to join the play as passengers with you**. Shy children sometimes become involved in group play if the teacher joins, too. "Come on, Jennifer, let's get our tickets and climb on board William's train before it leaves the station!" **You can stay with the play until the players feel com-**

+   **fortable and then extract yourself.** Although it may be tempting for you to stay longer because it is so enjoyable playing with the youngsters, remember that children gain most from dramatic play when they do it on their own.

Another day, you can ask the chidren what it is like to ride on a school

+   bus. **Would they like to set up their own school bus,** just as they did their train? Another time, children who enjoy playing with miniature cars in the Block Center can set up **their own pretend car** in the Dramatic Play Center with the driving bench and chairs. **Before** the same vehicle play becomes involved with **riding in a pretend airplane, be sure the children have some**

+   **sort of real experience with planes** at an airport, museum, or park. Dramatic play like this is an excellent followup experience for a field trip.

Keep your eye on this play as it progresses. If children do not think of it themselves, you can suggest that **they might want to pack a bag before**

+   **they go on their trip**. Be ready by having bag props available for everyone: airline bags, book bags, athletic bags, or knapsacks. The shy participant can now do something more than merely sit in one of the vehicle's seats if he or she has to pack a bag. Purses and wallets are other props that children can use here.

• Leader and Follower Roles

Other social roles in dramatic play involve being a leader or following the lead of someone else. In order to begin dramatic play and keep it going, leadership is necessary. One or more play leaders need to emerge spontaneously from the group. The leader will set the stage for the play by suggesting the theme, setting the roles (sometimes assigning the roles), and filling in the details of the play as it progresses. This leader is accepted by the group and generally retained as long as the play goes smoothly or the leader is not too demanding. A common sequence in preschool dramatic play might go as follows:

Amy: Let's play "school bus." I'll be the driver.

Beth: No. You were the driver yesterday. It's my turn to be driver.

Amy: Okay. But I'm going to be the next driver.

Beth sits down on the driving bench and "starts the bus" with a loud "Br-r-r-room-m-m."

Beth: We're ready to go. Get the children on the bus. Tell them to hurry.

Amy: I'm not the teacher. (She sits down in a chair behind Beth.) Sheila, you be the teacher and get the children on the bus.

Sheila: I'm a passenger. (She sits in a chair behind Amy.) I'm going to the mall today to go shopping.

Beth: You can't go to the mall. This is a school bus. You're going to school. (Makes motor noises.)

Sheila: You better hurry or we'll be late to school.

Amy: Sit down in your seat, little girl. You have to sit down when the bus is in motion. If you don't sit down, I'm going to report you.

Sheila, who has remained seated all the while, now giggles. She stands up and then quickly sits down when Amy turns and gives her an angry look.

Typical of leadership roles in dramatic play, in this scenario more than one leader has emerged, and negotiation has to take place in order to settle who will be the driver. The original leader, Amy, agrees to wait until her time comes to be driver, but she will not agree to take an assigned role as teacher (so she says), although she acts as a teacher once Sheila has joined the play. In this brief play segment, Sheila has accepted a follower's role and agrees to most of the ground rules set out by both Beth and Amy.

It is obvious from this typical drama that leader and follower roles are not all that distinct among preschoolers. To be effective and keep the play going, leaders must practice a give-and-take style of leadership in which they recognize the feelings of others in the group and compromise when necessary. The most successful leaders are those who can perform both leader and follower roles with ease, who can accept the ideas of others yet have novel ideas of their own, and who are fun to play with. Some children seem perfectly happy being followers as long as they are not dominated too forcefully by the leaders (Trawick-Smith, 1988, 53–54). Children learn what works best in their particular group and how far they can go through many experiences in playing together. When a leader becomes too demanding and uncompromising, the play simply disintegrates, and the players leave.

When you consider the practice for real life experienced by child players in these spontaneous dramas, it becomes obvious that dramatic play has a vitally important role in the lives of young children.

• Superhero Play

Many children enjoy taking on the roles they see performed in television cartoons, especially those of the superheroes such as Batman, Robin, Superman, Wonder Woman, Spiderman, Dracula, Darth Vader, or whoever happens to be the featured star of the moment. Many preschool teachers are not especially happy with the prospect. They feel that too often, superhero play disintegrates into rowdy rough-and-tumble play that is not appropriate indoors in the preschool classroom. The question is twofold: Should superhero dramatic play be allowed in the preschool classroom? If so, what can young children gain from it?

The gains should be considered first. Cartoons teach children some very basic values that our society espouses: who is good and who is bad, what good people and bad people do that makes them good or bad, and what happens to you if you are good or bad. Cartoons deal in stereotypes. The characters are simple, one-dimensional figures who are either all good or all bad. The superhero is a good character who is good-looking, strong, loyal, helpful, unselfish, ready to fight against evil, and always the winner. The bad character is evil-looking, strong, selfish, disloyal, underhanded, sneaky, always challenging the good character, and always the loser. Cartoons such as this play the same role as fairy tales did in an earlier time. They are not supposed to be true-to-life. Instead, they teach values in a very exaggerated and forceful manner. However, if children can learn prosocial values from superhero play in the Dramatic Play Center, then perhaps you should consider it.

Does such play really have a place in the preschool classroom? If it can be kept from getting out of hand, if its inherent violence can be downplayed and controlled, the answer again may be "Yes," or at least, "Maybe." Children are going to attempt superhero play whether or not it is allowed. It speaks to something deep within them. Think of yourself as a young child. Were you attracted to such cartoons? If you have young children, are your own children attracted? If so, you realize that superheroes are powerful symbols, indeed, to young children. When you understand that such symbols can represent positive values in our society, then you may want to consider allowing superhero dramatic play in the classroom if it can be controlled and directed into prosocial channels.

Children's play researchers have noted that dominant themes in pretend play often include: capture and rescue, submit or vanquish, and attack or flee (Kostelnick, 1986, 5). If this is the case, then superhero play is not so far off base. But why do some of your children want to play the role of the bad guy? What can they learn from being Dracula, Darth Vader, or the Joker? They know already that these evil characters are going to be defeated by the superheroes. Think about being little, helpless human beings controlled by big, powerful adults, and you may have the answer. Young children want to try the negative roles, too—the ones that challenge the good guys, for they, too, want to challenge their adult "keepers." They realize that these "bad guys" are not going to win. They do not want them to win. Children want us, the teachers and adults in their world, to put the limits on negative behavior—their own and the bad superheroes.

If you decide to admit superhero play to your classroom, you need to channel it in the direction of prosocial learning with restrictions and limits. When it occurs, you can sit down with the children and talk with them about their superheroes. What are some of their humane, prosocial traits that can be admired? They are loyal to their friends. They are unselfish. They help the underdog. They stand up against evil. Can children be like that? How?

Do people have to use violence and fighting to bring about good things? How else can a person behave who wants to be a superhero? How should pretend superheroes behave in the classroom? What should they avoid doing? What should happen when things get out of hand? If you can talk with your children about values and behavior, if you can establish limits ahead of time about what is allowed and what is not allowed, then it is possible that superhero play can help your children learn to practice prosocial helping behavior.

• • • • • • • • • • Dramatic Play Activities to Promote Emotional Development

As with other activities in the self-directed learning environment, children learn these social roles more effectively when they do them on their own. Dramatic play is not always smooth and happy. Often, there is haggling and disagreement. Teacher intervention may solve problems temporarily, but children learn how to control emotional outbursts and to interact with peers best on their own rather than having an adult solution imposed.

One of the most common types of conflict in dramatic play at this age involves children trying to get their own way. Young children are at an egocentric level of their cognitive development, in which each one of them acts as if he is the center around which everything revolves. Since not everyone in a group situation can have his own way, there is great potential for disagreement and conflict during dramatic play.

We have already noted that the most effective leaders find ways around this conflict in order to keep the players appeased and the play going. Some children are unable at first to allow another person's desires to take precedence over their own. Why should they? After all, their feelings are the ones that count, they may believe. They seem unable to see things from another child's point of view.

That is the point of dramatic play: to see things from another character's point of view. Children who insist on having their own way and are unable to accept another child's position soon find themselves on the outside of the play. A noisy conflict does not seem to resolve anything, they find. It may bring the teacher down on the group with her own solution, but when the teacher leaves, the children are on their own again and may refuse to play with the child who gets his or her own way through argument or bullying.

On the other hand, left to themselves, children are often able to work out very creative solutions to conflict. When the disagreement centers around a desirable role and who will play it, negotiation and give-and-take enter the picture on the part of experienced players. As with Amy and Beth, they work out the problem of who will be the driver without resorting to arguing or refusal to play. Other children learn how to negotiate and compromise by watching how experienced players handle problems. Then they find out what works and what does not work by trying it themselves.

The teacher can best help children to consider various solutions to dramatic play conflicts by activities conducted outside the Dramatic Play Center. For instance, she can **read stories centered around play conflicts**
+   and afterwards **talk with the children about how they were resolved**. In the book *A Lion for Lewis* by Rosemary Wells (1982), little Lewis is playing dress-up in the attic with two older children who always force him to play an inferior role that he does not want. He has to be the baby when the other two are mother and father. He is the sick child when they are doctor and nurse, and maid when they play king and princess. Instead of fighting with the other two or leaving the play, Lewis creates his own dynamic role by putting on a lion suit that he finds in a trunk and playing a role even bigger and more important than theirs.

Children are intrigued by Lewis's solution to "who gets the best role." They sometimes offer other solutions of their own:

1. He could be a giant baby who makes the mother and father mind him.
2. He could be a maid who finds a treasure and gets richer than the king and princess.
3. He could be a pretend maid who is really the biggest king of all.

Another book that offers the same possibilities for discussion of who gets the best role or who is in control is *Much Bigger Than Martin* by Steven Kellogg (1976). It is the story of Martin's little brother, who dislikes playing inferior roles with his brother so much that he tries to grow into a giant by eating too many apples. When this solution only makes him sick, he tries another one: building a pair of stilts!

Your children can have another good **discussion of what else Martin's**
+   **little brother can do to get a better role** when the two brothers play pretend games. Given the chance to discuss them and try them out, young children's solutions to dramatic play problems are often more effective and more creative than anything an adult can dream up. Even the followers in the group learn something about resolving conflict without aggression or punishment.

It is, then, **important for the children to have real practice with their**
+   **ideas about resolving conflict in the Dramatic Play Center itself**. The more

experience they have in playing spontaneous, self-imposed or self-accepted roles, the more opportunity they have to see things from a different point of view: their character's. When children play pretend roles, they put themselves in their character's place. They are mother or father, and they find that they have to act like a mother or a father. They learn not only what is acceptable for mothers or fathers to do and say, but they also learn how their peers respond to such a person. Young children can be brutally frank with one another, but in pretend play, this is how they learn to play roles in an acceptable fashion. This is how children learn to overcome the negative aspects of their egocentric natures by seeing things from another point of view.

• • • • • • • • • • Dramatic Play Activities to Promote Cognitive Development

Some of the problem-solving methods mentioned above could just as well come under this heading of cognitive development. Children need to be cognitively mature in order to see things from another person's point of view or to problem-solve in the manner suggested in the section about emotional development. They also need **practice problem solving in real situations in order to discover what works and what does not work,** as suggested above.   +
Obviously, child development occurs in a holistic manner, with a particular curriculum activity contributing to many aspects of a child's development.

Another important contribution that dramatic play can offer in promoting children's cognitive development involves helping them understand concepts or general ideas about their world and how it works. **Dramatic play can serve as a followup activity to** field trips the children take, **helping them to conceptualize** and understand the things they experienced on the   +
trip.

A field trip to the fire station is one that many preschool programs make. Children see the trucks, the ladders, the hoses, the "cherry-picker" crane for tall buildings, the alarm bells and sirens, the firemen's boots, coats, and hats, and sometimes a Dalmatian dog mascot. When they return to the classroom, they will want to talk about the things they have seen. Perhaps **photos of children on the fire trucks** have been taken that **can be placed in the Dramatic Play Center**. The teacher can **read a fire station book** to stimulate more discussion and thinking about the field trip. Finally, **fire station props** can be placed in the Dramatic Play Center for the children to use in   +
taking roles and pretending about their experience.

A book that is always a favorite with children is *Curious George at the Fire Station,* edited by Margret Rey and Alan J. Shalleck (1985). Preschool children really enjoy the antics of the little monkey, George, who explores the fire station from top to bottom, gets into mischief with the fire bell, but

Dramatic play helps children to conceptualize and to understand how things work in their world.

saves the day by rescuing one of the Dalmatian puppies. After reading the story, you can put out fire station props, such as several fire hats (from toy stores, or paper fire hats from party supply stores), a fire chief's cap, a bell, some boots, raincoats, and a short length of hose. If the children saw a Dalmatian dog at the station, you may want a stuffed Dalmatian dog prop as well. **Children can use the driving bench and chairs for their fire truck** if they want, or they can make up their own plot.

Another field trip with dramatic play possibilities is a visit to a pizza shop, where children can watch pizza being made. Back in the classroom, they will want to make their own pizza from a package mix or from scratch, using an illustrated recipe chart. **Have three different groups of children making their own pizza** so that everyone can be directly involved. **Dramatic play followup** can take place with props such as pizza pans, measuring cups, bowl, flour sifter, pizza cartons, chef's hats, and aprons. Or the children may want to have a pizza restaurant setup with chairs and tables with red checkered tablecloths. Be sure to read a book such as *Curious George and the Pizza,* edited by Margret Rey and Alan J. Shalleck (1985). Again, George gets into mischief with the pizza dough, but saves the day by making a pizza delivery over a locked gate.

Another Curious-George-inspired field trip and dramatic play followup can be a **visit to a nearby laundromat**. Adults may not find such a trip all that interesting, but children certainly do. Read the book *Curious George at the Laundromat,* edited by Margret Rey and Alan J. Shalleck (1987) back in the classroom. In this story, George investigates the washing machines and creates a flood of soapsuds when he dumps in a whole box of detergent. **Children can explore the properties of soapsuds and bubbles in the Science Center and at the water table.** They can **really wash the doll clothes** and hang them on a line with clothespins to dry. Then they can **pretend about the laundromat in the Dramatic Play Center** if you put out props such as cardboard-carton washing machines, clothes and clothes baskets, measuring cups, and empty detergent containers.

• • • • • • • • • • **Dramatic Play Activities to Promote Language Development**

Every role-playing situation with which the children are involved affords them opportunities for language development as they listen to the conversation around them, participate in the give-and-take of negotiations, and speak for the character they are portraying. As Catherine Garvey has noted, "Carrying out the make-believe is largely a matter of communication" (Garvey, 1977, 86). Children involved in dramatic play often have to speak not only for their own character but also for pretend characters. If they are leaders, they have to give directions, to plan for action, to add new details, and to explain the plot or its changes to other players as they go along.

Because almost every kind of pretending affords children opportunities for speaking and listening, it is important that preschool programs **allow**
+ **enough time for children to become deeply involved in dramatic play**. Garvey's research reveals the following types of pretend action to be most popular:

Treating-healing	Cooking
Averting a threat	Dining
Packing	Repairing (of car)
Taking a trip	Telephoning
Shopping	

(Garvey, 1977, 92–94)

Props make a difference in dramatic play. If there are no telephones in the center, there will be little telephoning. To promote this type of conversational language production, **you need two telephones for children to call**
+ **and answer with**. Some programs have **pretend telephone booths** as well. Realistic, child-size toy phone booths are available commercially. Children derive as much or more pleasure from **making their own classroom phone booth from a large, cardboard carton**. They may want to **visit a real phone**
+ **booth** to try it out before making their own.

Written language should be visible in the Dramatic Play Center as well. **Have real calendars on the walls.** Have **real phone books and a note pad near the toy telephones**. Have a **magazine rack for magazines and newspapers**. Children can pretend to read and write. Someone can pretend to be
+ the **newspaper deliverer** and **bring the daily paper** to the housekeeping area. Look around your own home. What other written language is visible that children could use in their pretend play?

+ **Can children make up stories about their dramatic play experiences?** To motivate this sort of storytelling, read to a small group of children *In the Attic* by Hiawyn Oram (1984). It is the story of a little boy who climbs the ladder of his toy fire truck into a magical attic full of adventurous mice, an exotic garden, and other worlds that he visits on a fabulous flying machine. What worlds can your children see in the pictures? What other worlds can they invent?

• • • • • • • • • • Dramatic Play Activities to Promote Creativity

Most dramatic play episodes call on children's creativity to get them started and keep them going. If you want to stretch their imaginations even farther, **take them on a wild and wonderful trek around the classroom or**
+ **around the block** outside. To get the children in the mood, read to a small

group *The Trek* by Ann Jonas (1985), about the little girl who walks to school and imagines that she is on an African safari with wild animals in every yard, tree, and puddle she passes.

Take this same small group of children on a similar trek. Have them pack a bag or knapsack to take along. Then, proceed slowly and cautiously with yourself as the leader. What kinds of animals or other imaginative creatures can you see in the shapes of the bushes and trees? **Pretend to see elephants in the schoolyard, tigers in the bushes, parrots in the trees.** What   +
exciting incidents can occur? You might have to hide behind a tree if a rhino charges! Phew, a narrow escape! Watch out for the monkeys in the trees! They are throwing fruit!

If your safari is a success, you will want to invite other small groups on other days until everyone has had a chance. On the next repeat trip, encourage the children to join in the pretending. What fabulous creatures do they see?

To motivate the children to make up more of their own creative adventures, **read similar stories based on wildly imaginative plots**. *The Giant*   +
Jam Sandwich by John Vernon Lord (1972) is the story of Itching Down, where 4 million wasps flew into town and the people decide to catch them by creating a giant jam sandwich. In the book *Pigs* by Robert Munsch (1989), Megan opens the gate to the pigpen just a little bit against her father's instructions, and wap-wap-wap-wap-wap, the pigs thunder out to take over her house, the school, and the school bus, which they eventually drive back home to their pen. Can your children make up wild stories of their own about the giant guinea pig that bursts its cage or the block tower that grows by itself right up through the ceiling? Creative pretending helps children develop their imaginative powers, which in turn strengthens their ability to play pretend roles with others in the Dramatic Play Center.

• • • • • • • • • • The Teacher's Role in the Dramatic Play Center

Just as the Dramatic Play Center itself consists of two separate parts—a housekeeping/family area and a generic sitting room area—so the teacher's role in the center is twofold. She must set up the family area in a permanent way to entice children to enact the roles they are most familiar with: that of mother, father, brother, sister, baby, and grandparent. Thereafter, she will be observing children to see which ones participate in cooperative group play, which ones play parallel to a play group, perhaps waiting for an opportunity to join it, and which ones are solitary players doing their pretending apart from the group. In addition, the teacher will be observing the levels of interaction that her children demonstrate.

• Observing Interaction Levels

Do young children manipulate the medium in dramatic play as they do in art, music, writing, with blocks, and with other new materials? In other words, do they go through the stages of manipulation, mastery, and meaning? The answer seems to be a guarded "Yes," although dramatic play is such an all-encompassing and complex type of endeavor that we realize many factors are at work in children's pretending. If children's pretending involves physical objects, then we can apply the 3-M formula.

When young children first begin to pretend and play roles at around the age of two or two-and-a-half, they play bits and pieces of roles, such as putting the baby doll in bed and putting a blanket over it; or getting out the broom, sweeping the floor, and putting the broom away; or getting out the dishes and setting the table.

They do not seem to be able to get beyond these limited actions, perhaps because they are developmentally unable as yet to conceptualize the roles more fully. Even coaching on the part of other, more mature children has little effect. Instead, the younger children play the same bits over and over again in the same way, as if they were practicing them—just like children at the mastery level of interaction.

On the other hand, children ages three and four who are developmentally more mature but who have not done such pretending before show definite tendencies first to *manipulate* the materials by playing around with them, and then later to use the materials in a more mature fashion. They may first use an object such as a stethoscope, for instance, to blow into or shout into, as if it were a microphone rather than a doctor's examining instrument. Their involvement with children who are more experienced with dramatic play eventually helps them correct such inappropriate actions, and they are finally able to *master* their roles with objects.

Eventually, they may use props not only as they were meant to be used, but also by applying their own *meaning* in purely original ways. This may mean pretending that a flashlight in certain situations is an implement for squirting water, for example. Children at the highest level of fantasy do not need real objects at all for their dramatic play, but can create pretend objects out of thin air.

As play researcher Garvey has noted:

> We have seen that, in the early stages of play with objects, pretending is tied to the perceptual or physical properties of objects. It seems to be the case, however, that once a child reaches a level of cognitive maturity that permits him to operate with roles and plans, he becomes less dependent in his pretending on the real properties of objects. (Garvey, 1977, 96)

Teachers can record such observational data on the Child Interaction Form. If a group of children together are engaged in a dramatic play episode, then all their actions and dialog can be recorded on the same form. Plans for individuals can then be formed based on interpretation of the data as recorded under "Accomplishments," "Needs," and "Plans" for the various children.

• Facilitating Dramatic Play

Sometimes dramatic play disintegrates or gets out of hand. If children seem unable to solve the problem themselves, the teacher then has a third role to play: that of facilitator. As such, she has several options. She can:

1. Redirect the play;
2. Extend the play;
3. Take a role in the play herself;
4. Stop the play and talk to the children in terms of the three-part caring theme of the class.

If she chooses to redirect the play, the teacher can suggest to the players another direction to take with their pretend situation. For example, if the doctor play has gotten out of hand, with children fighting over the stethoscope or about who is going to give shots, the teacher can say something such as, "It is time for the doctor's office to close for the day. He needs to pack up his bag and go home. He'll have to call a taxi because his car is broken. Is there anyone here who drives a taxi or can fix a car?"

On the other hand, the teacher may choose to extend the play by inserting an exciting new idea that bypasses the trouble with the stethoscope but keeps the play going. For example, she might say: "Here are the four new laser scopes you ordered, doctor (gives "doctor" four cylinder blocks). The hospital would like you and your assistants to try them out on your patients, and see if you can see right into their bodies with them to find out what their sickness is. These laser scopes are a new invention and you are the first medical people to use them. Be careful with them as they are very fragile."

You need to know your children and how they respond to suggestions in order to decide how to salvage dramatic play that has gotten out of hand. By taking a role in the play yourself, children will generally either calm down or leave the play. If the play resumes in a peaceful manner, you can excuse yourself in the same way as you inserted yourself.

Sometimes it is necessary to stop the play. If children are so out of control that they cannot take suggestions for redirecting or extending the play, the teacher may need to step in and stop the play completely. This is the time to talk calmly but firmly about the three-part caring theme emphasized by the program: that in this classroom we care for ourselves, we care for one another, and we care for our surroundings and materials. "Jackie, I can't let you hit Robbie. In this classroom, we care for one another. We do not hit others. If you feel angry, you need to tell Robbie how you feel. If you are too angry to talk, then you need to leave the Dramatic Play Center until you feel better."

If everyone is involved in the turmoil, you may need to stop the play and calm them down right then and there by reading an appropriate book: "This sounds like a squabble over who's turn it is. Did you know that real doctors also have problems over turns? Yes, they do. Let's all sit down right here and I'll read you a story about one doctor that had such a problem. Little Gloria was that doctor's patient, and she did not like the doctor to give her a physical examination. So guess what she did? She gave the doctor a physical examination instead! How do you think he liked that? This is a book about it called *Your Turn, Doctor*" (by Deborah Robison, 1982).

You will have books such as this on tap for such a disruptive situation because you are aware of the kinds of conflicts that commonly occur among preschool children. If you show children that you care for them in this manner and will help them to stay in control, they will be better able to resolve their own dramatic play conflicts when the time comes.

IDEAS+
in CHAPTER 11

1. *Setting up the Dramatic Play Center*
   a. Have a family area available to stimulate family role playing. (p. 249)
   b. Cups, pots and pans, and cooking utensils can be hung on a pegboard with an outline or cutout of the item for matching and classifying by the children. (p. 249)
   c. Hang dress-up clothes separately on hooks; hang hats on pegboards or a hat tree; store purses, belts, wallets, shoes, and jewelry on shelves with illustrated labels. (p. 249)
   d. Have a second "room" in the Dramatic Play Center as a generic sitting room for use in different play themes. (p. 250)
   e. Have parents contribute empty shoe boxes, bags, and old shoes for a shoe store setup. (p. 250)
   f. Use a toy cash register for any store setup. (p. 250)
   g. Consider a combination space shared with the Large Motor Center for a "house-gym." (p. 250)
   h. Have a cardboard box playhouse or a tent. (p. 250)

2. *Promoting social development*
   a. Dramatic play on a travel theme can include shy children in the undemanding role of passengers. (p. 251)
   b. Initiate train play by reading a theme book and setting up a train with a driving bench and chairs. (p. 251)
   c. Invite onlookers to join the travel play with you as passengers. (p. 252)

   d. Extract yourself from the play when the players feel comfortable. (p. 252)

   e. Help to initiate a school-bus play theme. (p. 252)

   f. Give children a real experience with planes or airports before involving them in an airplane theme. (p. 252)

   g. Have the children pack a bag before they take their pretend trip. (p. 252)

   h. Channel superhero play in a prosocial direction with limits. (p. 255)

3. *Promoting emotional development*

   a. Help children deal with dramatic play conflicts by activities conducted outside the Dramatic Play Center. (p. 256)

   b. Read stories centered around play conflicts and discuss with the children how they were resolved. (p. 256)

   c. Discuss with children how smaller children can get better roles. (p. 256)

   d. Give children real practice with their ideas of resolving conflict in dramatic play. (p. 256)

   e. Give children practice in real play situations to discover what works and what does not work for them. (p. 257)

   f. Have dramatic play serve as a followup to field trips. (p. 257)

   g. Stimulate field trip followup play with photographs in the Dramatic Play Center and theme stories. (p. 257)

   h. Put out field trip props for use by the children. (p. 257)

   i. Use the driving bench and chairs as a fire truck. (p. 259)

   j. Stimulate pizza shop play with a field trip and then making of three pizzas by three groups of children. (p. 259)

   k. Stimulate laundromat play with a field trip. (p. 259)

   l. Have children explore the properties of soapsuds and bubbles in the Science Center and at the water table. (p. 259)

   m. Have children wash the doll clothes and hang them on a line. (p. 259)

   n. Put out props such as cardboard washers for laundromat pretending. (p. 259)

4. *Promoting language development*

   a. Allow time enough for children to become deeply involved in dramatic play. (p. 260)

   b. Have two telephones in the Dramatic Play Center. (p. 260)

   c. Make a phone booth from a cardboard carton. (p. 260)

   d. Have calendars on the wall, phone books and note pads near phones, and magazines and newspapers in the family area. (p. 260)

   e. Have children make up stories about their dramatic play episodes. (p. 260)

5. *Promoting creative development*

   a. Take children on an imaginative safari around the block. (p. 260)

   b. Pretend to see elephants in the yard, tigers in the bushes, and parrots in the trees. (p. 261)

   c. Motivate creative play themes by reading stories featuring imagination. (p. 261)

REFERENCES CITED

Garvey, C. (1977). *Play.* Cambridge, MA: Harvard University Press.

Kostelnik, M. J., Whiren, A. P., & Stein, L. C. (1986). Living with he-man: Superhero fantasy play. *Young Children 41* (4), 3–9.

Trawick-Smith, J. (1988). 'Let's say you're the baby, ok?' Play leadership and following behavior of young children. *Young Children 43* (5), 51–59.

OTHER SOURCES

Abraham, K. G., & Lieberman, E. (1985). Research report: Should Barbie go to preschool? *Young Children 40* (2), 12–14.

Bergen, D. (Ed.). (1988). *Play as a medium for learning and development, A handbook of theory and practice.* Portsmouth, NH: Heinemann Educational Books.

Johnson, J. E., Christie, J. F., & Yawkey, T. D. (1987). *Play and early childhood development.* Glenview, IL: Scott, Foresman and Company.

CHILDREN'S BOOKS

Jonas, A. (1985). *The trek.* New York: Mulberry Books.

Kellogg, S. (1976). *Much bigger than Martin.* New York: The Dial Press.

Lord, J. V.(1972). *The giant jam sandwich.* Boston, MA: Houghton Mifflin Company.

McPhail, D. (1977). *The train.* Boston, MA: Little, Brown.

Munsch, R. (1989). *Pigs.* Toronto, Canada: Annick Press Ltd.

Oram, H. (1984). *In the attic.* New York: Henry Holt and Company.

Rey, M., & Shalleck, A. J. (Eds.). (1985). *Curious George at the fire station.* Boston, MA: Houghton Mifflin Company.

Rey, M., & Shalleck, A. J. (Eds.). (1985). *Curious George and the pizza.* Boston, MA: Houghton Mifflin Company.

Rey, M., & Shalleck, A. J. (Eds.). (1987). *Curious George at the laundromat.* Boston, MA: Houghton Mifflin Company.

Robison, D. (1982). *Your turn, doctor.* New York: Dial Books for Young Children.

Wells, R. (1982). *A lion for Lewis.* New York: The Dial Press.

TRY IT
YOURSELF

1. Set up the Dramatic Play Center to include a family/housekeeping area with appropriate props as described in this chapter and a second sitting room area for other play themes.

2. Observe and record the levels of social play that your children demonstrate according to Parten's levels (see Chapter 2).

3. Help onlookers or solitary players become involved in dramatic play by inviting them to share an undemanding role with you.

4. Record several episodes of dramatic play that give evidence of leadership and following roles.

5. Take children on a field trip and follow it up with dramatic play activities using appropriate props and a story.

LARGE MOTOR CENTER

JANIE IS A JUMPER

(Action chant)

Janie is a jumper,	
See her hop-hop-hop;	(jump in place three times)
Bonnie is a bumper,	
See her bop-bop-bop;	(jump forward three times)
Phillip is a flier,	
See him loop-the-loop;	(turn in place, arms outstretched)
I can go still higher,	
Watch me fly-the-coop!	(run away, flapping arms like wings)

• • • • • • • • • • • Large Motor Activities in the Early Childhood Classroom

Running, jumping, and climbing are large motor skills closely associated with young children, the very essence of early childhood, most people readily agree. Striding, gliding, and galloping are locomotor skills that young children seem to accomplish almost without effort. Whirling, twirling, and bending are whole-body movements that preschool youngsters perform with verve and vigor. Is it really true? Are all young children so skilled and so energetic about body movements? Do all preschoolers participate in large motor activities with such ease and excitement?

Not everyone can, and not everyone does. We are beginning to realize that our society is becoming a sedentary one. More people are spending more hours in activities that require little movement: watching television, playing video games, sitting at computers. Young children reflect the attitudes and practices that they have experienced in their environment. They learn a great deal from older sibling and adult role models.

In addition, many children's free movement is being restricted as city streets and parks become unsafe. Where are children to practice the skills of running, jumping, and climbing? Today more than ever, it is the early childhood classroom that must provide such activities. It is the preschool program that is being called upon to guarantee young children their natural birthright of growing up with strong and healthy bodies.

The Large Motor Center in an early childhood classroom thus takes on an importance it may not have experienced before. As a crucial component of the self-directed learning environment, it must be set up to appeal to children's own interests in motor skills. As an essential element in the Appropriate Practices Curriculum, it will include child-initiated activities to enhance development of particular large motor skills. The center will be available for children's daily use, exactly as the other classroom learning centers are.

What about an outdoor playground or an indoor gymnasium? They also have an important role in children's development of large motor skills because of the many running, jumping, climbing, balancing, swinging, sliding, and riding skills that cannot be practiced as freely in the classroom. Outdoor and gym time need to complement the daily program wherever possible, but these do not substitute for large motor activities within the classroom. Children need in-class large motor experiences on a daily basis. In the developmental scheme of things, the focus is truly on the large motor skills for preschool children. It is the foundation for much of the rest of the child's development to follow. Parents and teachers alike want that foundation to be a strong one.

Setting Up the Large Motor Center

The Large Motor Center of the preschool classroom contains equipment and materials to promote the development of many physical skills such as:

Walking	Crawling	Throwing
Running	Creeping	Catching
Galloping	Balancing	Riding
Jumping	Bending	
Hopping	Climbing	
Leaping	Creative movement	

Flexible, multiple-use equipment is best. A multi-use climber is as important indoors as out. A junior-gym or house-gym that includes a ladder going up to the fenced-in platform on top and a slide going down provides challenges for several children at a time in using the large muscles of the arms, legs, feet, hands, and torso. These gyms come in a variety of sizes and configurations. Some have a section with a tunnel attached to the climbing platform through which a child crawls to go down the slide. Some have a door or crawling hole at the base. Most are made to fold up for easy storage.

House-climbers also serve as dramatic play areas, with children playing on top and underneath the platform as well as on the ladder and sides. One version, built in an A-frame shape, is called an Alpine house-gym. A smaller, solid-wall version of the house-gym has steps going up to a platform with railings, a wooden slide going down, and a crawling hole underneath. Vinyl and foam-filled floor mats should be placed under and around such climbing equipment to cushion falls.

Some programs prefer to use nesting climbers that can be stacked out of the way when not in use. They are tubular climbers in triangular shape that can stand alone or be used in combination with another climber, with a bridge between two, or with a sliding board. Still other programs prefer large, hollow, heavy-plastic climbing cubes with holes in tops and sides.

Children (with your help) **can create their own climbing-crawling-sliding apparatus** if the Large Motor Center contains a set of snap-together   +
or push-together materials. Plastic Snap-Wall sets include waffle-like walls with circular openings, steps, slides, railings for platforms, tunnels, and ramps. Walls are snapped together into child-size cubes with tunnels erected from one cube to another or steps and slides fastened to their tops. Other climbing materials include large vinyl foam-blocks in a variety of colors and in square, round, and ramp shapes that can be pushed together and held in place with hook-and-loop fasteners.

Most preschool programs do not extend their classroom large motor facilities much beyond the climbing equipment mentioned above. The Appropriate Practices Curriculum, on the other hand, fills the Large Motor Center with a variety of activities at particular stations within the center. These stations are discussed under each of the skills to follow. In addition, the center can display **pictures of children** involved in climbing, crawling,   +
jumping, and running. If you do not have a source for such pictures, take them **from a play-equipment catalog,** enlarge them on a copy machine, and   +
mount them attractively on the walls of your center.

· · · · · · · · · · **Activities to Promote Specific Large Motor Skills**

· **Walking**

"All preschool children surely know how to walk, don't they?" you may ask. Take a look and see. You will note that not all of your children walk the same way. Depending on their size, their center of gravity, their development, and their personalities, children walk in many styles and with varying degrees of ability and confidence. Many taller, more mature girls stride along like adults. Younger children who still retain some of the top-heaviness of toddlers may walk with less agility. Some children seem more awkward in their movements than others. Physically impaired children have locomotor difficulties.

Thus, your Large Motor Center should at all times feature materials and activities to promote walking—a basic skill for all human beings. Walking comes in different forms. Your children should be able to: step, tiptoe, tread, tramp, hike, stroll, saunter, march, prance, stride, strut, clump, shuffle, trudge, slide, and glide. Keep your activities personal and fun for the children, and everyone will want to become involved.

Where can children walk inside the classroom? In the Large Motor Center itself, **they can walk up and down steps** if you have commercial equipment   +
such as a rocking boat that inverts to up-and-down steps, or a step-and-slide climber, or a nursery gym with steps. It is not necessary, though, to purchase commercial equipment. Creative teachers can devise all kinds of

walking activities. For instance, children can **walk or march in place** when

+ you lead them **in action chants** such as those at the beginning of each chapter.

For an always-available walking activity that children do on their own,

+ you can designate one area of the center as the **walking rink** and section it off with a rope attached to chairs or with masking tape on the floor. Not only does such an area promote walking, but it also controls large motor movement that might otherwise get out of hand with more exuberant walkers! Your rink can be a square or circle large enough for one or even several children if you have sufficient room.

Children can take a ticket from an envelope attached to the rope or the wall that designates which motion they will perform in the rink: **red tickets**

+ **for walking, blue for jogging, yellow for hopping, purple for tiptoeing.** Have a stick-figure drawing of the motion on each ticket. Children then perform their motion inside the area of the rink and return the ticket when they are finished. How long they stay in the rink is up to the children. If you **mount a chart with their names** on the wall in the area, they can **put a peel-**

+ **off colored sticker** after their name each time they perform an action. Children love to fill up the chart with as many different colored stickers as possible.

+ Another week, **use the walking rink for animal walking.** Have tickets with animal pictures on them: elephants, ducks, cats, deer, rabbits, and kangaroos. Let children move as they think these animals would move. Still

+ another week, use the walking rink **for dinosaur walking.** Children have a special attraction for these extinct giants. To get your youngsters started with dinosaur movements, read them a simple dinosaur book such as *Giant Dinosaurs* by Erna Row (1973) that features the trachodon, tyrannosaurus, triceratops, stegosaurus, brontosaurus, brachiosaurus, and diplodocus. Do not be fooled by these so-called "difficult" names. Young children love to roll them around on their tongues. At this time, you will also feature miniature toy dinosaurs in the Block Center, dinosaur music in the Music Center, and dinosaur software in the Computer Center.

What if your children want to continue their walking fun outside the Large Motor Center? Can they do their high-stepping elsewhere? They can if you have **cut out footprints from colored contact paper and make a**

+ **walking trail around the room** with them. Make the footprints have the same color-coding as your tickets, and place the footprints as they would look for walking, jogging, hopping, and tiptoeing. The children can help.

+ Children enjoy **ice skating and skiing** as well. The walking rink activities can include these gliding, sliding skills during one of the winter months. Bring pairs of double-unit blocks from the Block Center to be used as skates and skis. Preschoolers can balance on a pair of blocks and slide along the floor. Bring in some ski poles from children's toy skis, or have the children use a pair of brooms from the Dramatic Play Center as ski poles.

Children can **go on hikes or climb mountains** in the walking rink if they   +
want to stretch their imaginations as well as their muscles. Fill up knapsacks for them to wear on their backs as they hike. Have walking sticks in
the Large Motor Center to add to the drama. What other walking activities
can you or the children dream up? What about **walking with crutches?**   +
Bring in a pair of children's crutches and let them practice.

• Running/Riding

Children need to practice the skill of running indoors as well as out. Once
again, you can promote yet control the activity if you provide a special space
for it. **Have a running pad** in the Large Motor Center where children can   +
run in place. This can be one of several stations in the center where children
take a ticket and do the exercise required, just as they do with the walking
rink. For the actual pad, you can use a doormat or some other rubberized,
nonskid mat. Mount a chart of children's names nearby and let them paste
a peel-off sticker on the chart after they do their running.

If you have the space, **consider having a running/riding ring.** This can be   +
the circle-time circle if you have an actual circle marked on the floor. It can
also be a roped-off circle in the Large Motor Center with a length of rope
looped through the backs of chairs that are formed into a circle. The size is
immaterial. It can be big enough for one or for three or four. You would
probably not want space for more within the classroom itself. Children especially like this type of circle. They can help you set it up, even on a daily basis
if need be. Like swimmers swimming laps, the **children can run rings**   +
around the inside of the circle. They can keep track of their own rings and
take a number from the basket you provide that tells the number of rings
they have run. Thus, a large motor activity can promote cognitive skills as
well. (Accuracy in counting is not the point at this stage of their development.)

How else can children move in the running/riding ring? How about **galloping on a horse around the track**? For this kind of movement, you may   +
want to supply your riders with several stick horses. They are available commercially, or make your own from a cut-down mop or broom. The galloping
movement is as close as many preschoolers will come to skipping—a more
complex skill not expected of children younger than six or seven years old.

Try to discourage horse races in the ring because of their potential win-   +
lose element (fine for horse races, but destructive for the preschoolers who
lose; all the children who participate in your riding ring are winners). Why
else would someone ride in a ring if not to race? What about **a horse show**?   +
Children can help make their own stick horses and then show them off in
the ring. What about **a rodeo**? For inspiration, read to a small group of in-   +
terested participants the book *White Dynamite and Curly Kidd* by Bill Martin, Jr. and John Archambault (1986). It is the spine-tingling adventure of

a rodeo bull rider, Curly Kidd, and his wild ride on the bull, White Dynamite, as his little child, Lucky Kidd, looks on. Lucky Kidd tells the story with wonderful rhyming sound words on the full-color pages of the book, keeping readers and listeners on the edge of their seats until the ending surprises everyone. Can children make stick bulls (like stick horses) for a pretend rodeo? What kinds of movements would a rodeo bull make? What about a bucking horse? This type of activity is especially appropriate wherever rodeos are a part of the children's culture.

Children can perform in the Large Motor Center running/riding ring for any number of weekly or monthly events: a **motorcycle rally** with children riding stick motorcycles they have made; a **car show** with children driving stick cars; a **kangaroo hop** with children seeing how far they can jump (with their two feet together) around the ring; or a **camel trot** with riders crossing the desert. The only limits to ring-running or -riding are your and the children's imaginations. Remember to bring the **large, wooden riding vehicles** into this area for at least one day a week.

• Jumping/Hopping/Leaping

Here is another station in the Large Motor Center. **Have a jumping pad** where children can jump up and down, two feet together, on some kind of pad, cushion, or miniature trampoline. The station can be sectioned off with chairs, rope, or merely masking tape and a sign. Or you could have steps where children can walk up one side and jump off the other onto a pad.

More elaborate kinds of jumping can take place in the Large Motor Center if you make proper arrangements. If you read children the book *Jump, Frog, Jump* by Robert Kalan (1981), be prepared to **have a frog pond** with a lily pad, a log, a net, an island, and a basket. These can be made by marking out the various areas on the floor of the center with masking tape, or better still, by using a series of vinyl mats for the pad, the log, the net, the island, and the basket. Let children jump from one pad to the other as you read this cumulative tale. If you cannot locate the book, make up your own frog-jump tale.

Jumping skills can also be promoted by **having your own basketball jump station** in the Large Motor Center. Mount a round basket (with the bottom out) or a ring of some kind to the wall in the center, high enough so that children will have to jump up a little in order to put a ball in it. For a ball, use a sponge or foam ball that is light and not bouncy. This is not a basketball game, but a jumping station. Again, place a chart with children's names nearby, where they can put a colored sticker next to their name after they have completed the basketball jumping.

Children can also hop on one foot and then the other if your activities en-

courage this movement. **Have a hopping pad as yet another station in the Large Motor Center.** Some teachers prefer a **footprint hopping trail** with   +
self-sticking vinyl footprints of two colors (e.g., red for the right foot, blue for the left foot) mounted on the floor in a trail for hopping first on one foot and then on the other. If children have difficulty hopping on one foot, have them hold onto the back of a chair while they practice.

Leaping activities can occur in the Large Motor Center if you tape off a section of the area for such an activity. Because leaping is a skill that carries a child across a space from one side to the other, make your leaping inviting for children by giving them something intriguing to leap across. You can designate a **leaping lizards lodge or a leapfrog locale as a station** where a   +
different kind of leaping activity takes place each week. One week, tape a section of blue posterboard to the floor as a river that the children must leap across, taking off on one foot and landing on the other. Children can also leap across pretend mud, sand, or snow. Again, put up a name chart for colored stickers.

• Balancing/Bending

Children can practice the skills of balancing and bending in the Large Motor Center if you set up **a balancing/bending bower as a station.** Again   +
on a weekly basis, include a particular balancing or bending activity for them to practice on their own. One week, **have a balance beam or walking board as a bridge across a taped-down blue posterboard river** for children   +
to cross by walking forward, sideways, and backward. They might try to carry a little suitcase as they walk across the balance-beam bridge. Another time, they can try carrying a little bucket in each hand as they cross the bridge.

For a bending activity, **place a pole or broom between two chair backs and have children duck under the fence.** Another week, have objects (e.g.,   +
pebbles) at the bottom of a bushel basket that children have to bend over to retrieve. Another bending activity can be **a pick-up-chips** or put-down-chips **game** in which children take a container of colored plastic chips and   +
bend over to place them on self-sticking vinyl stepping-stones of the same color as the chips. When they have finished placing the colored chips on the proper stepping-stone, they can go around and pick up the chips for the next child, giving them yet a second bending experience. Each time they complete a set of activities, let them peel off a sticker to place by their name on the chart.

Each week, you can substitute a new bending activity for the children that they can do on their own. For instance, try **panning for gold with gold-painted pebbles that you place here and there on the floor of the station and a pie pan for the children to collect their gold in.** Base your activities   +

on topics the children are pursuing in other centers of the classroom. When they are reading about dinosaurs or playing dinosaur computer games, **have a dinosaur food-gathering expedition** in which children must bend over to collect in a basket or bucket the cutout pieces of food you have scattered here and there around the floor of the bending bower. Such activities should lead you and your children into devising similar creative experiences based on curriculum interests and needs.

• Crawling/Creeping

Although we often use the words interchangeably, *crawling* refers to the movement of propelling the body forward with arms and legs when it is flat on the floor. *Creeping* refers to the forward body movement done on hands and knees with the body raised above the floor. Your Large Motor Center can afford children an opportunity to promote these skills on their own if you **set up a crawling chamber as a station.** In addition to the crawling spaces provided by commercial climbing equipment, you can also purchase fabric tunnels that are collapsable and easily stored, as well as vinyl-pad tunnels.

Many teachers prefer to make their own crawling/creeping materials. **A large, cardboard carton can be cut out with an opening at each end large enough for children to crawl through.** Call it a cave or a car tunnel, and have the children help you paint it an appropriate color. **Tunnels can also be made of pairs of adult-size chairs laid down opposite each other** with their backs touching to serve as the roof of the tunnel. Cover the chairs with a blanket for a more interesting effect. Children can pretend to be bears creeping into their dens or cars driving through a tunnel in the mountain. **Sing a song together when children creep and crawl.** How about *The Bear Went **Under** the Mountain?*

If yours is a large-city program, take the children on a subway field trip, and then **make a subway tunnel** in your crawling chamber upon your return. The children themselves can be the cars of the subway train as they creep through the tunnel. Another week, they can be explorers crawling though a mountain cave. Still another week, they can be scuba divers swimming through an underwater cave or exploring a shipwreck. For added interest, place some objects (such as gold pebbles) inside the tunnel or ship for the children to discover. **A tent too small to stand up in also promotes creeping/crawling movements,** as does a homemade card-table tent with a blanket over it for the walls.

• Climbing

Climbing activities are popular with children because of the excitement they offer and with teachers because of the variety of children's large motor skills they promote. Children exercise arms, hands, shoulders, legs, and feet, as well as practice bending, twisting, balancing, pushing, and pulling skills. The commercial climbers, waffle blocks, and foam blocks previously mentioned are popular in classrooms that can afford the space and monetary commitment. Homemade climbing materials can be just as effective and perhaps more appealing to the children if they have a hand in setting them up.

Add a climbing corner as a station in the Large Motor Center. Plastic milk-carton crates that are often used for storage can also be used for climbing. Place them on the floor, open side up, and tie them together in a line or in a maze for children to climb in and out of one by one, like an obstacle course. Again, children can add a peel-off sticker to their name chart every time they complete the crate climb. Or have an envelope in each crate from which a child can extract a card of the same color as the crate. He or she can then collect climbing cards one at a time, afterwards returning them to their color-coded envelopes. Climbing thus becomes a cognitive activity as well as physical one.

A small closet can serve as a climbing corner by **removing the door and fastening rungs** across the door opening or inside from bottom to top with a pad at the bottom to cushion falls. **Large, hollow blocks belong in a climbing corner** rather than in the Block Center. Children can build child-size huts, forts, steps, and walls, climbing up and down and in and out of their structures.

• Throwing/Catching

Children ages three through five are at the beginning of their throwing-catching skills. Some still use two hands to throw an object, just as they did as toddlers. Others throw one-handed in a pushing movement. Children need practice in throwing objects both overhand and underhand in order to develop this complex skill. If you **use lightweight, nonbouncing objects such as bean bags, sponge balls, yarn balls, foam balls, and perforated plastic balls in a confined space,** you afford children the opportunity of throwing as hard as they want. **Set up a throwing booth as a station** in the Large Motor Center to encourage children to practice this skill on their own.

Place a small table or low counter for holding the throwing objects two or three yards from the wall. Against the wall, place a target. Make it something colorful and interesting: a tall, flat cardboard carton painted with an animal face with a wide-open mouth (a large hole) to fill with food; or a bright basket or plastic hoop fastened to the wall; or a small bucket covered with colorful cloth or paper standing on the floor against the wall; or a hanging sheet of cardboard with several large holes outlined with colorful circles.

Have children stand behind the counter to throw the balls or bean bags into the target. Children can sign up for turns, take a ticket, or wait at the

Even three-year-olds can jump and throw a ball into a basket when it's at their height, and take great pride in doing so.

counter for a turn, thus giving them yet another opportunity to practice social turn-taking skills.

Your throwing booth can become a "feed the animal" experience whenever you are featuring animal activities in the other learning centers. Put out animal food (bean bags) on the counter of the throwing booth, and have an animal "mouth" against the wall for them to throw the food into. A circle with animal ears, eyes, nose, and a large hole for a mouth drawn on a cardboard carton can serve as the animal for the children to feed. Bean bags can be thrown overhand or underhand into the mouth. Homemade bean bags can be made of banana-shaped pieces of yellow cloth filled with dry beans and sewn together to represent bananas for a monkey; green bean bags can be catnip for a cat; white bean bags can be bones for a dinosaur or alligator.

Catching is often a more difficult skill for preschoolers than throwing. Their reflexes are not as developed as they will be by the time they reach kindergarten. Nevertheless, preschool children appreciate the opportunity to practice catching as well as throwing if you **set up a catching coop as a station** for two children to use together. To help them control their catches in the beginning, have each child wear a catching mit on his nonthrowing hand. Sew or glue a strip or two of hook-and-loop fasteners to the palm of a regular mitten. Glue strips of the other half of the fastener to a foam ball. Children can throw the ball to one another or up to a target against the wall, trying to catch it when it comes down. The two children will also be practicing the social skills of give and take as well as language skills as they talk with each other during the activity.

• Creative Movement

Creative movement may be occurring in various parts of the classroom: perhaps in the Music Center as children explore with their bodies the sound and movement of wind; perhaps in the circle-time circle when the whole class moves creatively to "dinosaur clump" music. Creative movement can also be an individual large motor activity at a station in the Large Motor Center. **Fasten a hula hoop to the floor, or place masking tape down in a small ring in a space that you designate as the dancing ring.** Locate two dancing rings next to each other if you want two individuals to practice dancing movement at the same time.

What will the dancers do? If you read a story to a small group about a certain type of movement or dance and then place a tape player near the dancing ring, one or more children can try doing dancing movements to music while staying within the ring. The book *Ayu and the Perfect Moon* by David Cox (1984) is a simple, beautifully illustrated story of the Balinese girl Ayu, who dances the Lelong dance in the village square when the moon is full. The pictures show Ayu practicing the dance, being dressed in dancer's clothes of red and gold with a golden crown on her head, and finally doing the dance with her feet and hands and eyes.

+ **Make a paper crown for your dancers, and let them move to music as Ayu did or as they would like to,** staying inside the dancing ring. You can use taped flute music or music from the movie *The King and I*. Such tapes are often available from the public library. **A child from the Music Center**
+ **can also play on a xylophone while a dancer moves within the ring.**

+ Dancing ring movements are especially well suited to **a child in a wheel chair** who may only be able to move the upper part of his body. For another
+ activity, **put a chair in the dancing ring and have each child try dancing** to music played as they sit in the chair. Can you think of other creative movement ideas for an individual to perform within the dancing ring? Group movement and dancing can take place at circle time in the classroom or in the gymnasium.

+ **Props** such as a hat, cap, crown, feather headdress, cape, paper wings, flag, streamers, or "jet-pack" may be all that a child needs **to motivate him-**
+ **or herself to move to the music** you provide for the dancing ring. Try a new dance every week, and soon, this station will become one of the most popular ones in the Large Motor Center. Children enjoy the challenge of dancing in one spot within a ring once they have tried it. In addition, such an activity promotes creativity as children invent their own movements to go with the music and the props.

• • • • • • • • • • • **The Teacher's Role in the Large Motor Center**

Most classrooms obviously do not contain space enough for all the stations described to be set up at the same time, nor should they be. Two or three stations at a time are the most your children can use to best advantage. How will you know which to provide of the ones described:

Walking rink	Leaping lizards lodge
Running pad	Balancing/bending bower
Riding ring	Crawling/creeping chamber
Jumping pad	Climbing corner
Frog pond	Throwing booth
Basketball jump	Catching coop
Hopping pad	Dancing ring

+ The **particular stations you set up will depend upon the needs and interests of the children, based on your observations**. As you do in each of the other learning centers in the classroom, you will be observing individual children to determine their large motor abilities. In this case, the 3-M formula of manipulation, mastery, and meaning is not as important as the actual physical skill development of walking, running, jumping, hopping, leaping, balancing, bending, climbing, crawling, creeping, throwing, catching, and moving creatively.

Observe individuals on the playground, in the gymnasium, and in the classroom, recording on note cards their ability, first of all, to walk and run with ease and confidence. If some of the children exhibit developmental lags in these areas, set up stations in the Large Motor Center to promote these skills. As children progress in these abilities, other stations can be added and the original stations put aside for the time being.

In addition to children's developmental needs, **your rationale for including particular stations can involve the children's own interests as well as the integration of large motor experiences with other classroom activities.** The throwing booth is a popular station in some classrooms because   + certain children like to throw. The frog pond may become the focus of jumping activities because of the live frog in the Science Center terrarium. The riding ring may increase in popularity when a rodeo or car race comes to town.

How long should a station remain set up in the Large Motor Center? This is a teacher's judgment call. So long as the station is serving the needs of the children and curriculum, it can remain. However, because we realize that young children learn best when they are challenged by activities slightly above their abilities and that young children participate more frequently when activities and materials exhibit some novelty, you will want to **add intriguing new stations to the Large Motor Center when interest in present activities begins to lag. Keep track of the numbers and names of children**   + **using the various stations on a daily basis.** Use this information at the   + weekly planning sessions to determine when to add or eliminate a station.

On the other hand, do not eliminate a new station just because few children are using it. **If there is a need for a jumping pad,** for instance, **but few children are using it, it is up to you and your staff to stimulate children's interest in jumping.** Read them a book such as *Moon Jump* by Mustapha   + Matura (1988). It is the story of Cayal, who loved to jump so much that he eventually jumped all the way up to the moon. **Transform your jumping pad into the surface of the moon by taping to the floor a laminated circle with craters drawn on it.** Have a man in the moon as a separate cutout, taped to   + the floor nearby to watch the children jump. How high can they jump? Let them tell the man in the moon. Children enjoy engaging their imaginations like this, and your jumping pad should take on a new life when everyone tries a "moon jump"!

Thus, it is up to you and your children, as well as their interests and needs, to determine the activities you will include in your Large Motor Center and when to change them. Physical skills in young children do not develop overnight. It takes time. Give your children the time and the opportunity to try out the various large motor skills on their own. If the activities you provide are interesting enough, children will happily take the time to practice each of these skills.

IDEAS +
in CHAPTER 12

1. *Setting up the Large Motor Center*
  a. Use flexible, multiple-use equipment. (p. 270)
  b. Have children create their own climbing-crawling-sliding apparatus. (p. 271)
  c. Mount pictures of children involved in large motor activities enlarged from toy catalogs. (p. 271)

2. *Promoting walking*
  a. Have children practice walking up and down steps on equipment such as a walking boat. (p. 271)
  b. Lead children in walking or marching activities in place with action chants. (p. 272)
  c. Set up a walking rink station in the Large Motor Center with chairs and a rope or tape on the floor. (p. 272)
  d. Have children take colored tickets for walking, jogging, hopping, or tiptoeing. (p. 272)
  e. Mount a name chart on the wall for use with peel-off stickers. (p. 272)
  f. Use the walking rink for animal walking. (p. 272)
  g. Make a walking trail around the room with contact paper cutouts. (p. 272)
  h. Children can ice skate and ski on unit blocks. (p. 272)
  i. Children can go on hikes in the walking rink wearing knapsacks. (p. 273)
  j. Let children practice walking with crutches. (p. 273)

3. *Promoting running*
  a. Set up a running pad in the Large Motor Center. (p. 273)
  b. Have a running/riding ring as a station. (p. 273)
  c. Have children run rings and take a number that corresponds. (p. 273)
  d. Have children gallop on stick horses around the ring. (p. 273)
  e. Try to discourage horse races. (p. 273)
  f. Have a rodeo with stick bulls or bucking horses. (p. 273)
  g. Have a motorcycle rally or car show. (p. 274)
  h. Have a kangaroo hop or camel trot. (p. 274)
  i. Bring large wooden riding vehicles to this area. (p. 274)

4. *Promoting jumping, hopping, leaping*
  a. Set up a jumping pad as a station. (p. 274)
  b. Have a frog pond for jumping. (p. 274)
  c. Set up a basketball jump station (p. 274)
  d. Have a hopping pad station or a hopping trail. (p. 275)
  e. Set up a leaping lizards lodge station. (p. 275)

5. *Promoting balancing, bending*
   a. Set up a balancing bower station with a balance beam or a walking board. (p. 275)
   b. Place a pole between two chair backs for ducking under. (p. 275)
   c. Have a pick-up-chips bending activity. (p. 275)
   d. Pan for gold in the bending bower. (p. 275)
   e. Gather dinosaur food in the bending bower. (p. 276)

6. *Promoting crawling, creeping*
   a. Have a crawling chamber as a station. (p. 276)
   b. Have a large cardboard carton or pairs of chairs act as a car tunnel. (p. 276)
   c. Sing a song as children creep through the tunnel. (p. 276)
   d. Make a subway tunnel. (p. 276)
   e. Have a tent or card-table tent with a low opening. (p. 276)

7. *Promote climbing*
   a. Add a climbing corner with plastic milk crates as a station. (p. 277)
   b. Remove the door of a small closet, and fasten rungs across the opening from bottom to top. (p. 277)
   c. Put large, hollow blocks in the climbing corner. (p. 277)

8. *Promoting throwing, catching*
   a. Set up a throwing booth as a station with lightweight, nonbouncing bean bags and balls. (p. 277)
   b. Have a feed-the-animal bean bag activity in the throwing booth. (p. 279)
   c. Set up a catching coop for two children to use together. (p. 279)

9. *Promoting creative movement*
   a. Set up a dancing ring as a station for creative movement. (p. 279)
   b. Have a paper crown for a Balinese dancer. (p. 280)
   c. Have children do creative movement while sitting in a chair or a wheelchair. (p. 280)
   d. Have a child from the Music Center play the xylophone for a child in the dancing ring. (p. 280)
   e. Use props such as hats, caps, crowns, feather headdresses, and so on to stimulate creative movement. (p. 280)

10. *Changing the Large Motor Center*
   a. Observe individual children to determine which stations to set up. (p. 280)
   b. Other stations can be set up based on the children's interests and curricular activities. (p. 281)
   c. Add new stations when interest in present activities begins to lag. (p. 281)
   d. Keep track of numbers and names of children using stations on a daily basis. (p. 281)
   e. Where particular stations are necessary but not being used, stimulate children's interest in them by reading an appropriate book. (p. 281)
   f. Transform your jumping pad into the surface of the moon. (p. 281)

OTHER SOURCES

Beaty, J. J. (1992). *Skills for preschool teachers.* Columbus, OH: Merrill Publishing Company.

Cherry, C., Godwin, D., & Staples, J. (1989). *Is the left brain always right?* Belmont, CA: David S. Lake Publishers.

Javernick, E. (1988). Johnny's not jumping: Can we help obese children? *Young Children 43* (2), 18–23.

Sullivan, M. (1982). *Feeling strong, feeling free: Movement exploration for young children.* Washington, DC: National Association for the Education of Young Children.

CHILDREN'S BOOKS

Cox, D. (1984). *Ayu and the perfect moon.* London, England: The Bodley Head.

Kalan, R. (1981). *Jump frog, jump.* New York: William Morrow and Company.

Martin, B., Jr., & Archaumbault, J. (1986). *White Dynamite and Curly Kidd.* New York: Henry Holt and Company.

Matura, M. (1988). *Moon jump.* New York: Alfred A Knopf.

Rowe, E. (1973). *Giant dinosaurs.* New York: Scholastic, Inc.

TRY IT
YOURSELF

1. Observe each of the children in the class, on the playground, or in the indoors Large Motor Center to determine whether they walk and run with ease and confidence.

2. Set up the Large Motor Center to include three stations to promote three different skills as described in the chapter. (At least one station should feature walking or running if your observations show this as a need.)

3. Stimulate children to pursue the activity at one of the stations you have set up by reading them a book as described.

4. Observe and record the numbers and names of children using the stations in the Large Motor Center on three different days.

5. Change the stations to interest more children based on your observations.

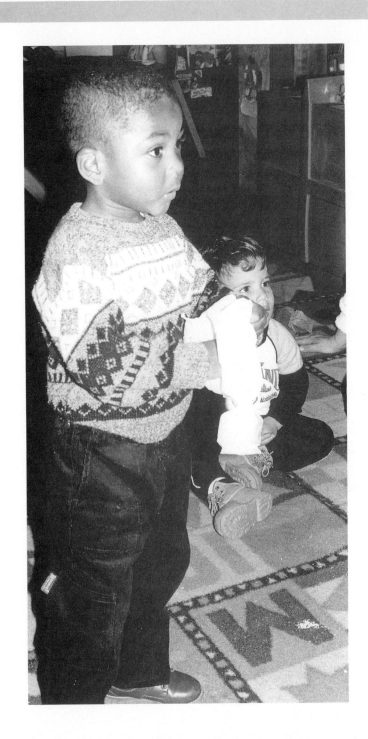

PLANNING FOR INDIVIDUALS

LEARNING LADDER

Let's climb up the ladder,
One step up;
Where we start won't matter,
Two steps up;
Every rung goes higher,
Three steps up;
What if we should tire?
Four steps up;
There are friends to go up,
Five steps up;

They won't let us slow up,
Six steps up;
Now the air is clearer,
Seven steps up;
Look, the top is nearer!
Eight steps up;
Oh, we're up so high now!
Nine steps up,
Maybe we can fly now!
Ten steps up: Whee-ee-ee!!!

• • • • • • • • • • • Planning for Something to Happen

An old cliché states that "if you want something to happen, you must plan for it to happen." Furthermore, you can add, "If you want something wonderful to happen with the children in your classroom, then you must make wonderful plans." It is true. Although your program can proceed without a great deal of formal planning once you have set it up, you cannot expect particular results to occur unless you have made plans for them to occur. Setting up your classroom into the ten learning centers as described in the previous chapters is the foundation for such ongoing planning. It speaks to the principal theme of the Appropriate Practices Curriculum: "Let the environment do the teaching."

Now it is up to you, your staff, and your children to plan particular activities for individual children, based on their needs and interests, that will promote their development of physical, cognitive, language, social, emotional, and creative skills. Such planning is not a chore but a challenge: the directions for a marvelous learning adventure that you and the children can pursue together. Making such plans with staff members and children can be as exciting as carrying them out.

• • • • • • • • • • Yearlong Plans and Monthly Themes

At the beginning of the year, you and your staff can discuss the overall topics you will be dealing with throughout the year. Focus on the children   +
themselves and the things that make a difference to them personally. Such topics may include:

The child: his or her family, home, body, pets
The neighborhood: buildings, stores, services, people
The environment: schoolyard, trees, air, weather, birds
People who help: firefighter, police officer, mail carrier, doctor, librarian

Current events: space shuttle, new highway, ice jam in river

Next, you need to **consider how each of the learning centers can con-**
+ **tribute to these overall topics.** Choose which of the centers to begin with,
+ and **map out a list of possible themes for the ten or twelve months** of the
year during which your program operates. Some programs choose to start
with the neighborhood as the first topic because children need to and want
to learn about this new place where they will be during the day. In that case,
you may want to begin with a Block Center theme for the first month such
as "Buildings in Our Neighborhood."

The teacher in charge of the Block Center can take small groups of children on a walk around the school and the neighborhood, bringing back instant print photos of the buildings with the children looking at them. These
photos can be displayed in the Block Center to encourage building of any
kind that the children want to do. Remember that many children are not at
the mastery or meaning level of building, especially at the beginning of the
year, so they may not be ready to build representations of buildings.

Plans need to be made at the same time about how the other nine centers
can contribute to this overall theme of "our neighborhood" during the first
month. Here are some possibilities:

Computer Center: Have the program "Stickybear Opposites" available
for the children to use. Its graphics include scenes and objects that children
may see in the neighborhood such as: stairs, ladder, seesaw, hill, fence,
wall, pump, road, cars, airplane, bridge, stoplight, box, house, plant. At
some point, sit with the children who are using the program and ask them
which of the objects they saw on their field trip around the neighborhood.
You can make a list and mount it in the Computer Center and the Art Center. Make it fun by **asking the children to help you find out about the**
+ **things in Stickybear's neighborhood.** Later in the month, the children can
use the program "Stickybear Shapes" and try to find circles in Stickybear's
neighborhood.

Art Center: Have scissors and magazines available at some point during
the month. Children may want to tear or cut out pictures similar to the
things they have seen in the neighborhood. Some may want to **find pictures**
+ **of things in Stickybear's neighborhood.** They could paste together a collage
of the neighborhood pictures. Another week, you can bring in a large cardboard carton, cut out a door and window, and then put out paints for the
children to use in painting their house.

Music Center: The children can sing a song about their house or their
neighborhood. Make up the words to a well-known melody such as *Go In
and Out the Windows.*

Go round and round the building,
Go round and round the building,

Go round and round the building,
As we have done today.

Go up and down the sidewalk,
Go up and down the sidewalk,
Go up and down the sidewalk,
As we have done today,

They can make motions with hands and body or actually move around in a circle or a follow-the-leader line.

Story Center: Books about houses can be read by the teachers to small groups of children during the month. Such books as *This Old House, Shaker Lane,* and *Building a House,* as discussed in Chapter 3, can be used.

Writing Center: The children in this center can go outside with the teacher and look for *signs* in the neighborhood. The teacher can write down the words on the signs spotted by the children or take instant print photos of them. Back in the Writing Center, the teacher can **print these signs on posterboard.** Children can try to find and match the letters on the signs from their sets of magnetic letters or alphabet blocks.

Manipulative/Math Center: Let children **build houses and other buildings of Stickybear's neighborhood** from sets of table blocks, interlocking blocks, or bristle blocks. Be sure to take a photo of their buildings along with the builders for display in the center.

Science Center: This center can challenge the children to **find out what growing things there are in the neighborhood.** If it is a city neighborhood, the children may see plants growing in someone's window, trees in a park, a dandelion in a sidewalk crack, or weeds on a vacant lot. Instant print photos can record the findings. Children's questions and comments can help lead the teacher in charge of this center to particular followup activities.

Dramatic Play Center: This center can feature people the children see in the neighborhood. Bring in clothes and props and have a neighborhood get-together for children to dress up like the people they have seen: The mail carrier, police officer, street cleaner, taxi driver, or house painter can **have a pretend neighborhood picnic in the center.**

Large Motor Center: What kind of movements did the children discover on their field trip around the neighborhood? Was someone walking a dog? Riding a bike? Driving a truck? Pushing a baby buggy? **The walking ring can feature baby-buggy-pushing** for a few days—or riding on large wooden vehicles. Drivers of the vehicles can wear a truck driver's cap or taxi driver's hat.

• • • • • • • • • • Learning Center Themes

In like manner, each of the ten learning centers can feature an overall monthly theme to be used in planning for the entire curriculum. Some possible themes to select from are:

Block Center
"Buildings in our Community"
"The Fire Station" (or airport, library, zoo, hospital)
"Constructing a Building"
"Building Roads and Bridges"
"Safety in the Street"
"Visit to a Farm" (or ranch)
"What's in a Museum?"
"Launching a Space Shuttle"

Computer Center
"Working in a Computer Center"
"Space Control Center"
"Spaceship Operation"
"TV News Station" (or weather station)
"Artist's Studio"
"Visit to a Newspaper Office"
"Dinosaurs Live Here"
"Can You Move through a Maze?"
"Make a Mask for Halloween"
"Putting Animals Together"
"People's Faces"

Manipulative/Math Center
"Making a Collection"
"Counting Cars and Trucks"
"What Makes a Million?"
"Tickets on Sale"
"Mailing Letters"
"Measuring the Room"
"Guess Your Height and Weight"
"Building a Race Car"
"Card Trading Center"

Story Center
"Talking Animal Stories"
"Adventure Books and Stories"
"Books and Stories About American Heroes"
"Curious Creature Stories"

"Pets, Pets, and More Pets"
"Stories to Make You Hungry"
"Nighttime Stories"
"Mystery Stories"

Writing Center
"How a Book Is Made"
"Writing Letters to Santa"
"Classroom Newspaper"
"The Greeting Card Shop"
"The Sign Shop"
"Postcards Printed Here"
"Alphabet Letters Are Everywhere"
"Scribbles Are Natural"

Art Center
"Painting the House"
"The Colors of the Rainbow"
"The Colors of a Rainy Day"
"Red Is Best"
"An Art Gallery of Pictures"
"The Artist of the Month"
"Purple People Eater"
"Statues Start Here"

Music Center
"Shoes Are Special"
"Sounds of Spring"
"Drums Can Talk"
"Our Strumming Band"
"Sing a Song of Self"
"Clap Your Hands"
"Puppets Can Sing"
"Pet Songs We Know"

Science Center
"Looking Near and Far"
"Our Bodies Are Wonderful"
"Homes for Pets"
"Catching Snowflakes"
"What Makes a Shadow?"
"How to Hug a Tree"
"We Need Water"
"Plant Pets"

Dramatic Play Center
"The Doctor Is In"
"Sally's Shoe Store"
"Our Super Supermarket"
"Polly's Pets"
"The Train Station"
"Going on a Bus"
"Our Pizza Parlor"
"The Fire Station"

Large Motor Center
"Creature Crawling"
"Mountain Climbing"
"A Rodeo"
"Ice Skating Rink"
"Tracking Mr. Big Foot"
"Exercise Stations"
"Moon Jump"
"Feed the Animal"
"Dancing Rings"

• • • • • • • • • • Child Input into Theme Planning

Themes like this can evolve from the children's own interests as they build with blocks, take field trips, try out new ideas, or gain information about topics of interest. A **teacher working with a group of children in the Block Center,** for instance, **can ask them which theme that particular center could sponsor for the next month.** Listen carefully to what the children say, and make a list of their ideas. They may also have their own ideas for activities they would like to pursue that will carry out the theme. Be aware that you need to follow through on some of the children's suggestions once you have involved them in the planning. Let them know that not every suggestion can be followed. They may want to vote. What an exciting experience it is for them to have input into their classroom's operation!

On the other hand, such themes can come from staff planning as you brainstorm ideas or consider topics that will stimulate children to explore on their own. While child input is valuable, it is the classroom staff that has the overall responsibility of meeting the needs of all the children.

• • • • • • • • • • Monthly Planning Sessions

+   **Set aside time to plan for the month ahead.** A particular afternoon can be selected, say, the last Friday in the month. This is the time for the entire staff to gather to talk over what has occurred with children and activities over the past four weeks and to make plans for the next month. Many program directors find that having **one staff member in charge of particular learning centers for a month at a time** works best.

Early childhood programs often have two or three staff members per classroom: a teacher, an assistant teacher, and an aide or volunteer. When this is the case, the learning centers can then be divided up, with **each adult in charge of three centers for a month at a time** and one of the teachers keeping an eye on a fourth center.

In programs in which space is at a premium, **learning centers can sometimes be combined spacewise** and still provide separate activities for the children. For example, the Computer Center can be combined with the Manipulative/Math Center or with the Writing Center. In another arrangement, the Story Center can be combined with the Writing Center. Staff members still need to be in charge of each area for a month at a time. The staff member who is **the computer "expert" should share expertise with the other staff members** so that they, too, can enjoy this activity with the children.

Staff members can choose or be assigned to the centers. The lead teacher may decide to start out the year herself with "Buildings in the Neighborhood" in the Block Center. Other staff members can then brainstorm and add ideas about how their particular centers will support this neighborhood theme week by week. Flexibility should be the keyword. Not every plan works successfully. Some need refinement. Some need rethinking. The monthly planning session is the time to discuss such issues.

Planning the Weekly Schedule

Once a monthly theme is determined, the staff members can begin designing overall weekly plans and detailed daily plans for the learning centers they will oversee. First of all, **each learning center needs to consider how it can contribute to the overall monthly theme during four different weeks.** For the month of October, for example, one program chose "Stories to Make You Hungry," sponsored by the Story Center. The Story Center staff member brought out **a number of children's books about food as a starting point for staff discussion.**

The staff members had in mind choosing a different fruit or vegetable for each week, having some sort of field trip (weekly if possible), having a weekly cooking activity, and culminating in a visit to a pumpkin farm and the carving of a jack-o-lantern for Halloween. As they looked at the storybooks and talked together, they decided on the following subthemes and activities for the four weeks:

Week 1: Apples
Story: *Apple Pigs* by Ruth Orbach
      Applebet by Clyde Watson
      Eating the Alphabet by Lois Ehlert
Field Trip: To the supermarket down the street to buy apples
Cooking: Making apple-and-cinnamon snacks
      Making applesauce

Week 2: Pears
Story: *Each Peach Pear Plum* by Janet and Allan Ahlberg
      Don't Forget the Bacon by Pat Hutchins
      Eating the Alphabet by Lois Ehlert
Field Trip: To a supermarket down the street to buy pears
Cooking: Making pear-and-peanut butter snacks

Week 3: Pumpkins
Story: *The Biggest Pumpkin Ever* by Steven Kroll
      The Mystery of the Flying Orange Pumpkin by Steven Kellogg
      The Vanishing Pumpkin by Tony Johnson
      Eating the Alphabet by Lois Ehlert
Field Trip: To a pumpkin patch to buy three pumpkins
Activity: Carving jack-o-lanterns

Week 4: Spaghetti
Story: *Daddy Makes the Best Spaghetti* by Anna G. Hines
      Cloudy with a Chance of Meatballs by Judi Barrett
      Strega Nona by Tomie de Paola
Cooking: Making spaghetti and later having a family night with
      spaghetti supper

The fourth week's "spaghetti" idea came from the teacher in charge of the Story Center for October who wanted to share a favorite Halloween story of hers with the children: *Strega Nona*, about the good witch whose helper starts the magic pot making spaghetti but cannot get it to stop. One of the fathers had offered to come in and make spaghetti for the class, so this seemed an opportune time to have a family night supper that the children could help to prepare, with apple and pear salad on the side and three lighted jack-o-lanterns for decorations.

The **next phase of their planning involved deciding on specific activities for the learning centers.** Each of the learning centers was already set up and operating, so these would be additional activities within the centers to support the monthly/weekly themes as well as to help individual children accomplish their own learning goals. Because this program operated half-days for five mornings a week, the teachers planned some activities that would go on for more than one day, giving all the children a chance to participate.

Each of the three teachers wrote the description of an activity on a card for each of her three learning centers and hung the cards on a hook on the Daily Schedule. On the back of each card was a transition activity she planned to use to help the children move from one location to the next. All the transition activities were kept the same for a week at a time within the learning center so that the children would learn to know them.

The activities for the first week, "Apples," included:

Block Center:
Pictures of farm buildings displayed (house, barn, silo).

Accessories: Figures of people, farm animals, tractors, trucks.

Transition: Block pick-up game—Sing *Old MacDonald Had a Farm* ("and on his farm he had some blocks . . . with a block, block here, and a block, block there"). Pick up block at every "block" word, put in small wagon, and deliver to block shelf.

(Same activities every day)

Computer Center:
Introduction to computer program by reading *Eating the Alphabet* by Lois Ehlert (M–F).

Using the computer program "Stickybear ABC" (M–F).

Mon: Can children find the apple graphic?

Tues: Can children find the grape graphic?

Wed: Can children find the orange (fruit) graphic?

Thurs: Can children find the vegetable graphic?

Fri: Can children find the yellow (color) graphic?

Transition: Take an alphabet letter from the teacher's grab-bag; when teacher calls letter child is holding, he or she can go to wash up for snack.

Manipulative/Math Center:
Have a different set of sorting material on table every day to support apple theme.

Mon: Take small group to supermarket to buy apples, sugar, and cinnamon; afterwards, help cut up apples into slices for dipping into sugar and cinnamon mixture for snack time.

Tues: Set of little plastic fruit counters; sort into cups with pictures on them of apple, orange, lemon; help slice apples for snack.

Wed: A tray of teddy-bear counters in various colors; sort out all the orange bears into an orange box; slice apples for snack.

Thurs: Collection of buttons of all kinds and colors; sort out orange buttons and yellow buttons and drop into slot on orange box and yellow box.

Fri: Wooden shapes box and pieces to sort and put into slots of the
right shape; talk about circles.

Transition: Say chant together using different child's name until all
are gone—

"One apple, two apples, three apples, four,

Betty, put your game away,

Then go out the door."

Story Center:

Each week have on a table the three books about fruits and food
previously mentioned. Groups can switch books each day for three
days; teacher can read stories to individuals when requested.

No transition planned.

Writing Center:

Have three-dimensional alphabet letters out; let children try to match
letters to outline of letters on posterboard; on some days, have out
magnetic letters with metal backing board.

Transition: Sing *Alphabet Song* while picking up and putting away
letters.

Art Center:

Mon: Make "apple pigs" as described in the storybook of the same
name, or with apples, toothpicks, marshmallows, and pipe-cleaners.

Tues: Same as Monday.

Wed: Make play-dough together; play with small rolling pins.

Thurs: Color play-dough red with food coloring; use small rolling pins
and round cookie cutters.

Fri: Red play-dough with ice-cream scoop and melon baller to make
"apples" of different sizes.

Easels out every day with red, yellow, orange paint.

Transition: Clean up area and take a circle card in red, yellow, or
orange; teacher calls color card holders to wash up for snack time.

Music Center:

Children can listen to music on tapes every day.

They can learn to tape record their own songs.

They can sing with the teacher to the tune of *The Farmer in the Dell:*

"Come to our apple feast,

Come to our apple feast,

Come man, come bird, come woolly beast,

Come to our apple feast." (adapted from the sign in the story *Apple
Pigs*)

Transition: When it is time to get ready for snack time, they can sing:

"Get ready now for snack,
Get ready now for snack,
Ann and Barb and Andrew, too,
Get ready now for snack."

Science Center:

On Thurs. and Fri. do cooking activity with interested children on
concept of "cooking changes things": make applesauce for snack.
No transition planned; snack may be later on these two days while
applesauce cools.

Dramatic Play Center:

Set up supermarket with empty food containers from home, plastic
fruits, paper sacks, toy cash register; children who went on field trip
to supermarket on Mon. can help operate store.
No transition planned.

Large Motor Center:

The following stations set up for the month: "Step-up-and-down" (set
of steps up against wall); "Walking Ring" circle with colored tickets for
walking, tiptoeing, hopping, and jogging; "Apple Throw" (basket
fastened high on wall with red yarn balls to throw into it; children
need to climb up on stool afterwards to retrieve balls from basket).
No transition planned.

• • • • • • • • • • Plans for Individuals Based on 3-M Observations

The basis of your planning for individual children is the 3-M observa-   +
tions you and the staff have made of children's interactions with materials
and with one another in the learning centers. You have recorded information about the children's three levels of activity interaction (manipulation,
mastery, and meaning) as well as their three types of social interaction (solitary play, parallel play, and cooperative play). Now you must record interpretive information on the back of the Child Interaction Form under the
headings: "Accomplishments" and "Needs." Only then will you be able to fill
in the third item on the form, "Plans." In order to make plans for individual
children that will satisfy their observed needs, you must interpret the data
you have recorded on the face of the form.

• • • • • • • • • • Interpreting Recorded Information

The children's levels of interactions, along with their actions and words,
are the basis for information recorded on the reverse side of the form under
"Accomplishments." Next on the reverse side of the form comes "Needs." It

is here that the observer must interpret the data in order to determine a child's needs. In addition to the recorded data, the interpreter should use knowledge of the child's ordinary behavior in the classroom.

For example, Leslie is four years old and has attended this particular program for the past three months. She spends a great deal of time in the Science Center with the animals. She watches the fish in the aquarium, making comments or asking questions about them. She feeds the guinea pig, helps clean out its cage, and likes to pick it up and carry it around. She is the one who named it Whistler for the noise it makes. However, everything she does in the Science Center is by herself in a solitary manner.

The teacher checks on the data recorded about Leslie in the other centers as well as asking the other staff members about Leslie's interactions. She finds that Leslie enjoys painting at the easel in the Art Center; plays by herself in the Dramatic Play Center, often dressing the dolls, feeding them, and taking them for a ride in the baby buggy; and plays table games by herself in the Manipulative Center. Leslie has never been observed playing in the Block Center, the Computer Center, or the Writing Center. She sometimes looks at books by herself in either the Story or Science Centers.

The teacher decides to put together a cumulative record of Leslie's interactions for purposes of interpretation and planning. After reviewing previously recorded data about Leslie and talking with other staff members, she completes the Child Interaction Form on the following page.

From this data, the teacher makes the following interpretation on the back of the Child Interaction Form:

Accomplishments

Strong interest in animals, animal stories, animal names; in painting; in matching games; in feeding animals and dolls; in looking at books.

Speaks in expanded sentences to teachers, animals, sometimes dolls; articulates clearly.

Is at mastery level in dramatic play, matching games, and art; at meaning level in science animal activities.

Needs

To interact with other children, talking to and playing with them.

To try out activities in Block, Computer, and Writing Centers.

To advance to meaning level in art, dramatic play, and math games.

• • • • • • • • • • Planning for the Individual Child

In making plans for an individual child such as Leslie, the teacher takes into consideration both her accomplishments and her needs. Then, she lists possible **activities that will use Leslie's interests and accomplishments to help her fulfill her needs.** To involve Leslie in playing with other children, for instance, the teacher decides it might be helpful for her to start

FIGURE 13–1	Child Interaction Form

Child _____Leslie W._____ Observer _____D. B._____

Center _Dram. Play, Manip., Story, Art, Sci._ Date _____9/15 - 11/15_____

CHILD INTERACTION FORM
With Materials

Manipulation Level   Actions/Words
(Child moves materials around
without using them as intended.)

Mastery Level   Actions/Words
(Child uses materials as *Dram. Play: Dresses & feeds dolls; rides dolls in buggy.*
intended, over and over.) *Manip.: Plays lotto, pegboard, number matching games.*
Story/Sci.: Looks at books, esp. animal stories.
Art: Paints at easel - lines, circles, scribbles. (Fills many sheets.)

Meaning Level   Actions/Words
(Child uses materials in
new and creative ways.) *Sci.: Watches fish in aquarium. Asks, "What's that
one's name? Can I feed him?" Feeds guinea pig, talks to it: cleans
cage; carries guinea pig around: names it "Whistler" for the noise it makes.*

With Other Children

Solitary Play   Actions/Words
(Child plays with
materials by self.)
*Plays by self in Art, Sci., Dram. Play, Manip. & Story Centers; talks to fish,
guinea pig, dolls & teachers; seldom talks with other children.*

Parallel Play   Actions/Words
(Child plays next to others with same
materials but not involved with them.)
*Did one group art project — painting a cardboard carton to be used
for house in Dram. Play, but worked parallel to others without talking.*

Cooperative Play   Actions/Words
(Child plays together with
others and same materials.) *Participates in group singing, finger plays &
circle games when led by teacher; sometimes talks with other
children during these games; knows words to songs & games.*

In making plans for an individual child, the teacher takes into consideration both the child's accomplishments and her needs.

with one other child. If this works, the teacher will watch to see whether she makes connections with other children as well, or whether the teacher may need to help her get involved in group activities. The teacher then proposes on paper several ideas that will be discussed at one of the daily summary sessions or weekly planning sessions and may be implemented in the days to follow:

1. Change classroom job chart to teams of two children for each job instead of only one child; add jobs of "feeding fish" and "washing doll clothes" to chart along the jobs of "feeding Whistler," "cleaning Whistler's cage;" two children will need to sign up for each job and work together.

2. Suggest that Leslie learn to play the computer program *Stickybear ABC* to see how many animals she can find; this is a good beginner's program; two children use the computer at once; if Leslie gets interested in using the computer, bring in *Stickybear Opposites.*

3. Bring in books *The Guinea Pig ABC* and *Guinea Pigs Far and Near* to the Story Center or Computer Center when Leslie is using the ABC and Opposites programs.

4. Suggest that Leslie take a photo of Whistler with the class instant print camera and make her own book about him in the Writing Center with the teacher's help.

· · · · · · · · · · · **Weekly Planning Sessions**

Plans for Leslie as noted above will more likely be discussed and agreed upon at the weekly planning session. They will then be implemented for as long as necessary. The Child Interaction Form will be returned to a weekly planning folder for its results to be discussed next week. Did the plans work out? Is Leslie interacting with at least one other child? Should the plans continue to be implemented for another week, or should other ideas be considered?

Planning sessions like this not only provide the opportunity for the entire staff to have input on the accomplishments and needs of individual children, but also to make **an ongoing evaluation of the plans for individuals.** Are the plans working out? Should they be continued? Are new plans necessary? The staff looks back at the needs of the child as indicated on the Child Interaction Form. Then they decide whether these needs are being addressed by the plans. If not, new plans are made for the child.

· · · · · · · · · · · **Learning Goals for Individuals**

Some programs prefer to make long-range plans for individuals in each of the classroom learning centers. After the child has been in the program long enough for the staff to become acquainted with him or her, the teachers look over recorded data on the child and decide on a set of learning goals. These are referred to at the monthly planning sessions that follow and added to or changed as the year progresses. A sample set of "Learning Goals for Joel," dated October 1, reads as follows:

Block Center
Joel is at the manipulative stage; help him progress to mastery of block building.

Computer Center
Joel does "piano-playing" of keys; find program that he can master; pair him with child who knows program.

Manipulative/Math Center

Can he count with counters rather than just playing with them?

Story Center

Help him learn to sit still through a whole story.

Writing Center

Interest him in using this center; he has not used it so far.

Art Center

Interest him in using this center; he has not used it so far.

Music Center

Joel listens but does not participate in songs; help him become involved.

Science Center

Joel shows great interest in insects and animals but doesn't stay still long enough to accomplish project; help him work with a partner on an insect project.

Dramatic Play

Joel seems to avoid this center; involve him with a partner playing the role of a scientist or jungle explorer; his language skills need developing; more practice in conversation.

Large Motor Center

Joel loves to run in the running rink; give him many experiences; have him help others to accomplish running games.

Learning goals such as these are kept in Joel's folder from month to month. They **are shared with staff members at planning sessions and with**
\+   **parents at parent conferences.** The goals are then updated when appropriate at the monthly planning sessions. Thus, the program stays responsive to the needs and interests of individuals.

• • • • • • • • • • The Total Group: Circle Time

Is there any place for a total group activity within the self-directed learning environment? Yes, very definitely. **It is important for individual chil-**
\+   **dren to feel a part of the total class** as well. Your plans should call for **activities that lend themselves well to the performance of the entire**
\+   **group of children together,** such as songs, fingerplays, storytelling (not book reading, which is better done in small groups), musical games, creative movement and dancing, large motor games, and circle time.

Because circle time itself provides the framework for any or all of these activities, many program directors schedule a daily circle time within which such activities can take place. If **circle time** is scheduled **at the beginning of the daily session,** its purpose is **to welcome the children** and help them make the **transition from home to school** as well as to **introduce them to the activities** available in the various learning centers. If scheduled in the **middle of the day,** circle time often serves as **a change of pace** to speed things up or slow them down and to help children focus on what comes next. Circle time **at the end of the day helps children to recall** what they did, **to clarify** any questions or concerns they might have, and to help them **make the transition from school to home** with a goodbye song or chant.

Whenever it is held, circle time should be planned to help the children focus their attention and interest on the activities at hand. Research has shown that the most successful circle-time activities are stories and music; the least successful are show-and-tell and opening exercises (McAfee, 1985). Whatever is planned, it **should start with a high-interest activity that involves the total group,** thus engaging everyone's attention. **Then, a calming activity** such as a fingerplay or story can slow things down and help to focus the children's attention on what individuals have to say.

In the Appropriate Practice Curriculum, **this sort of total group activity can help to pull together at the end of the day all the separate activities performed by individuals and small groups** in the learning centers, as children volunteer to report on what they have accomplished during the day. Teachers also can give the children information about the activities that interested the teachers most. This interchange thus helps to summarize the day's accomplishments for both children and teachers. Teachers should note such comments for use during the daily summary session.

• • • • • • • • • • •The Daily Schedule

The Daily schedule in the self-directed learning environment is a general plan of time use and activity order that occurs on a day-to-day basis. Its components can be illustrated on a Daily Schedule Chart with cutouts or drawings, as suggested in Chapter 1, so that the children can understand what is happening in their program. **Beside each of the learning center names is a hook** for staff members to **hang color-coded cards with a description of the activity** in their particular learning center, **along with the transition activity** they plan to use to help children move from one component to another of the Daily Schedule. The schedule in a half-day program can include the following components:

Arrival	Story time
Free choice (learning centers)	Outdoor or gym
Snack	Closing circle

A full-day program can include:

Arrival	Story time
Free choice (learning centers)	Lunch
Morning circle	Rest time
Snack	Free choice (learning centers)
Outdoor or gym	Closing circle

Although the order of the components generally remains the same, **the length of time that each component uses may vary** somewhat from day to day, depending on the type of activities, the children's interests, and spur-of-the moment changes.

· · · · · · · · · · **Daily Summary Session**

At the end of each day, the teachers in charge of the various learning centers take their activity/transition cards off the hooks of the Daily Schedule Chart and **bring the cards along to the summary session.** In addition to discussing individual children, as mentioned previously, **the staff also evaluates the activities** in the various learning centers. Were they carried out successfully by the teachers and the children? How did the children respond? Should there be any changes for the next day? **Ideas and changes are noted on the cards,** and these cards (or new ones) are returned to the hooks in preparation for the next day's activities. **At the end of the week, the cards are placed by subject in a file box.**

The use of activity file cards like this thus captures the spirit of the moment, encourages creative ideas, and helps curriculum planning to be a challenge for the teachers, not a chore. For ideas that work especially well, **some staff members award themselves a star** on their file cards, calling attention to activities they may want to use in the future.

Because each staff member has direct input into daily, weekly, and monthly planning, each tends to give more time and energy in making such plans. **Ideas also blossom when each staff member is responsible for what happens on a daily basis** in his or her particular learning center. When staff members develop excitement about the activities they have proposed and confidence in their ability to carry them out, the whole program takes on a new life. The self-directed learning environment thus applies to staff members as well as to children. And **when teachers are enthusiastic about the curriculum, the children reflect the same zest about their learning.** The classroom thus becomes a stimulant for everyone, and the ripples of excitement started by self-direction spread out into the lives of each child and each teacher involved.

IDEAS+

in CHAPTER 13

1. *Making yearlong plans*

    a. Discuss overall topics with the staff at the beginning of the year. (p. 287)

    b. Decide how each learning center can contribute to overall topics. (p. 288)

    c. Make a list of possible themes for ten or twelve months. (p. 288)

2. *Deciding how learning centers can contribute to a neighborhood theme*

    a. Ask children to help you find out about things in Stickybear's neighborhood in the Computer Center. (p. 288)

    b. Cut out pictures of things in Stickybear's neighborhood in the Art Center. (p. 288)

    c. Print signs in the Writing Center of actual signs found in the outside neighborhood. (p. 289)

    d. Build buildings with table blocks in the Manipulative/Math Center. (p. 289)

    e. Discover on a field trip what growing things live in the school neighborhood. (p. 289)

    f. Have a pretend picnic in the Dramatic Play Center for "people in the neighborhood." (p. 289)

    g. Feature "baby-buggy-pushing" in the walking ring. (p. 289)

3. *Having children contribute to theme planning*

    a. Ask children which theme their particular learning center can sponsor for the next month. (p. 292)

4. *Conducting monthly planning sessions*

    a. Set aside time to plan for the month ahead. (p. 292)

    b. Have one staff member in charge of particular learning centers for a month at a time. (p. 293)

    c. Have each staff member in charge of three centers at a time. (p. 293)

    d. Combine certain learning centers if space is a problem. (p. 293)

    e. Share expertise with one another (e.g., computer expertise). (p. 293)

5. *Planning the weekly schedule*

    a. Decide how each learning center can contribute to the theme. (p. 293)

    b. Bring children's books on the theme to your planning session. (p. 293)

    c. Decide on specific activities for learning centers. (p. 294)

6. *Making plans for individuals based on 3-M observations*

    a. Base planning for individual children on 3-M observations. (p. 297)

    b. Use the child's interests and accomplishments to help fulfill his or her needs. (p. 299)

7. *Conducting weekly planning sessions*

    a. Do an ongoing evaluation of plans for individual children. (p. 301)

    b. Develop learning goals for individuals to be shared with staff and parents. (p. 302)

8. *Conducting circle time*

    a. Help children feel part of the total group. (p. 302)

    b. Have activities that lend themselves to total group involvement. (p. 302)

    c. Use circle time to help children make the transition from home to school, to introduce new activities, to clarify activities, and to make the transition from school to home. (p. 303)

    d. Start with a high-interest activity that involves the total group, followed by a calming activity. (p. 303)

9. *Planning the Daily Schedule*

    a. Have the staff record activities and transitions for their learning centers on cards on the Daily Schedule Chart. (p. 303)

    b. Use various lengths of time for scheduled components, depending on types of activities. (p. 304)

10. *Conducting daily summary sessions*

    a. Spend time at the summary session at the end of the day to share information about children and plan for the next day. (p. 304)

    b. Evaluate the various activities in the learning centers. (p. 304)

    c. Note changes on Daily Schedule Chart cards. (p. 304)

    d. File cards by subject in a file box at the end of the week. (p. 304)

    e. Award a star on cards for outstanding activities. (p. 304)

    f. Be enthusiastic about the curriculum, and children will reflect the same attitude. (p. 304)

REFERENCES CITED

McAfee, O. D. (1985). Circle time: Getting past 'two little pumpkins.' *Young Children 40* (6) 24–29.

CHILDREN'S BOOKS

Ahlberg, J., & Ahlberg, A. (1978). *Each peach pear plum.* New York: Viking Penguin.

Barrett, J. 1978. *Cloudy with a chance of meatballs.* New York: Atheneum.

Barton, B. (1981). *Building a house.* New York: Viking Penguin.

De Paola, T. 1975. *Strega nona.* Englewood Cliffs, NJ: Prentice-Hall.

Duke, K. 1983. *The guinea pig ABC.* New York: E. P. Dutton.

Duke, K. 1984. *Guinea pigs far and near.* New York: E. P. Dutton.

Ehlert, L. 1989. *Eating the alphabet.* San Diego, CA: Harcourt Brace Jovanovich.

Hines, A. G. 1986. *Daddy makes the best spaghetti.* New York: Ticknor & Fields.

Hutchins, P. 1976. *Don't forget the bacon.* New York: Greenwillow Books.

Johnston, T. 1983. *The vanishing pumpkin.* New York: G. P. Putnam's Sons.

Kellogg, S. 1980. *The mystery of the flying orange pumpkin.* New York: The Dial Press.

Kroll, S. 1984. *The biggest pumpkin ever.* New York: Scholastic, Inc.

McGraw, S. (1989). *This old new house.* Toronto, Canada: Annick Press Ltd.

Orbach, R. 1976. *Apple pigs.* New York: Philomel Books.

Provensen, A., & Provensen, M. (1987). *Shaker lane.* New York: Viking Kestrel.

Watson C. 1982. *Applebet, an ABC.* New York: Farrar, Straus, and Giroux.

CHILDREN'S COMPUTER PROGRAMS

Weekly Reader Software
Middletown, CT 06457
  Stickybear ABC 1982 (Apple, Atari)
  Stickybear Opposites 1983 (Apple, Atari)
  Stickybear Shapes 1983 (Apple, Atari)

TRY IT
YOURSELF

1. Map out a list of themes for ten months; then take one month's theme, and plan how each of the ten learning centers can contribute to the theme with appropriate activities and materials.

2. Write out a set of plan cards for each of the ten learning centers for one day in the month you planned in number 1. Include an appropriate transition activity on the back of each card.

3. Observe or participate in one of the learning centers during the day, recording on the Child Interaction Form how children responded to activities; then join in a summary session at the end of the day, contributing to the discussion with your observational data, and write up learning center plan cards for the next day.

4. Observe and record information about one of the children for three days. Afterwards, make up a "Learning Goals" list for this child for one month and share it with the staff.

5. Participate in a total group circle time, and lead one of the activities.

Chapter 1

COME IN

D. J. Zeigler

Walk up the side walk knock at the door

Peek through the win-dow gaze at the floor

Hand on the door knob should you go in?

O - pen the door wide come right in!

Chapter 2

TEACHER

D. J. Zeigler

Good morn-ing tea-cher, how do you do, good morn-ing tea-cher,

I'm fine too; good af-ter - noon tea-cher I want to state, good

Af-ter-noon tea-cher I feel great!

Chapter 3   **BLOCK CENTER**

D. J. Zeigler

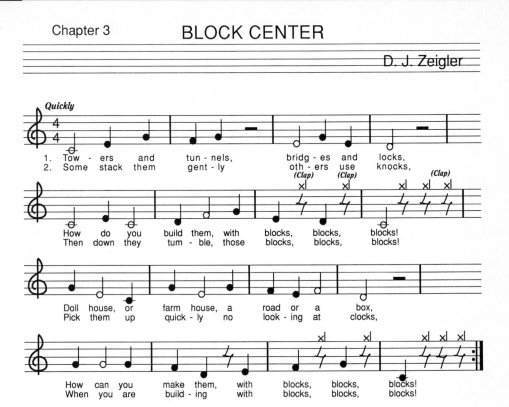

Chapter 4   **COMPUTER CENTER**

D. J. Zeigler

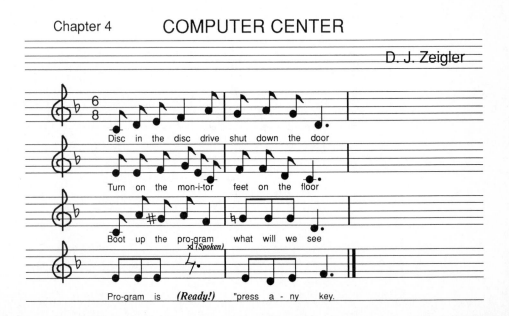

Chapter 5

NUMBERS

D. J. Zeigler

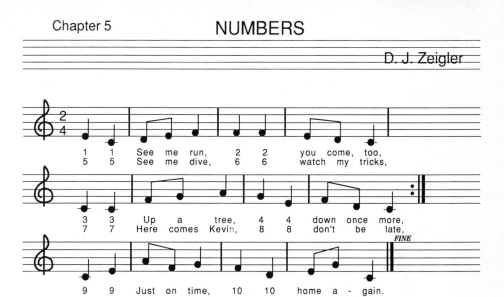

1   1   See   me   run,   2   2   you   come,   too,
5   5   See   me   dive,   6   6   watch   my   tricks,

3   3   Up   a   tree,   4   4   down   once   more,
7   7   Here   comes   Kevin,   8   8   don't   be   late,

FINE

9   9   Just   on   time,   10   10   home a - gain.

Chapter 6

BOOKS

D. J. Zeigler

Come   in   come   in   said   the   li-brar-y   door;   I

O-pened   it   wide   and   saw   books   ga-lore.   Tall   skinny   books   up

High   on   the   shelf,   lit-tle   fat   books   that   stood   by   them-selves.   I

O-pened   one   up   and   sat   down   to   look,   the   pic-tures   told   sto-ries   what   a

Won-der - ful   book!

Chapter 7

LETTERS

D. J. Zeigler

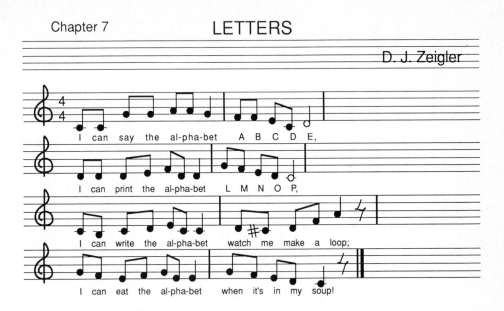

I can say the al-pha-bet A B C D E,

I can print the al-pha-bet L M N O P,

I can write the al-pha-bet watch me make a loop;

I can eat the al-pha-bet when it's in my soup!

Chapter 9

MAKING MUSIC

D. J. Zeigler

Can you whis-tle, whis-tle, whis-tle, can you

Hum hum hum can you shake it like a this-tle can you

Strum strum strum can you tap your fin-gers light-ly can you

Drum drum drum can you move a - round po-lite-ly can you

Run run run!

Chapter 10   **PETS**

D. J. Zeigler

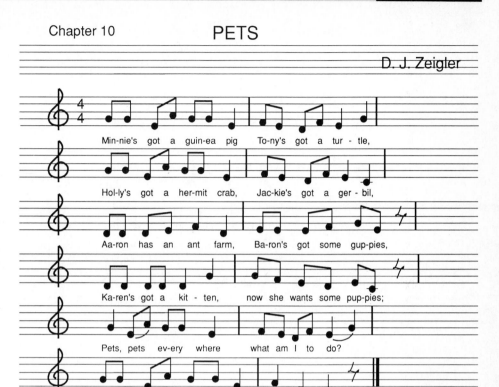

Min-nie's got a guin-ea pig To-ny's got a tur - tle,

Hol-ly's got a her-mit crab, Jac-kie's got a ger-bil,

Aa-ron has an ant farm, Ba-ron's got some gup-pies,

Ka-ren's got a kit - ten, now she wants some pup-pies;

Pets, pets ev-ery where what am I to do?

I don't need an - oth - er pet I've got you!

Chapter 11   **WHO AM I?**

D. J. Zeigler

Who am I, let me see, I'm won-der wo-man on T - V

I'm a dan-cer on the stage, I'm a rock star all the rage; to-

day I'm the mo-ther who pours the milk,

Yes-ter-day a prin-cess dressed in silk, to - morrow I don't know what I'll do,

I don't know -- do you? *(Spoken)*

Chapter 12   **JANIE IS A JUMPER**

D. J. Zeigler

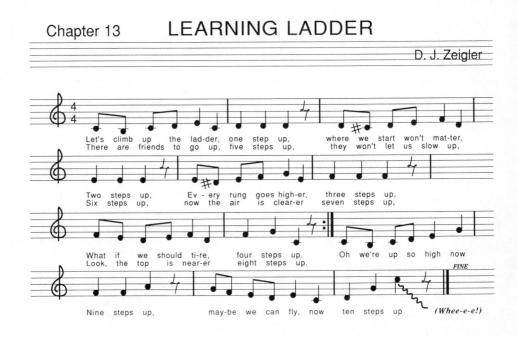

Ja-nie is a jum-per see her hop - hop - hop;

Bon-nie is a bum-per see her bop - bop - bop;

Phil-ip is a fli - er see him loop-the - loop,

I can go still high - er watch me fly the coop!

Chapter 13   **LEARNING LADDER**

D. J. Zeigler

Let's climb up the lad-der, one step up, where we start won't mat-ter,
There are friends to go up, five steps up, they won't let us slow up,

Two steps up, Ev - ery rung goes high-er, three steps up,
Six steps up, now the air is clear-er seven steps up,

What if we should ti-re, four steps up. Oh we're up so high now
Look, the top is near-er eight steps up.

FINE

Nine steps up, may-be we can fly, now ten steps up *(Whee-e-e!)*